THE ROAD TO
SPIRITUAL FREEDOM

ALSO BY HAROLD KLEMP

Animals Are Soul Too!

The Art of Spiritual Dreaming

Ask the Master, Books 1 and 2

Autobiography of a Modern Prophet

The Call of Soul

Child in the Wilderness

A Cosmic Sea of Words:
The ECKANKAR Lexicon

ECKANKAR's Spiritual Experiences
Guidebook

ECK Masters and You: An Illustrated
Guide

ECK Wisdom Temples, Spiritual Cities,
& Guides: A Brief History

Is Life a Random Walk?

The Living Word, Books 1, 2, and 3

A Modern Prophet Answers Your Key
Questions about Life, Books 1 and 2

Past Lives, Dreams, and Soul Travel

Soul Travelers of the Far Country

Spiritual Exercises for the Shariyat,
Book One

The Spiritual Exercises of ECK

The Spiritual Laws of Life

The Temple of ECK

Those Wonderful ECK Masters

Welcome to the Wonderful World of
ECK! Your Membership Guidebook

The Wind of Change

Wisdom of the Heart, Books 1, 2, and 3

Your Road Map to the ECK Teachings:
ECKANKAR Study Guide, Volumes
1 and 2

Youth Ask a Modern Prophet about
Life, Love, and God

The Mahanta Transcripts Series

Journey of Soul, Book 1

How to Find God, Book 2

The Secret Teachings, Book 3

The Golden Heart, Book 4

Cloak of Consciousness, Book 5

Unlocking Your Sacred Puzzle Box,
Book 6

The Eternal Dreamer, Book 7

The Dream Master, Book 8

We Come as Eagles, Book 9

The Drumbeat of Time, Book 10

What Is Spiritual Freedom? Book 11

How the Inner Master Works, Book 12

The Slow Burning Love of God,
Book 13

The Secret of Love, Book 14

Our Spiritual Wake-Up Calls, Book 15

How to Survive Spiritually in Our
Times, Book 16

The Immortality of Soul Series

The Awakened Heart

The Awakening Soul

HU, the Most Beautiful Prayer

The Language of Soul

Love—The Keystone of Life

The Loving Heart

The Spiritual Life

Touching the Face of God

Truth Has No Secrets

Spiritual Wisdom Series

ECK Wisdom on Inner Guidance

Spiritual Wisdom on Conquering Fear

Spiritual Wisdom on Dreams

Spiritual Wisdom on Health and
Healing

Spiritual Wisdom on Karma and
Reincarnation

Spiritual Wisdom on Life after Death

Spiritual Wisdom on Prayer, Meditation, and Contemplation

Spiritual Wisdom on Relationships

Stories to Help You See God in
Your Life

The Book of ECK Parables, Volumes
1, 2, and 3

Stories to Help You See God in Your
Life, ECK Parables, Book 4

This book has been authored by and published under
the supervision of the Mahanta, the Living ECK Master,
Sri Harold Klemp. It is the Word of ECK.

MAHANTA

THE ROAD TO SPIRITUAL FREEDOM

HAROLD KLEMP

MAHANTA TRANSCRIPTS

BOOK 17

ECKANKAR
Minneapolis
www.Eckankar.org

The Road to Spiritual Freedom,
Mahanta Transcripts, Book 17

Copyright © 2016 ECKANKAR

Printed in USA

Compiled by Mary Carroll Moore
Edited by Patrick Carroll, Joan Klemp, and Anthony Moore

Cover painting by Becky Morris
Text illustrations by Cynthia Samul
Spine photo and text photo (page xii) by Art Galbraith

Library of Congress Cataloging-in-Publication Data

Names: Klemp, Harold, author.
Title: The road to spiritual freedom / Harold Klemp.
Description: Minneapolis : Eckankar, 2016. | Series: Mahanta transcripts ; Book 17 | Includes index.
Identifiers: LCCN 2016023935 | ISBN 9781570433412 (pbk. : alk. paper)
Subjects: LCSH: Eckankar (Organization)--Doctrines. | Liberty--Religious aspects--Eckankar (Organization)
Classification: LCC BP605.E3 K56475 2016 | DDC 299/.93--dc23 LC record available at https://lccn.loc.gov/2016023935

♾ This paper meets the requirements of ANSI/NISO Z39.48-1992 (Permanence of Paper).

CONTENTS

FOREWORD

*T*he teachings of ECK define the nature of Soul. You are Soul, a particle of God sent into the worlds (including earth) to gain spiritual experience.

The goal in ECK is spiritual freedom in this lifetime, after which you become a Co-worker with God, both here and in the next world. Karma and reincarnation are primary beliefs.

Key to the ECK teachings is the Mahanta, the Living ECK Master. He has the special ability to act as both the Inner and Outer Master for ECK students. The prophet of Eckankar, he is given respect but is not worshipped. He teaches the sacred name of God, HU. When sung just a few minutes each day, HU will lift you spiritually into the Light and Sound of God—the ECK (Holy Spirit). This easy spiritual exercise and others will purify you. You are then able to accept the full love of God in this lifetime.

Sri Harold Klemp is the Mahanta, the Living ECK Master today. Author of many books, discourses, and articles, he teaches the ins and outs of the spiritual life. Many of his talks are available to you on audio and video recordings. His teachings lift people and help them recognize and understand their own experiences in the Light and Sound of God.

The Road to Spiritual Freedom, Mahanta Transcripts, Book 17, is a collection of his talks from 2000 to 2006. May they serve to uplift you on your journey home to God.

To find out more about Harold Klemp and Eckankar, please turn to page 353 in the back of this book.

Sri Harold Klemp, the Mahanta, the Living ECK Master shows each Soul Its own path to spiritual freedom in this lifetime.

1
GIFTS STRANGER THAN FICTION

here was an article in the *Wall Street Journal* on the editorial page. The National Institute for Health Care Research did a new study of 126,000 people that found a statistically significant link between churchgoing and life span. You're 29 percent more likely to live longer if you're a churchgoer than if you sleep late on Sundays.

This applies to people who go to church, people who go to temple; it doesn't matter what building they worship in.

THE UPSIDE TO CHURCHGOING

Here are some of the benefits of churchgoing, or regular worship: lower rates of cancer, heart disease, and mental illness and fewer bouts of depression. Believers generally have lower blood pressure and stronger immune systems.

The editorial asked, What's the connection between regular religious observation and outliving the local atheist club president? They discovered that churchgoing will let you outlive the local atheist club president; the question is *why*.

Churchgoing will let you outlive the local atheist club president; the question is why.

The doctor who put together this study speculated that religion confers certain benefits that are not found in the secular world. Religion gives a conservative creed that cultivates moderation or abstinence. It also provides a social network that sustains believers in these values. And it provides a strong belief system that gives hope in the face of hardship.

These things combine to protect the faithful from making dangerous choices and to relieve stress. So there is a real upside to worship services. The benefits are mental, emotional, and spiritual health.

The benefits are mental, emotional, and spiritual health.

LOOKING AT THE BIGGER PICTURE

Sometimes we look at things in too small a way.

John Doremus's radio program, *Patterns in Music*, airs in Rochester, Minnesota. It's on five nights a week, Monday through Friday. I listen to him sometimes before bedtime as I'm wrapping up my day.

One evening he was telling a story about a speaker who was in front of a business group. On an easel was a big pad of white paper, and the speaker took his pen and made a little dot on the paper. He asked for a volunteer to tell him what he saw there.

One of the people in the audience raised his hand. "A black dot."

The speaker went through the audience, asking the other people, "What do you see?" Most of them just shrugged their shoulders and said, "A black dot."

Then he asked, "Doesn't anyone see the big pad of white paper?"

It shows the tendency of human nature to focus on the small, unimportant things and let the big things go.

WATER FOR JOCELYN'S MOTHER

In *Herbs: The Magic Healers*, by Paul Twitchell, there is a statement about the benefits of doing the Spiritual Exercises of ECK. This also applies to any sort of worship that a person does, either personally or in a group, including prayer.

It says: "Health and happiness means to be rid of fatigue and disease. To have a good appetite, good memory, good humor, and precision in thought and action. To be free from anxiety and fear. To have a great capacity for survival over illness and anxieties. To have joy, long life, and great spiritual adventures."

In this connection, I'd like to mention Dr. Batmanghelidj's book *Your Body's Many Cries for Water.* I mentioned it at the last seminar, and an ECKist named Jocelyn wrote me. She's a writer in the Montreal area.

Jocelyn wrote an article about *Your Body's Many Cries for Water* for a French magazine in Quebec, and it was published in the December 1999/January 2000 issue.

The article got a large response. One of the readers asked Jocelyn, "Do you know that you are raising the consciousness of these readers?" Because many of the people had no idea of the value of something as simple as water.

But there was also a benefit much closer to home.

Jocelyn's mother was in her early seventies. She was having problems with dizziness and confusion. She went to the hospital, the doctors examined her, and they seemed very happy to have found a gray spot on her brain. They looked it over and said, "It looks like epilepsy—seizures." The doctors prescribed a drug.

Herbs: The Magic Healers, by Paul Twitchell says: "Health and happiness means to have good humor, joy, long life, and great spiritual adventures."

But when Jocelyn's mother took the drug, she felt depressed and dopey. And worse, the doctor told her, "You can't drive anymore."

The mother's poor health had started back when she was forty years old. Back then she had digestive problems, and she went to the hospital to have them taken care of. The doctors had told her it was a problem with her esophagus. They went in to look at it and found out that the esophagus had become so dry it was like parchment. When they tried to operate and fix it, they accidentally damaged it more, because the membrane was so delicate.

Things went from bad to worse. By age fifty, Jocelyn's mother had bone degeneration; osteoporosis had set in. The doctor told her, "The bones are drying out."

By the time Jocelyn's mother reached age seventy, the doctors had begun to tell her that the brain, like these other parts of the body just mentioned, was also drying out.

The mother was desperate for a solution. So she turned to her daughter for advice because her daughter has an interest in health matters.

Shortly before, Jocelyn had read *Your Body's Many Cries for Water*.

The basic premise in the book is that many of the problems people have are based on chronic dehydration. They just need more water. Her mother admitted that most of her life she had taken very little water because she just didn't like the taste of city water.

If you have health problems, I recommend you read the book.

The book gives advice about how much water to take and also how to increase one's salt intake. Otherwise all the salt is leached out of the body.

If you have health problems, I recommend you read the book. But if you decide to put its advice into practice, that is something you should do under the care of your doctor; have him or her check you over before, during, and after.

Jocelyn's mother was one of the fortunate ones. She increased her water intake for about two weeks. At that time, her migraines stopped. Her angina stopped. She went back to the neurologist two months later. She wanted to drive. The doctor saw that she was in better condition than before, and he said, "When we did those tests, we suspected epilepsy, but we had some doubts."

Jocelyn says her mother is now in a group for elderly people. She enjoys dancing, conversations, and traveling with her new friends. With water in her diet, she can now control her digestive problems. But more importantly, she's taken charge of her health. She's now able to preserve her autonomy and dignity. These two things are very important to her.

EYES-OF-THE-FUTURE WAKING DREAM

Everyone knows about sleeping dreams. You go to sleep, something happens, you wake up, and you say, "What a dream!"

A waking dream is different. It's something that happens in everyday life. It's a parallel. Something about a common, everyday event that stands out and brings things into focus for you. You say, "You know, that answers a question I had."

A widow of seventy-five went to a big grocery store, and as she was walking in she noticed four kids out front. They were about eight or ten years old. One of the little girls was holding a dog.

The widow remembered when she was that age with a pet. She went into the store, shopped, came out, got in her car, and started to drive away. While

A waking dream happens in everyday life. It brings things about a common, everyday event into focus for you.

waiting her turn to leave the parking lot, she saw the four children again. As she watched them, a boy waved to her and came up to her car.

"Do you want to see the eyes of the future?" he asked the woman.

Before she'd gone into the store, the woman had been looking over her life. She had been a widow for only a short time. She was looking at life alone now. She had asked the ECK, the Holy Spirit, "What's next? What's next in my life?"

Now, a half hour later, a little boy comes up to her with some papers in his hand and asks, "Do you want to see the eyes of the future?"

Without a moment's pause, the widow said, "Yes."

The boy handed her two sheets of paper. On the front of the first page, one of the children had drawn a great big eye. That's all.

The boy said, "Look at page two."

The woman looked at page two. There were the names of the children and a little message: "The eyes of the future are helping pick up trash and doing the right thing."

The woman had been wondering what she should do with her life, what she could do as a seventy-five year old, what she could do that would matter to life. She kept the papers and gave the kids a commemorative coin as a way of saying thank-you. They could take it home to their mother. They could say, "Look, someone did understand what we were doing. Someone understood that it was important, and we got this coin to prove it."

The woman realized she was already doing what the message had said. When she took her dog out for a walk, if she saw trash, she picked it up.

This was a lesson for her. When you ask, How can

The children had written a little message: "The eyes of the future are helping pick up trash and doing the right thing."

I serve Spirit and people best? chances are you're already doing it in some little way.

It just takes something to bring it to your attention.

The woman is a member of an ECK dream class. She took the two sheets of paper with her and showed them to the other ten members of the dream class. At first they had a hard time understanding the waking dream. But then she gave her little example, and they could see what spiritual significance this had for her.

In this way, it was important. As she's out walking her dog, picking things up, she's doing the right thing. She'd had a question about the future and how to fill a useful role as an instrument for Divine Spirit, and within the hour, the ECK brought her the answer through these four children.

BUCKWHEAT TREASURES

It's the simple things in life that are the most beautiful and the most important.

"Lewis," from Colorado, was to attend two business meetings in a town about three hours away. Just before he got in the car, he noticed he had a flat tire.

But no problem. Lewis owned a little tire inflator. He took it and tried to inflate the tire. The tire inflator broke. Louis said, "No problem. I'll call the American Automobile Association." So he called them to come fix his tire.

The AAA representative said, "There will be an hour's delay."

"Oh, great," said Lewis. "There goes my day."

He got on the phone and called the people he was supposed to meet with in the city three hours away. They rescheduled the two appointments for the next week.

It's the simple things in life that are the most beautiful and the most important.

By this time, the tow-truck driver had arrived. He inflated the tire. "This'll hold you until you can get to a service station," he said. Then the driver started writing up the ticket for having made this service call.

As the driver was writing up the ticket, he began talking about his father.

After a while, Lewis asked him, "Is your father still living?"

"No," said the driver, "he passed on." Then the driver, whose name was Charlie, launched into a story.

Well, Lewis figured, *what the heck. The meetings are off anyway. My gift to this man will be just listening, letting him talk as long as he wants to.*

So Charlie began to tell many stories about when he was a farmer back in Pennsylvania before he moved out to Colorado. He told story after story about the neighbors, how they got along, and all their different interactions and relationships.

One story particularly struck Lewis.

Charlie said that way back when Charlie was farming, he used to raise buckwheat and sell it to Pillsbury. This was a time when consumers used buckwheat for pancakes and other such things.

But as time passed, the consumer's taste switched to other flours—the lighter flours like wheat—and buckwheat fell out of favor. So Charlie had to find some other cash crops to make a living. He also raised beef cattle.

One day Charlie told his father, "I've got this piece of land out there. I can't grow a thing on it. All it's got is briars. I'd sure like to use that land."

His father said, "Why don't you just sow some buckwheat?"

Well, *Lewis* figured, my gift to this man will be just listening, letting him talk as long as he wants to.

"Buckwheat?"

"Sure. It's good for the land."

Charlie thought it over. "Whatever I plant there comes up unhealthy; it doesn't have any value to it," he said.

"Try buckwheat," his father said. "Nothing tames wild land like buckwheat. Just give it a try."

So Charlie did. To his surprise and delight, the buckwheat came up fine. Over the following years, he continued to plant buckwheat. And he found that buckwheat did a very interesting thing to the soil: it changed its composition. The soil became productive again.

After Charlie left, Lewis thought about this story in relation to his own job.

Lewis worked in education. He began thinking, *There must be a lot of buckwheats out there—something that has little value in itself, but it can transform other things.*

"If I can find the buckwheat that will transform some of the educators that I'm trying to serve in the school system, that would be a real gift," he said. "If I can bring a better attitude to some of the public schools that I serve, this would truly be another gift." Lewis looked at all these things. He decided that somehow he must look for the catalyst.

So the challenge is the same for you. If you're creative or energetic, look for the buckwheat in your own life to transform something. Now this buckwheat is going to look useless to you, but there's a hidden treasure in it. And somehow, in some way, it can create a miracle with something else that is not doing too well in your life.

Look for the buckwheats.

He began thinking, There must be a lot of buckwheats out there— something that has little value in itself, but it can transform other things.

THE SPIRITUAL MEAT OF STORIES

I was out driving two weeks ago. Sunday services were on, and there was a minister on the radio. His sermon wasn't particularly good, and his voice was pretty much like mine. Right away, I was all ears.

A speaker is always supposed to be very dynamic. But as I've explained before, I don't want to appeal to the emotions of people with flamboyance. Basically, it's a cheap trick. It gets people all worked up into a lather, and when they go home, a big vacuum comes in.

They need spiritual meat. They need something to help them throughout the coming week.

So, this minister was telling stories. He told one story after another, and each story had a nice point to it. The stories took place in the Minneapolis area. This man made up for his lack of dynamic speech with good stories.

I thought, *How nice. This man is doing a favor to his audience. He's telling stories with spiritual principles.*

We like to flatter ourselves that we've had a hand in this because ECK videos have been showing in the Minneapolis area for a good ten years. I get reports of people of other religions who watch and enjoy the videos. Basically, they are half-hour excerpts from talks I've given.

A simple story sticks better than pure philosophy. You can take a story home and figure out what that story means to you.

A simple story sticks better than pure philosophy. You can take a story home. And you can pretty much figure out what that story means to you; you don't need someone else to tell you.

When I tell you stories, I tell you what it means to me and to someone else, perhaps the original teller of the story. But it may mean something entirely different to you. I tell six, seven, eight, or nine stories, and maybe only one of them means something to you. But during the coming weeks, the story might flash through your mind, flit through it like a butterfly. You'll say, "That reminds me. What's going on here is just what he said to look for when he told that story."

In this way, a story sometimes gives a spiritual benefit that carries further than philosophy.

JANE'S LUNCH-LINE MIRACLE

"Jane" has been an initiate of Eckankar for many years. One day she and her sister had a disagreement about a family matter. They had some warm words. The next day Jane was still carrying the argument around with her.

"Why can't that blockheaded sister of mine see it my way?" she said to herself. "It would have worked out better for everyone." Thoughts typical of most of us if we get ourselves worked up about something.

That day she took her son to McDonald's to get some lunch. Jane said that 99 percent of the time, she's in a sunny mood and always feels good. But when she walked into McDonald's that day with her son, a little black cloud was raining down on her. She knew it, but she couldn't shake it.

They got in line. Ahead of her, a man was straddling two lines. He had one foot in one line and the other foot in the other line.

Jane, not being herself, said, "Excuse me. Are you here or there?"

The gentleman turned to her and said, "My child, I am everywhere."

Oh, great, thought Jane. *Please don't send me an ECK Master in disguise now.*

She said, "I'm not myself today. Thank you."

Jane, not being herself, said, "Excuse me. Are you here or there?" The gentleman turned to her and said, "My child, I am everywhere."

The stranger continued kindly: "I love you and respect you, and God loves you."

This answer floored her. It got her back on track. She started looking in her purse for a HU card, as if an ECK Master would actually need one, if that's who it was.

By the time she found the HU card, the man was gone. ECK Masters do that; they're there and then they're gone. Sometimes it's simply the awareness of a high state of consciousness that comes into an ordinary stranger. And from the mouth come these holy words.

This, too, was a waking dream. It was the Voice of God speaking directly to Jane, reassuring her of Its love.

It was one of those gifts of Spirit—stranger than fiction and even more common.

The stranger continued kindly: "I love you and respect you, and God loves you." It was one of those gifts of Spirit—stranger than fiction and even more common.

NIKKI'S TIMELY WATCH

"Nikki," from New York, worked as a property manager for a local construction company. She showed model apartments to prospective renters.

One day, she was in her office, and she saw a car drive up. The car sat outside for a long time. Over the next half hour, Nikki saw a man struggle out of the car and very slowly and laboriously make his way to her office.

It turned out he had multiple sclerosis. He could barely walk. His speech was a simple mumble.

Nikki took the man on the tour. Now when the man first arrived, Nikki had checked her watch. She saw there was plenty of time before she had to pick up her son from school. But now the tour was going longer and longer, and the whole experience became a real test of Nikki's patience.

But the Inner Master, the Mahanta, kept saying, "Just have patience. This will be your gift to him."

Nikki remembered: That morning she had declared herself a channel for the ECK, the Holy Spirit. She'd said, "Make me a channel for you, Mahanta, and for divine love. Let everything that I do today be in thy name. Let it help others in some spiritual way." And here, nearly at the close of the day when she was just about ready to leave, had come the man with MS.

But Nikki looked at her watch, and everything seemed fine. There was still plenty of time.

So she continued the tour, and while they were walking, the man had a chance to talk. Through his mumbling, Nikki was able to get his story.

Since he'd become ill, his family had lost patience with him, and the stress in the family house was making his condition even worse. "I've got to get out of the house to save my life," he told Nikki. "That's why I'm here."

The tour ended, and the man made his way out to his vehicle again, laboriously climbed in, and drove off. Nikki went back to her office and sat down. Just as she did, the phone rang.

It was her son calling from school. He was very upset. "Mom, do you know what time it is?" If any of you are parents who have been late to pick up a child, you've heard that.

Nikki looked at her watch. "It's four o'clock."

Her son said, "It's five o'clock. You're over an hour late."

She took a closer look at her watch and saw it had stopped. Nikki realized that the ECK had stopped her watch simply so that she would allow enough time for this gentleman to be able to unload his

> *Nikki remembered: That morning she'd said, "Make me a channel for divine love."*

spiritual burden during the tour. If her watch had been going, she would have rushed the tour and hurried him along as much as possible so that she could pick up her son from school.

She found that the ECK, in stopping her watch, was in control of all things. She summed it up like this:

"I'm so grateful for the gift of the Mahanta's love," she said. "I think that people who leave ECK must have never really known that love. Otherwise, how could they ever leave that circle of friends?"

BEING IN A CIRCLE OF FRIENDS

People come and go in ECK. Many years later, many lifetimes later, they find their way back to ECK again.

That's a good question. It comes up. People come and go in ECK. When they come, I'm happy for them; and when they leave, it's a mixture of both happiness and sadness on my part.

I'm happy they came for as long as they did because I see that these Souls have come to get as much of the outer or temporal teachings as they can hold at that time. Then when they're filled, they go on to another path in their quest, their spiritual shopping. They go from window to window, looking at the offerings in all the different religious stores, hoping somewhere that they can find just the item that will make them feel happy and contented inside.

Many years later, many lifetimes later, they find their way back to ECK again. Maybe for a short stay, maybe for a longer stay. But generally it's a longer stay because life has taught them more about loving. They've learned more about divine love.

Divine love comes through our friends, our family, our pets. It comes through in appreciation of the things that nature provides—the sunsets, the desert, the forest, the sky, the sun, the moon, the birds, and the other animals and beings and creatures.

A Bike Ride Stranger than Fiction

There was an article in a West Coast newspaper, *The San Jose Mercury*. It was titled "A Bike Ride Stranger Than Fiction."

Two young men, twin brothers, decided to go to one of the large parks in California. It was a wild place. They were going to take their mountain bikes and make a forty-mile loop, going along ridges and up and down trails. They wanted to see if they could reach a certain summit. After reaching the summit, they would head back to the ranger station where they had parked their truck.

Before their ride, they stopped at the ranger station to check in. They told the rangers of their plan in case anything happened.

The ranger said, "If your truck is still parked out here by our station in the morning, we'll come looking for you."

This was a foreshadowing of what was in store for them.

So the two brothers, full of adventure, set out on their bike trip—going fast, pedaling up and down hills and ravines.

The park had coyotes, wild boar, birds, hawks, and all kinds of other creatures. In the dark areas of the forests, there was a considerable amount of danger.

After a while they became very, very tired. Should we press on to the summit? they asked themselves. Will we be able to make the summit and get back to the ranger station before dark? They realized that they had planned poorly, underestimating their trip. The ride was a lot harder than they'd thought. They were near exhaustion now, and they still had a long way to go. But they decided to go for the summit.

The ranger said, "If your truck is still parked out here by our station in the morning, we'll come looking for you."

So they went up a high summit trail and, finally exhausted, they got to the top. There was a great view. They admired it briefly, then said, "Now we better get out of here." Off in the distance at the next ridge, they could see a rainstorm coming in. It was hard enough riding their bikes on the trail as it was. All they needed was rain turning the trail to mud.

But the rain hit, and so they began slogging through the mud. The brothers were so exhausted, they began thinking it was the end. But they struggled on a little more.

They both fell down in the mud—flat on their backs, unable to move. "Well, it's been a good life," one of them said.

Then things got worse. They had lost the trail. It was too much. They both fell down in the mud—flat on their backs, unable to move. "Well, it's been a good life," one of them said.

So they lay there as comfortably as possible, exchanging stories of the adventures they'd shared.

Suddenly one of them looked up. An old man was standing in front of them. He had a walking stick in his hand and an old rain cap on his head. But the most striking feature was his long white beard.

The man looked at them and said, "What are you doing?"

The twins answered in unison, as twins often do. They said, "We're going to die." It was said as a joke, but not really. They thought they'd come to the end.

They lay in the mud, flat on their backs, looking up at the man, too exhausted to move. "Where'd you come from?" they asked him.

The old gentleman didn't answer them directly. He said, "I am a caretaker."

"Where's the trail back to the ranger station?" they asked.

The man's eyes had a gentle, compassionate look. He pointed. "That's the way home," he said.

And just a few yards away was the trail they'd been looking for. They hadn't seen it.

The old man said, "You guys are not ready to die."

They all smiled at that.

Finally refreshed, the young men got up, got on their bikes, and headed down to the trailhead a few yards away. They turned to wave to the old gentleman, but he was already gone.

When the two brothers got home, they were starved. One of them, the writer of the article, went to a fast-food place and ordered three of their largest hamburgers and fries. After he got home, he stuffed it all down, cleaned himself up—got the mud off—and headed for his warm, soft bed.

That night came the gift stranger than fiction. The writer had a dream. In this dream the stranger, the old man, the caretaker, appeared to him.

The young man said, "What are you doing in my dream?" He was very possessive about his dreams.

The old man said, "I wanted to tell you that you have more adventures ahead of you and to be thankful."

"Thankful for what?"

The old man said, "You are a wild spirit and have a big heart." Smiling then, the old man continued, "Be thankful for every minute you are here."

The young man challenged him. "You mean wander the hills alone like you?"

The old man said, "No. Be the caretaker of your life."

When the dreamer awoke, he was filled with a contentment and happiness that he'd not felt for a long time. The conclusion he reached from all this: We are all caretakers for ourselves and each other.

That night came the gift stranger than fiction. The writer had a dream. The stranger, the old caretaker, appeared to him.

Take every step with grace, for life is a precious adventure. "And most of all," he said, "never give up."

He'd met the ECK Master Fubbi Quantz.

SOUL'S MISSION

What's the purpose of service?

So often you'll hear me say, "Soul's mission is to serve life." Some people who have yet to get more of the experience of divine love in their own life—in this life or some previous one—say, "How dull. It doesn't sound like a very interesting thing to do. Life comes but once. We should make the best of it. And what is this 'serve life, serve God' stuff?"

Basically, it's helping people. It's helping them do the things that they need to make life easier for them.

And in so doing, you are working for the Holy Spirit. In so doing, you are working for the good of other people. And in so doing, you are doing much good for yourself.

FINDING GOD'S LOVE

Some people have such a strong desire for truth they will let no number of miles stand between them and a chance to hear it.

The Shariyat-Ki-Sugmad, Book Two, says this about service: an ECKist resolves to "aid all sentient beings to reach the ECKshar, the enlightenment, or supreme consciousness."

ECKshar is an ECK term that just means a high state of consciousness. It's beyond cosmic consciousness. It's an initiation into a higher state of recognizing God's love.

I think back to the early years in ECK and see even today when some people have such a strong desire for truth that they will let no number of miles stand between them and a chance to hear it.

I know I did myself. And my wife, Joan, did too.

When we heard about ECK, that was life. Suddenly things clicked. Others like us have the same experience. Some people have a similar experience when they join a new church—when a Catholic becomes a Baptist, a Baptist an Anglican, a Jew a follower of Islam, or whatever.

When we heard about ECK, that was life. Suddenly things clicked.

Everything is possible. Soul comes in a form, in a body, that is suited for Its best spiritual unfoldment at that time.

To accomplish the goal of receiving more wisdom and more spiritual freedom, that Soul sometimes has to jump a lot of walls and climb and crawl through many briar patches, because that's the way of it.

And so my love is with you. And I am always with you. May the blessings be.

ECK Summer Festival, Montreal, Quebec, Canada, Saturday, June 17, 2000

There is a way to do things. So often, it's not what you're doing as how you're doing it, how you approach it in your heart.

2

THE FOOLISH
OF GOD

*S*ometimes I look at the members of Eckankar from one country and those from another country. How different the life experiences of an individual in each place are!

In many places in Africa, as well as in Europe, there is a great deal of upheaval. You have to look very hard sometimes to realize that it's the right place for a person to be at that time. But it's the place and the time for Soul's spiritual unfoldment. Which is sometimes a very interesting time. Old forms are thrown away. Old ways of doing things give way to the new.

That period of change is very hard on people. Often people must leave their homes, lose family members. It's during times of great upheaval that a person feels, ironically perhaps, closer to life than at any other time.

We think everyone is foolish but us.

WHO ARE THE FOOLISH OF GOD?

We think everyone is foolish but us.

We're wise, considerate, kind, all-knowing—not

21

all the time, but often enough that we can recognize a problem when we see it.

But the fact is God puts those people in our path whom we need to bump shoulders with. The people in our life are those who need to be here for our spiritual unfoldment.

As soon as we learn the lesson that a person has to teach us and we've made the adjustments inside ourselves, we may go on to a new spiritual lesson.

God puts those people in our path whom we need to bump shoulders with for our spiritual unfoldment.

BUMPED OUT OF OUR GROOVES

We're telecasting this talk by satellite from the Temple of ECK in Chanhassen, Minnesota. In the last half hour before the talk began, everything went wrong.

I was getting in a car to come here, and the seat belt simply wouldn't reach. I did everything possible to make it reach. It wouldn't. I finally moved to the backseat. The seat in front of me had a very fuzzy backrest. When my legs brushed against it, I got fuzz all over the knees of my dark suit.

Then as we were driving here, we took a wrong turn. We went in another direction, then gradually got back on course. We made it to the Temple, but we were cutting it a little close on time.

Usually things go like clockwork for these talks because we plan so carefully. We each know what we're going to do so that everything can be done in a timely manner—without hurry, smoothly and peacefully. Today it was anything but smooth and peaceful.

One of the staff forgot the water glass. I said, "No problem." She was about to run off to find it in another part of the building. But a little plastic cup was near at hand. She asked, "Would one of these be OK?" I said, "It'd be great."

Before I came out here, I was talking with someone backstage. "It's been like this, upside down, for the last half hour," I said.

He gave me a blank look, then a knowing smile. "I know what you mean," he said. "I know just what you mean."

I asked, "Has it been like that for you too?"

He said, "Yes, it's been like that."

We had to make changes because changes were occurring. We had to adjust ourselves.

IS THERE ROOM FOR GOD?

When everything's going wrong, you just say, "The ECK, the Holy Spirit, has something going here, and time will tell us what it is." Sometimes the ECK bumps us out of our grooves. It says, "All right; you've got everything planned according to that little mind of yours. So you have it all worked out, do you?"

We smile and say, "Of course." Then the Holy Spirit shakes the dice, throws them, and says, "Now what are you going to do with this?" We're caught totally off guard. Then we do the best we can in the time that remains.

It usually means you end up letting one thing go, maybe more than once. If you have three minutes, maybe you're letting one thing go each minute. You find out what's really necessary.

That's how it is. The foolish of God. We are all foolish when we set ourselves against the divine order and the divine plan. Often we don't even know we're doing that. God and anything holy is very much removed from our daily life.

After all, you've got to get to work. You've only got twenty minutes, so you rush. And what do you find on

When everything's going wrong, you just say, "The ECK, the Holy Spirit, has something going here, and time will tell us what it is."

the freeway? Traffic's backed up. Then you get to work, and everything seems to be going against you.

So you throw up your hands and say something drawn from your childhood vocabulary—something you heard from people who noticed you were one of those foolish of God and you couldn't do a thing right. They exercised their vocabulary upon you, and you picked up some of these words. When things go wrong today, the easiest way to make yourself feel good is to practice them; and you practice them without God anywhere in mind, because somehow God doesn't fit in all this. Too remote, too distant. If there's time for God, it'll be tonight at bedtime. Give God a few minutes tonight, if we're not too tired.

Then tomorrow, start all over again. Maybe it's a better day, so maybe we can use some of the kinder language that we have also learned over the years. We can be more charitable, more friendly with our coworkers, because it's a good day.

Whether it's a good day or a bad day, seldom does the presence of God enter into it.

But whether it's a good day or a bad day, seldom does the presence of God enter into it. Too busy; there's no time. Got to pick up the kids. Got to get food for dinner. Got to get to the bank.

You might say it's different now because a lot of this is done on the computer. Yes, banking's done on the computer. We can buy food online, but usually you don't; it's not workable enough yet.

The computer takes time too. It takes time to boot up the computer, to sit there and wait while all the messages come on. You may get sidetracked. Or you've got to nurse the programs along and clean out files. Something might crash, and then you're into a couple of days' delay.

Life is a trade-off, and often it seems there isn't much room for God.

ONLY ONE LIFE?

The stock market has been up, and lately it's been sliding, here in the United States anyway. Since maybe 50 percent of working families have some stake in the stock market, it's almost as if people's god has become mammon—not the true God, but another false god.

But what would you expect of the foolish of God?

That's how we make our way through life—not just one life, but many lifetimes—stubbing our toes, bumping into the doorpost because we didn't aim quite right.

What does Eckankar offer? I often think about this. I mention it all too seldom. Whatever happens today, whether it's wrong or right in our minds, will happen again tomorrow. It won't be exactly the same. It'll rhyme, sort of like almost the right word but not quite. Yet it all works together to make something harmonious.

But what about this life, compared to your last life? Is it any different?

And how long will this go on? How long?

In some areas of the world, life is pretty good. There isn't the destruction of war, the upheavals that destroy houses and buildings and people on a great scale. We say it's a pretty good life. And we may think, *One life, that's it; then I'm out of here.*

But it's not that way. There are more people in the world who have an understanding of reincarnation and karma than do not. This is a shock to a Christian society. In a society such as this, people think we have one life here and the rest of eternity is over there.

Some of you know in your heart—not just as a

What does Eckankar offer? Some of you know in your heart there is something more to the scheme of life.

belief in your mind—that there is something more to the scheme of life. There must be a reason why some people are born poor, for example. A student of Eckankar, considering the life of Gandhi of India, once said, "It can't be that anyone who is not Christian is damned. Look at this good man Gandhi. He can't be damned for all eternity simply because he grew up in a different culture. Would God be so unmerciful and so cruel?"

Some say yes, and some say no. What do you think?

LEARNING FROM ALL LIFE

"Bennett" grew up in Africa, lived in Europe for a bit, then came to the United States. After he arrived here, he lived in New York City.

Bennett was very disappointed with American women. He thought they were shallow—probably because he wasn't getting anywhere with them.

One day, Bennett met a friend on the street, and he expressed this opinion to his friend. He said, "How could anybody want to become friends with an American woman? They have nothing to offer."

"All people we meet have something to teach us if we would but learn," his friend answered.

Bennett thought about this for quite a while. And he realized that it was so. All the people around us are here to teach us something.

Bennett asks, What can I learn from this person? to understand what lesson life is trying to teach him.

Now Bennett asks, What can I learn from this person? What is the Mahanta trying to teach me through this person? In other words, he stopped looking at the problem and he's now looking for a solution. This is a big thing.

Instead of trying to judge another person as being one of those foolish ones of life, he learned to just accept him. To understand what lesson life is trying to teach him through this person.

Often, we come from a certain culture with certain trappings, beliefs, and taboos. We bring our baggage with us when we go to another country. And we expect that everybody there should do things the way we do. We, the foolish of God, think that's perfectly normal—that a whole country should bend and do things our way.

That's like the American who goes to France expecting French waiters to speak English to him. I have news for him.

I've enjoyed the many times that I've been able to come to Europe, to The Hague, London, Paris, Switzerland. Everywhere the people are different from anywhere else. They look a little different; they act a little different.

KARMIC LEDGER

If you grew up in a family with a lot of kids, maybe you got into hitting each other, as siblings do. Your parent would try to find out who was at fault. But then you would point a finger and say, "He started it." This worked until your brother pointed back, saying, "I did not. He started it." And the argument started all over again.

That's what happens lifetime after lifetime too.

In this life, we rub someone the wrong way, or they rub us the wrong way. It's really not important what rubs someone else wrong; what is important is what rubs me wrong. That's one part of karma.

The other part is where everything is kind, harmonious, smooth, and good. That also counts in the great ledger book.

The other part of karma is where everything is kind, harmonious, smooth, and good. That also counts in the great ledger book.

After this lifetime, when the karmic accounting is done, the Lords of Karma look in the ledger. "Hmmmm," they say, "let's see. He's going back to another lifetime because he hasn't learned how to get off the circle of reincarnation. But he's done pretty well this lifetime. He's got some credits coming." So this individual gets born into another life. Nice family, life of ease, all sorts of good things. If he values education or a good family, he can have that.

But for another person, when the Lords of Karma look in the great ledger book and tally things up at the end of his lifetime, they say, "Why, this man has some debits." Then he may come back carrying a big burden on his shoulders.

Other people will say, "What an unfortunate person." Yes, unfortunate, it's true. But what we fail to realize—and do not want to realize because it doesn't fit our thinking—is that person is born the way he is for some spiritual reason. We're all born the way we are for a certain spiritual reason.

We're all born the way we are for a certain spiritual reason.

CREATURES OF OUR OWN CREATION

About 95 percent of people are unhappy with the way they look. But most of them have chosen whatever body form was available to them based on the credits and debits they had earned. They're given a choice. The Lords of Karma say, "Even though you've got a debit in your ledger, you can have the choice of any one of five bodies, spread out over several decades and several different cultures. What do you want?"

So you pick one. Maybe it isn't the greatest choice on earth, but we're all the creatures of our own creation.

These ideas are shocking to some. They'll say, "That is not so. It cannot be so." Looking at it from a purely social perspective, there are people who can't believe that a person was born with a disability because of some spiritual reason. It never enters their minds.

When you see someone who's carrying a burden that most people aren't carrying, just remember: Even the people who seem to have no burdens at all are carrying burdens. These burdens are simply karma—cause and effect. Where does this karma come from? From ourselves.

HOOKING UP WITH THE LIGHT AND SOUND

At some point we can wrap it up. We can be done with it and get off the wheel of reincarnation and karma.

How? Somewhere along the line of lifetimes, an individual must find someone who can hook him up with the Voice of God. This is the Light and Sound of God, the two aspects of the ECK, the Holy Spirit.

There is a way. In Eckankar, it happens during the Second Initiation, which comes after two years of study of the ECK discourses. It's a landmark. It says that this Soul need never return to earth again.

For many people this is fine. They'll say, "If I can just get away from this earth and not have to come back to it ever again, I'll do whatever it takes."

Of course, there's more to the equation. There are planes above the earth plane that still are subject to karma and reincarnation—the Astral, Causal, Mental, and Etheric Planes. But they're at a higher, finer level than the Physical Plane.

HEAVENLY TRAVEL

In time, the earth-centered, self-centered human being will come to realize there are people in the

Somewhere along the line of lifetimes, an individual must find someone who can hook him up with the Voice of God.

physical universe besides those on earth.

There have been reports of flying saucers for years. This is one sign of life beyond earth. There are many different life-forms. Some of the people who come from another place to earth must use the lower vehicles of travel—spaceships. Higher spiritual beings come here by higher means, such as astral travel or mind travel. That's another way to get around, for those who have the ability.

In Eckankar, we teach Soul Travel. This is one of the aspects of the teachings of the Holy Spirit. Soul Travel simply means the ability to travel as Soul.

It's different than astral travel, which just occurs on the Astral Plane or below that level, on the Physical Plane. There's also causal travel and mental travel, or mind travel. Usually people who are able to do mind travel do it on the Mental Plane. This is where higher math such as calculus, high forms of architecture, and the like are developed by creative people here on earth.

Once people are able to do higher forms of travel, they don't want to waste it flitting around earth. Astral travel does the job if a car, plane, train, or bus won't.

TEACHINGS OF LOVE

"James" grew up in the South. His family belonged to a very rigid Baptist denomination. Although I call it "very rigid," I say this without any sort of criticism. Every group will have its more understanding people as well as its very rigid people. That's because people who gather under the banner of an organization are still individuals. They're at all levels of consciousness, of awareness, and they gravitate to where they're most comfortable.

In Eckankar, we teach Soul Travel. Soul Travel simply means the ability to travel as Soul.

James grew up in this family because he had a lot to learn. The only contact he had with Eckankar was when he was a small boy in the late sixties or early seventies. One of his uncles was an ECKist, and his father had no use for that man because he mistreated his family.

This is not the sort of person we are proud to call an ECKist, any more than Baptists would say about such people of theirs, "This is one of ours here. Put him in the spotlight." There are certain people who, because of how they treat others, do not belong on a pedestal. They treat others poorly.

People are people. Instead of judging someone by his religion, judge him by his behavior. Judge him not by his thoughts, but by his behavior.

It used to be in Eckankar that some people would come to me—before they learned better—and say, "I had a dream about so-and-so. They were invading my space. Do something."

I would just say, "What has that person done to you out here? Nothing? Don't even see him? He lives hundreds of miles away?" Then handle it where the problem occurred. Go to the inner planes. Work it out there.

I'm not an easy shoulder to cry on if there's no reason. But if there's a reason, I have a soft shoulder.

So when James asked his father, who had very limited exposure to Eckankar except for the brother-in-law, "What is Eckankar?" his father said, "It's Soul Travel and reincarnation." End of discussion.

Eckankar is a lot more than that. The teachings of ECK, as of any true religion, are about love—God's love for Soul.

The teachings of ECK, as of any true religion, are about love— God's love for Soul.

PEOPLE OF POWER, PEOPLE OF LOVE

All the good religions teach God's love for Soul. But it boils down to how does any individual within that religion act? Does the person act from power or from love?

You see, power's got a whole bunch of little tricks in the bag. Like controlling others. People with a mind-set of power like to control others. They like to have fame. They like people to notice them. They like to be rich because it sets them apart from the rest. They like to carry their charity out in public—using other people's money, of course. They feel it makes them more of a real human being, somebody who feels the pain of others. It's just a self-serving lie. It doesn't fool everybody, although it may fool most people. So those are the people of power.

Then there are the people with love. They act with kindness and charity to all. They act with diplomacy, if possible, but they will also defend their own.

People of love are not simply doves. They are birds of the air like, for example, eagles and hawks. They are well-balanced spiritual beings.

People of love are not simply doves. They are birds of the air like, for example, eagles and hawks. It depends upon what the situation calls for. In other words, they are well-balanced spiritual beings.

GOD IS EVERYWHERE

In time, James went to Sunday school. He had this urge to study the Bible. Years later, he admitted it was for power—if he understood everything in these scriptures, maybe it would give him a key, an edge. For what? Perhaps salvation. Perhaps to lead a better life. Maybe to be a little bit more holy than someone else he knew.

Three times a week, he went to church with his

family. When I was growing up, we also went to church a lot, sometimes twice a week, especially during Lent or Advent, as well as for a wedding or a funeral. But James went three times a week. And he studied the Bible because he loved the Bible.

One day in Sunday-school class, the teacher was making a point. He said, "Hell is the eternal separation from God." And James started thinking. (He shouldn't have been thinking. He was in Sunday school.)

"If God is omnipresent, and hell is a literal place, wouldn't God be there too?" James asked.

The teacher couldn't handle that directly. So he pointed out the window to a tree and said to the boy, "Do you think God is in that tree too?"

James said, "If God is omnipresent, then yes, God is in the tree."

This frustrated the teacher immensely. He looked at James and said, "Then is God in your chair?"

The boy said, "If God is omnipresent, well, then God is in my chair too."

The teacher became very upset. "This is silly," he said. "Let's get on with the lesson."

James had just been put down in class. And his ego was like a control person's, a power person's. So he went to the Bible, the final authority, and studied the topic of the omnipresence of God. He looked everywhere in the index, and before the next Sunday service, he finally found a mention in Psalms 139, verses 7 and 8. "Whither shall I go from thy spirit? or whither shall I flee from thy presence? If I ascend up into heaven, thou art there: if I make my bed in hell, behold, thou art there."

The next Sunday before services, James found the Sunday-school teacher and told him about

The teacher said, "Then is God in your chair?" The boy said, "If God is omnipresent, well, then God is in my chair too."

Psalm 139, verses 7 and 8. "What do you think?" he said.

The Sunday-school teacher said, "I'll have to look at this, and I'll get back to you."

Well, he never had a chance. James never went back to church or Sunday school, from what I can tell.

ASPECTS OF SERVICE

Years went on. The boy grew into a man, and all the time the teachings of ECK were always at arm's length from him. He knew of them. He had run into another ECKist at the convenience store where he worked. But the ECKist had a hard time with one of the principles of salesmanship that was required by the store. It was a tactic of trying to sell a customer more, lead him on to another sale.

For example, a customer in a clothing store might buy a suit and a shirt. A salesperson might say, "You'll need two shirts because what if one is in the wash?" Then the customer would buy more.

The ECKist had trouble with this. He felt it was controlling people.

This is the same problem I had in sales. I couldn't do it, because I hadn't learned the right way to do it. This does not mean that any ECKist who is in sales is suddenly to give up sales and go straight. There's a way to do this, and that is to serve the customer. A good salesperson will be looking for ways to serve the customer.

A good salesperson will be looking for ways to serve the customer.

In serving the customer's need for another shirt, perhaps the customer will be very satisfied with his purchase. "I'm going to work today," he'll say. "I've got this nice suit, nice shirt." Then the clerk will say, "And have you any ties to go with those shirts?" "Well, no." "Well, let me show you my wares."

There is a way to do things. So often, it's not what you're doing so much as how you're doing it, how you approach it in your heart. Are you trying to help someone? Are you trying to serve someone else or yourself?

So many of the organizations in our societies call themselves service organizations but are really "serve-us" organizations. The company is serving itself. But there are some companies that are more like "serve-you" organizations, and those are the ones you want to go to.

We try to do that in Eckankar. We try to serve you. Of course, there are times when either I or another person in Eckankar might come up short of your expectations. But maybe your expectations are not grounded to earth; maybe they are unrealistic. Or sometimes we can't fulfill your expectations because of some oversight, resource limitation, or misunderstanding. This is where charity and goodwill come in. Charity or goodwill is love, of a general nature, for all.

So often, it's not what you're doing so much as how you're doing it, how you approach it in your heart.

A LIFE-CHANGING EXPERIENCE

James grew up, and the teachings of ECK were always close at hand.

For most of his growing-up years, his parents had him enrolled in a very religious school that had no love at all. Fortunately, for his last two years of high school they switched him to another school where there was love. And when he was a senior in high school, when love had started to enter into the teachings that were available to him, he had an out-of-body experience. But James was not prepared for it.

It used to be that when people had an out-of-body

or near-death experience it was kept quiet. Talking about it would subject that person and his family to ridicule. But with the advent of television, people have become very comfortable with the subject of near-death experiences and going out of the body. They have become comfortable knowing about such things, but they don't know the experience itself. There's a world of difference.

For instance, movies sometimes show war at its most gruesome. But war veterans say, "War movies are really gory, but they don't capture the smells."

Experiences out of the body are of a higher sort. The best TV graphics may show a beautiful scenario where a being in white clothing comes walking out of the light. That's fine. But many perceptions one has during an out-of-body experience do not come through on the TV screen. And so it was for James. His experience brought him to ECK.

LISTENING TO SPIRIT

I've become very sensitive and respectful of the Holy Spirit and Its signs and signals. When It speaks in any area at all, I listen.

I've become very sensitive and respectful of the Holy Spirit and Its signs and signals, in regard to my spiritual direction as well as my health. When It speaks in any area at all, I listen.

In the same way, as we drove over here this morning, we had to listen and be very alert in figuring out new, creative ways to do one thing or another.

This is how life is. A problem comes up. Instead of saying, "It's not going according to plan," then becoming angry, we back off and ask, "What is there to learn here?"

People who become angry or have a problem with anger generally have an expectation of what others should do or how things should go. They have very strong expectations. In other words you're speaking of a mind that is very contained, very crystallized. When the unexpected happens, it throws all these little plans, like bits of paper, into the wind. The person becomes very upset, simply because he cannot flow with life. He cannot go with the direction of the Holy Spirit.

Soul in the high state is always having to think things out. A creative person thinks on his feet.

Soul in the high state is always having to think things out.

ECK European Seminar, The Hague, Netherlands, Saturday, July 29, 2000

The most incredible stream of love flowed from the horse to her. Mary realized this was the blessing of the Holy Spirit bringing comfort to her.

3

THE SECRET PATH TO GOD

*W*henever I run into something in the health field that's worth mentioning, I like to tell you about it. This is for those of you who are having health problems and have looked just about everywhere and need another way of doing things.

The book is *Energy Medicine*, by Donna Eden. I heard about it from an ECK initiate who has problems with electricity and multiple chemical sensitivities. The book came highly recommended by her because she found the information helpful.

You may find it helpful too. It shows different ways of using energy to strengthen the body's organs, chakras, and other things. It has a very good section on muscle testing—applied kinesiology. For those of you who do your own muscle testing, you'll find that it's another second opinion.

You may find the book Energy Medicine, by Donna Eden, helpful too.

HEALTH TIP ON HELPING YOURSELF

I've worked with health practitioners who have been very good at muscle testing. But sometimes when we go home, we eat something, and there will be a conflict with one of the remedies that the doctor gave us. It's something that the doctor's muscle testing did not or could not foresee.

The ECK teachings help you help yourself in life, in all areas. Because the spiritual life takes in everything.

But if you learn how to test yourself, you can test certain vitamins, remedies, and foods, and help yourself.

This is the whole point about the ECK teachings: to help you help yourself in life, in all areas. Because the spiritual life takes in everything, and this includes health.

COMING BACK TO THE BASICS

A couple of weeks ago I was reading an article in the *Wall Street Journal* about the concern of some mainline churches about their identity. Back in the 1960s, churches began to lose members. This was the new revolution, a new age. People just weren't going to church. The different church bodies then softened their approach to what and who they were.

And so arose the ecumenical movement, where churches of different faiths would basically put their arm around other religions and say, We are all one. This worked for a while.

By the 1990s, church leaders found that something had gone wrong. They did have more members, but they weren't the same sort of members they used to have. There was a difference. It took awhile for anyone to put their finger on the problem. And now just within the last few years, the church leaders figured out what had gone wrong.

When they went into the ecumenical movement, relaxed their standards and took up social missions, many of the new people they gained became members because of these social pursuits.

Some of the people in these churches, if asked, What makes your religion unique? honestly don't

know. They can't say. The most they can say is, Well
it's a religion.

Today, the church leaders are coming back to the
basics. They're teaching their doctrines. They're teaching about their founder, the founding, and the battles
that occurred to make their religion what it is today.
A whole new reeducation process is taking place in
the mainline churches.

Membership in the United Methodist Church
during those twenty years dropped 10 percent. The
Presbyterian Church (USA) dropped 22 percent. The
Evangelical Lutheran Church in America, since the
merger of three different branches in 1988, had no
growth at all. The Episcopal Church was down 23
percent.

There was great concern among the church leaders. They said, We're not fulfilling the mission of our
religion. The gains they had made at first were seem-
ingly significant. Later they realized they had gained
people who did not know what that religion was
about. In fact, children were being taught things not
in accord with church doctrine. During these last
twenty years, some churches had allowed books into
their Sunday schools that were not written by and
for their own people.

For this reason, we always ask the teachers of
ECK classes to use ECK books. Mainline religions,
which have done a lot of exploratory work in another
direction, say that coming back to basics is a wise
course.

*All religions are
from God.*

I mention this because all religions are from God.
Each religion serves a certain segment of consciousness.

All consciousness that exists is of God. When
people are following a path that allows others free-

dom and a choice to believe as they wish, this is a good path. This is a good path if it helps people in the principles of self-responsibility.

ECONOMY AND RELIGION

Recently, I read the viewpoint of someone who studies the stock markets very carefully. He has for nearly thirty years. And he's noticed a correlation between economic good times and growth or shrinkage of church membership.

He says that when people value paper currency—and everything that comes with it—very highly, their interest is almost completely in material things. Their interest in spiritual things fades. When the bank account is full, people feel invincible. But when the market sags and things go a little bit wrong, when there's a correction, people suddenly feel an economic vulnerability.

When the bank account is full, people feel invincible. But when the market sags people then often turn back to religion.

This man observed that people then often turn back to the basics of life—food, shelter, clothing. And religion.

In the United States, the stock market has been going up. It's been a bull market all through the 1980s and 1990s. And membership in the churches has fallen.

It may have fallen partly for the reason that the church leaders suspect—that they had watered down their teachings in the interest of gaining more members. But when they did that, they were reacting to people feeling money flowing throughout the economy again. As the money flows, people's need for the spiritual things of life diminishes.

In the late 1980s, the Japanese economy was flying high, everything was great. Everything the Japanese did with money was high wisdom itself. And then the

Japanese yen crashed. No one expected that. It was a complete surprise—to the general public, anyway. The government then printed money, so there was money. But people had been burned. Once they got their hands on money again, they stuffed it into their bedrolls, and they wouldn't spend it. Money stopped flowing.

It's well over twelve years later, and people are still feeling the pain from when their life savings were very much reduced. They're very cautious of spending money.

They said it couldn't happen in Japan. Everybody thinks it can't happen in other places. Yet history repeats itself. Or, as Mark Twain says, it doesn't repeat itself, but it rhymes. That's why people don't recognize it when it comes again.

A Traveler at the Pearly Gates

Someone sent me five of the most-often-asked questions about life. They are these: What happens when I die? What is the meaning and purpose of life? Have I lived before? How can I find help with life's challenges? Are heaven and hell real places?

Are heaven and hell real places?

Walt, from Hawaii, sent me a story awhile ago. A man had come to the end of his life. He found himself in the other worlds. He was walking along a road. Alongside him was his trusted, loyal companion, his dog, who had passed on years before. So the man's walking along and says to himself, "I must have passed on too."

They walked a long while, until on one side of the road they found this beautiful white wall. It seemed

Are heaven and hell real places?

to be made of the finest marble. The road led up a long hill, and this wall ran along beside it.

The man and his dog walked up the hill, came to the gates, and looked at them. They were of mother-of-pearl—beautiful. And the street leading up to the gate was of pure gold.

A man seated near the gates said, "This is heaven. But I'm sorry, pets are not allowed."

There was a man seated near the gates, at a table off to one side. The traveler asked him, "Where am I?"

The man said, "This is heaven."

"Boy, that's good," the traveler said. "Say, my dog and I have come a long way, and we're very thirsty. Do you suppose we could have a drink of water?"

The man said, "If you come in, I'll bring you some ice water. But I'm sorry, pets are not allowed."

The man's thinking to himself, *What a raw deal. Here's my dog, faithful, loyal all those years. Am I just going to turn my back on my dog and leave him out here?* So the man sadly turned his back on the pearly gates and the golden street, and he continued down the road.

After awhile he came to a dirt road. He followed it, and it came to what looked like the entrance to a farm. There was a gate in front, but it seemed as if it had never been shut. There were no fences alongside. Off to one side, there was a man leaning against a tree, reading a book.

The traveler called out to the man. "Where am I?"

"This is heaven," the man said.

"Well," the traveler said, "this is confusing. I just stopped up the road at the pearly gates, and the guy at the desk said that was heaven."

The man leaning against the tree said, "Nope, that's hell."

The traveler said, "We've traveled a long way. Do you suppose I could get some water?"

The man said, "Sure. There's a pump right over there."

It didn't show from the entrance, but off to one side there was an old-fashioned pump—the kind where you pour a little water in to get the thing working, then you pump, and water comes out.

"By the way," the traveler said, "my dog is thirsty too. What about my friend here?"

The man said, "There should be a dish right at the base of the pump there somewhere. He's welcome to share with you."

The traveler's thinking, *This is pretty good.* So he said to the man by the gate, "Does it make you kind of mad that up the road they're claiming to be heaven, and you're heaven here?"

The man leaning against the tree said, "No. We're just glad that they screen out the folks who give up their friends for a bit of material goods."

FOLLOWING THE SECRET PATH TO GOD

The initiates of ECK have an open invitation to send a monthly initiate report to me. I'd like to read a letter from a Higher Initiate who states very well who we are and what we stand for. And when I say *we,* I mean we as ECKists. Who we are and what we stand for.

This is about the secret path to God. The letter goes like this:

> Once we have the Second Initiation in ECK, we have it all. Everything has been given at that point. Soul is connected to the returning wave of the Sound Current. We have the presence of

The man leaning against the tree said, "We're just glad they screen out the folks who give up their friends for a bit of material goods."

the Mahanta. We know the HU and the spiritual exercises and disciplines of purification in ECK. That's our path to spiritual liberation in this lifetime.

The Outer Master has led us to the Inner Master. The Mahanta is the captain of Soul's ship. The rest is up to us. If Soul wants to go home to God badly enough, then we will take full advantage of the spiritual powers that we have been given as gifts to us from the Mahanta. We will use our secret word, experiment with the spiritual exercises, practice the joys of spiritual freedom through our disciplines. Thus will we discover the secret path to God that exists within each one of us.

At that point, everything else we do in ECK is service of some kind. We contribute to the culture of ECK through fellowship, study, and Vahana (missionary) works, so that others can find ECK and have the same awesome opportunity. Even simply attending an ECK event is giving service and supporting the ECK culture.

ECK is a mystery school. The journeys and consciousness that come in life and in the spiritual exercises are Soul's pure, golden ecstasy. Everything said in the ECK works is completely true. All the wonders, the joys, the tangible company of the Divine ECK.

The letter goes: "The journeys and consciousness that come in life and in the spiritual exercises are Soul's pure, golden ecstasy."

This is a very good letter. It tells people how to follow the secret path to God and gain spiritual liberation in this lifetime. It's said so very nicely: the why and the what-for of the ECK teachings, what they mean to you.

The mainline religions are trying to redefine who and what they are to the members. You already know that you have it, and you work with it every day. This letter very nicely encapsulates what the ECK teachings are.

COMING TO THE ECK TEACHINGS

The secret path to God follows many little trails before one actually comes to the teachings.

"Phyllis" was a young girl when her mother contracted a very serious illness. The family was made up of nonpracticing Jews, Catholics, and Lutherans. Twenty years later the mother finally passed on.

Two years before her mother's death, Phyllis was in a serious car accident. It threw her out of the body through the Third Eye, the Spiritual Eye. She went to a wonderful place that was somehow very familiar and comfortable.

Phyllis was out of the body. She went to a wonderful place that was very familiar and comfortable.

In this wonderful place, Phyllis was watching a series of small screens with four or five frames to each scene. There were many people in these scenes, in many different scenarios. What she didn't realize until later was that this was the ECK-Vidya, the prophecy of the future—the ancient science of prophecy.

Just as she was saying, "Well, that's very interesting," she came back into this world in a blinding flash.

Phyllis never told anyone about the experience. She tried to find answers in her church. In the last four years she had become a member of the Catholic Church. But she found no answers.

She began studying the writings of Elisabeth Kübler-Ross and near-death experiences. As she studied, she came to an understanding that maybe there was something more to existence than just a single lifetime.

Sometime after her mother died, Phyllis had a dream. This dream led to another out-of-body experience.

In the experience, a man spoke very loudly to her. "Soul does not repeat Itself," he said. Phyllis had no idea what he meant.

But as she was listening, through the next two hours of the experience, the man showed her a history of life on earth from the dinosaurs through to modern times. He showed her pictures and other things. When he had finished, Phyllis said, "I'll never remember this."

"Don't worry," the man said. "You will remember what you need to, and the rest doesn't matter."

SEVEN LESSONS

By this point Phyllis had a sense that there was more to life than a single lifetime. She knew there was something to reincarnation. This was as close as the feeling had come before her inner experience. But now she realized Soul does not repeat Itself, because Soul is eternal. Soul is Soul.

She realized Soul does not repeat Itself, because Soul is eternal. Soul is Soul.

It takes on many different forms throughout Its many lifetimes in the lower worlds, but at the end of each lifetime, Soul sheds that material form. When Soul comes back to get more experiences in the lower worlds, It will take on a new form. And this goes on, lifetime upon lifetime.

When Phyllis was nearly fifty years old, she found the ECK teachings and took the Second Initiation. She likes to write initiate reports. As so many of you have found, it gives you a chance to unburden yourself from the cares and the troubles that have come along to you.

The Second Initiation in ECK is very important.

It's like a plane approaching the sound barrier. Sometimes the ride gets rough, but when this happens you can remember that it's only Soul meeting Itself. It's Soul meeting the imperfections that need to be purified so that It can become a better and more clear channel for the Holy Spirit, the ECK.

Phyllis mentioned she had learned seven lessons up to that point. I would like to list them for you.

1. Her level of consciousness is equal to her level of acceptance.
2. Peace cannot be transmitted unless the other person is ready for it.

Phyllis was a painter in her youth, and she worked with jewelry. But after her first out-of-body experience in the car accident, she took up a whole new life. Gradually, she began counseling, training, and evaluating disabled children. She worked with them for many years. She has traveled all over the world, consulting with many professionals. She has helped so many people and families with disabled children.

In that first out-of-body experience when she saw all these little pictures, she was seeing into the future. She was seeing the people she would one day serve and work with. Now, many years later, she recognized that.

3. What appears negative in the beginning may have a completely positive ending later.
4. She is responsible for what she knows, and must be honest about what she doesn't know.

That's especially important for a counselor.

5. To be loving and give love is more important than being right.

Sometimes we say, "Is it true? Is it necessary? Is it kind?" Use those three criteria before speaking

What appears negative in the beginning may have a completely positive ending later.

in practically any situation.

    6. One does not struggle to convince others, but rather oneself.

    7. To listen quietly is the best teacher.

Now, these were the seven lessons she had learned so far after being in Eckankar for just a few years.

A HORSE'S GIFT TO MARY

"Mary" is from Trinidad. She's a longtime ECKist, grateful for the ECK teachings and the presence of the Mahanta, the Inner Master.

A couple of years ago, it seemed as if her life went to hell in a handbasket. Her marriage broke up; her only child, her son, went on drugs; and at the same time it looked as if the rest of her family had abandoned her.

On the drive to work one day, tears were coming down Mary's cheeks so heavily she decided to pull to the side of the road and cry.

On the drive to work one day, tears were coming down Mary's cheeks so heavily that she decided to pull to the side of the road and cry.

She happened to pull up by a field where young horses were grazing some distance away. She enjoyed their beauty, and as she cried, one of the horses put up his head and came galloping toward her. He came right up to the fence right by the car, and stopped. Then the horse brought up his head and looked Mary directly in the eye.

The most incredible stream of love flowed from the horse to her. And Mary realized this was the blessing of the Holy Spirit bringing comfort to her.

She hadn't been afraid at the approach of this galloping horse. She just was filled with love.

When Mary understood that a gift of love had been passed to her, the horse shook its head, snorted, and trotted back to the rest of the herd.

Animals had often been the means by which the love of the divine power came through to her. So she recognized this, too, as a blessing from the Holy Spirit. It was a gift from the Mahanta. And she realized that there is no need to speak about love with people, animals, or plants. Just be love. If you are love, the person or thing you love will know.

Some people will think this is stretching it a little bit—that God's love would come through an animal. But those of you who are pet owners—who have dogs and cats and birds—you know that God's love does indeed come through pets. But it also comes through other things.

ANTS ON THE MOVE FOR LOVE

A couple in Finland had a nice home. On the property were over three thousand currant bushes. Every day a colony of ants would march out to the bushes. The couple welcomed these ants going out there because the ants kept the vermin away; the vermin didn't want all these little ants crawling all over and biting them.

The ants and the couple got along fine—except for one problem. In a direct line between the ants' nest and the currant bushes there happened to be the couple's breakfast table. And the table couldn't be moved.

One day the wife talked to the ants. She said, "Could you please move your nest? I love you, but I don't want to step on you by accident as we're having breakfast."

A couple of days later, she and her husband were sitting at breakfast and they saw the ants carrying their eggs and all their other ant paraphernalia. They

One day the wife talked to the ants. "Could you please move your nest?"

were moving their nest. They moved many yards off to the north where they would no longer disturb the couple at their breakfast table.

The woman realized that her request had gone to the group Soul, the group entity.

There is a group thought-form, perhaps like the Borg collective in the *Star Trek* series. It's a group entity, and it runs all the Borg. There's a similar group entity for ants, dogs, cats, birds, and everything else.

The wife had addressed herself to the ant group entity with love. And the ants took her request in the spirit of love and moved together. The group entity had said, "It sounds like a fair request. It's done for the good of all of us. Pack up, move out." So they loaded their Conestoga wagons.

UNIQUENESS OF SOUL

The secret path to God is secret only in that the ECK teachings are custom-fitted for you. Each of you is unique.

As you're on the secret path to God, you will find many of these things to be a normal part of everyday life. Other people will call you crazy if you try to tell them. So don't tell them. When they're ready for this sort of knowledge, they'll come to it on their own. And when they do, they'll have no more luck at telling others.

It's secret only in that the ECK teachings are custom-fitted for you. Each of you is unique. You're it. There is not another one like you anywhere.

Tomorrow you will be slightly different from the person you are today. Your experiences between now and tomorrow will make you slightly different. And between lifetimes the change is even more significant.

But you are Soul. You are the eternal part of the essence of who you are.

This is the reason we do not say, I have a soul. We say, I am Soul; I have a body. This is one of those little secrets, and if you happen to mention it within hearing of someone else, he'll say, What sort of a strange twist are they doing on this?

The fact is you're giving it straight. They have the cords twisted. They'll have to unscramble those themselves in time. And life shall teach them how.

That's the way of it. That's how we learn.

"WHAT ARE YOU SINGING?"

Sharmaine, from Temple Services at Eckankar, sent me a number of stories that people had told her about their experiences with the ECK teachings on the secret path to God.

One of the stories was about "Bernard." He was working in a place with very loud machinery. He was running one such machine, and the sound became very wearing.

To blend it and harmonize it with himself, Bernard decided to sing *HU*, the sacred name for God, in tune with the machine. Some machines lend themselves very well to singing *HU*. HU seems to blend right in and become part of it.

As Bernard sang *HU*, a supervisor came up to him. "You're singing," the supervisor said.

Bernard said, "Yes."

"What are you singing?"

Bernard told him about HU, this love song to God. The man said, "Tell me more about it." Bernard told him more, then he said, "Listen, tomorrow I can bring you a brochure in Spanish about HU, and I'll bring you a book in English." The supervisor was Hispanic.

The next day, Bernard brought in the Spanish brochure and the English book. The man took the

To blend the machinery sound and harmonize it with himself, Bernard decided to sing HU, the sacred name for God.

brochure, looked at it, and said, "English book, no. Bring me Spanish book." Bernard had brought Paul Twitchell's *Stranger by the River*. But he said, "All right."

That evening he got a Spanish version of *Stranger by the River* to take in to work.

By the next morning, the supervisor had read the brochure, and he told Bernard, "I sang *HU*. I am dreaming. I am dreaming!" Because he hadn't been able to dream before that. Then Bernard gave the Spanish *Stranger by the River* to his supervisor, and the man said, "Thank you very much."

The following morning he came over to Bernard and said, "Very good book." For several mornings after that, each day he'd say, "Very good book."

Bernard found that even at work, even in a place where the machines run so loudly that it was sometimes hard to think, he was still able to tell others about the teachings of ECK and HU.

CLOSER TO THE MAHANTA

Susan and Rich are pets in the home of three cats. The cats run the household, for the most part. Susan and Rich give the cats love and help out where they can, trying not to get underfoot. They arrange themselves around the cats, and that's how things are in that household.

One morning at four o'clock, Susan woke from a deep sleep to purring in her ear. Simon, the boy cat, was very politely trying to wake her up. He wasn't in his spot. So Susan looked over at his spot, close to her chest, and there was his sister Bella.

Simon had apparently woken up and decided to go get a midnight snack. And while he was at the food dish in the kitchen, Bella saw that his place was empty. Brothers and sisters being what they are, Bella took Simon's place right next to Mom.

When Simon came back, he said, "You're in my spot! Get over, move!"

Of course, Bella just pretended to sleep. Paid no attention to him.

Simon's a very polite cat. He couldn't figure out quite what to do. He decided he'd go right up to Mom's ear and purr. Then if Mom woke up, just by chance, she would make things right.

Mom woke up, saw what the situation was, and did something entirely different. She moved over further in bed and brought Simon in close.

Simon was in heaven. This was the way it was supposed to be. He was back in his spot in Mom's arms, and Bella was over there somewhere. Fair is fair.

Very soon, Simon was sleeping and snoring, all contented. Husband and Bella were asleep. Their third cat was also asleep. But Susan was lying awake. At four o'clock.

"Mahanta, what's going on here?" she said.

The Inner Master, the Mahanta, sent this understanding to her. She realized that the ECK, the Holy Spirit, sometimes through the agent of the Mahanta, moves the individual out of his spot. When the individual comes back and says, "I can't get back to my spot," the Master says, "Not to worry. I've moved over for you. Come, be as close, and closer than ever." Then everything's OK.

This is the way it works in ECK too. Change is always coming to cause people discomfort. When change comes, people say, "Oh, no. Let's have it the way it used to be in the past—yesterday, five minutes ago—for heaven's sake, please."

The Master says, "Not to worry. I've moved over for you. Come, be as close, and closer than ever."

But no, it's time to move on spiritually.

In ECK you'll find, as a Second Initiate and up, that life will have you meet yourself. Because that's the only way you can walk forward on the secret path to God. So some of us meet ourselves and we wonder, *Could I really be responsible for all these effects going on now? Could I really have done anything to deserve this?*

Rest easy. Yes. You are meeting yourself. You might as well do it now, or do it over.

SPIRITUAL EXERCISE FOR THE ECK-VIDYA

I haven't given a spiritual exercise at these talks in a while. The reason is that there are a great number of them now. You can experiment with them. Custom fit them with the help of the Inner Master, the counterpart to myself as the outer teacher. Work with the spiritual exercises. Modify them.

The ECK-Vidya, the ancient science of prophecy, looks at the present and the future. It gives a good look at the forces that are behind the events that affect you today.

Sometimes you'll grope around a bit before you come upon one that feels right, is right. The test of the pudding is in the eating. Does the spiritual exercise work? Are you noticing more clarity in your inner experiences?

I'd like to give a spiritual exercise for the ECK-Vidya. It's simple. It's in three parts. You can do this exercise in addition to the regular spiritual exercise you're doing, or instead of it. Do this exercise for a couple of nights if you want to put attention on the ECK-Vidya.

A brief explanation of the ECK-Vidya: it's the ancient science of prophecy. Basically, it looks at the present and the future. It gives a good look at the forces that are behind the events that affect you today. It can also, when you're ready—and this is a big "when you're ready"—show you certain parts of the future toward which you are moving.

First sing the word *Shariyat* once slowly. This stands for the Shariyat-Ki-Sugmad, the holy bible of ECK. Two volumes are in print out here in the physical world. Just sing *Shah-ree-aht*. Then sing *HU*. Sing that word one time. HU-U-U-U. For the third part, sing *ECK-Vidya*. *Ehk-vee-dyah*. Like so. Then go to sleep as usual.

I recommend you keep a dream log or a dream journal. And write down important memories.

If you like you may send experiences—ones that are significant for you—in an initiate report. Write them down, at least for yourself, even if you don't mail the initiate report. But I do like to keep in touch with you out here too. So occasionally, once every few months or once or twice a year, put together the best of the best and say, "This is what happened." This is what you've learned on your own secret path to God.

You've got to walk the secret path to God yourself. No one else can do it for you.

There're so many things that cannot be said, and for that reason this is the ECK mystery school. It's the secret path to God. You've got to walk that path yourself. No one else can do it for you.

ECK Worldwide Seminar, Minneapolis, Minnesota, Saturday, October 28, 2000

Divine love sent a message through the squirrel to teach
Sarah this Law of Balance, this Law of Karma.

4
THE LANGUAGE
OF LOVE

ivine love is the thing that makes this world
go around. It's the stuff of which creation
is made.

Sometimes when things go so fast or we
have other needs, we like to take a rest stop. Joan,
my wife, and I were out grocery shopping a couple
of weeks ago. On the way home, after many errands
and with still more errands to go, I decided I needed
a rest stop. As soon as you get some gray hair, you
notice that it's a good idea to know where all the
restrooms are, just in case. The height of wisdom is
to use a restroom when you come to it, no matter how
often that is.

We came to a little shopping center with a nice
coffee shop. People come in because there are so many
different kinds of coffee and the restrooms are clean.
We've been there before.

We walked in and passed the little tables where
people were sitting, drinking tea and having a good
time talking with their friends. Off to the side of the
room were the restrooms—one for the men, one for the
women.

The men's restroom was open, but someone was

*Divine love is
the stuff of
which creation
is made.*

in the women's room.

We were in a hurry. I told Joan, "Nobody's looking; come in this one if you want to." She said, "OK." We're married, we're practical. Time is time.

As we were ready to come out, somebody was trying the doorknob.

I said to Joan, "This should be interesting."

I'm very neat about electricity and things like this. So as I was leaving the room, I turned off the light. I left the restroom first. A big man about half a head taller than me was standing there.

He gave me a lazy nod when I said hello, and then his head snapped back when Joan came walking out right behind me from this dark room. In high school, some of my classmates would do fake double takes. This one was genuine. The man's head went back in a real snap. He stood there, his jaw hanging down.

In a very gracious way I said, "She's my guest."

The poor man didn't miss a beat. He said, "I can see that."

Joan smiled sweetly at him.

Then nature called, and he had business to do, and we had more errands to run.

We walked back to the parking lot. We wanted to get out of there as quickly as possible. As we were getting in the car, I said, "This was a most interesting rest stop."

"For him too," Joan said.

Sometimes as vehicles for the ECK, the Holy Spirit, things that we do shake up old thought forms in people. I wouldn't do a thing like that on purpose, because sometime that man's going to say, "So that's who it was—and do you know what he was doing?"

> I said to Joan, "This should be interesting."

SHAKING UP OLD THOUGHT FORMS

In Latin class way back in high school, our professor taught us a saying that I've remembered. It was *necessitas non habet legem*. It means "necessity has no laws."

In ECK this is certainly true. The Holy Spirit will juggle rules and use us as vehicles to make a change in other people's consciousness. Of course, we ourselves are not out to do such a thing. We look for peace, quiet, and harmony, and we do not get that if we upset the people around us. So we take great care not to do that.

A SPEEDIER PATH TO GOD

I got a letter from a man who is married to a Russian woman. He doesn't speak Russian, but in his letter to me he talked about Easter time. It is one of the most important Russian holidays.

It begins like this: in the morning, the couple in a family kiss each other on each cheek, and then once lightly on the lips with great tenderness. They make a vow to say or do nothing negative all day long. And this then becomes a very special day in the life of the Russian people.

It occurred to him that if anyone ever asked, How is Eckankar a speedier path to God than another religion? he could say ECKists practice daily what most others practice weekly, and ECKists practice weekly what most others practice yearly.

How is Eckankar a speedier path to God? ECKists practice daily what most others practice weekly.

This is not to set ourselves above others. Heaven knows we have our own problems in Eckankar. Every organization has its shining lights—probably most of the membership. But there are always a few; these are the ones that other people in the church wish would go to some other religion and get their spiritual food there. But they seldom go. This is part of living, this is part of life.

The language of love. The Russian ceremony is certainly a language of love—first in the couple's tenderness, then in saying everything positive and thinking positive for the entire day. This is a pact with God.

The Russian ceremony is certainly a language of love in saying everything positive and thinking positive for the entire day.

This is saying, For one day in this year at least, I'm going to try to live according to the Law of Love. Because we know that God is love.

Earth is a place to learn spiritual lessons. *Learning lessons* implies that all lessons are not yet learned. Some lessons are still there to be learned.

LESSON FROM A SQUIRREL

"Sarah" has a garden in a community garden plot. People come together, and each gets a gardening box that's five by eight feet. In hers, Sarah plants lettuce, kale, broccoli, cucumbers, carrots, and everything else that she can think of. She just loads that box up. It's a small garden, but Sarah plants something in every square inch.

Sarah soon became acquainted with the squirrels. One of them was a little wreck of a squirrel—very much like one I used to know. Sarah called this squirrel Scruffy.

Scruffy had a patch of fur missing from his head and another from his back, and his tail was stripped as if it had been singed by a flame. There was also something wrong with his foot; perhaps he had a clubfoot.

But Scruffy was tough, and he had the marks to prove it.

It is that way with squirrels. They've got these

lovely fur coats, but they've got to be real adventurers
to go out there and be the head of the pack. It's going
to cost them in looks. They're very particular about
how they look in their fur coats.

Sarah knew the squirrels were going to eat her
vegetables. So she made a silent agreement with
them. She said, "If I bring you snacks every day, you
leave my garden alone."

Squirrels are very intelligent beings, and apparently they understood. Every day she would come
with a brown bag from the grocery store, and the
squirrels would gather around—Scruffy too. They
stood there, begging, very cute.

Scruffy was the cutest little beggar. He'd perform
a little act for her, like an entertainer: he'd run around
in circles and do all kinds of little tricks, and then
he'd go into his classic pose. He'd put one hand over
his heart and hold the other out as if to say, From
your heart, give me what you have. So Sarah would
reach into her bag and feed him nuts or peanuts.

This went on day after day. There was peace in
the garden. Peace forevermore.

Right next to Sarah's little garden box was another one which belonged to some children. Their
teachers brought them to the garden occasionally,
and the children would plant what they wanted. But
the children had no real interest in the garden because it took work and because things happen that
they didn't understand. Besides, plants grow so slowly;
it gets tiring waiting for them to come up.

Sarah took it upon herself to water the children's
garden plot, and it came along very nicely despite the
children's neglect.

One day Sarah noticed there was a little bare spot
in a far corner of her garden box. She noticed some

Sarah made a silent agreement with the squirrels. "If I bring you snacks every day, you leave my garden alone."

64   THE ROAD TO SPIRITUAL FREEDOM

nice collard greens in the children's box. *I'm owed something for watering their garden; otherwise there would be nothing,* she told herself. So she went to the children's garden and very carefully took out three little slips of collard greens.

The children would never miss three little slips of collard greens she reasoned.

The children would never miss them, she reasoned. If it weren't for her, their whole garden would be all brown.

Very carefully she planted the collards in her garden. They filled in that little space that she had neglected to jam full of other produce.

Time went on. Soon her cucumbers were growing. One day she saw three little cucumbers on the vine. *Pretty soon now,* she thought, *I'm going to have a nice, fresh garden salad. I'm going to invite a friend over, and we'll share it.*

Sarah came back a couple of days later. The cucumbers were almost ready; they were just about perfect.

She called her friend. "Come over to the garden plot," she said. "I want to show you my cucumbers. Then we'll pick up some of our other food from the garden. We'll go home and have a salad."

They got to her plot, and the cucumber plant had not one cucumber on it. They were all gone.

Sarah was upset. She walked around to the other gardeners and asked, "Why did you take my cucumbers?"

They all denied having any knowledge of her cucumbers.

After Sarah had made the rounds of the other gardeners, she was still hot under the collar. Scruffy came up to greet her, the same as always. He stood there, then he went into his little act. He did all his tricks, running around, chasing his tail. Then he went into his classic beggar's pose.

"Scruffy, what do you know about these cucumbers?" she said, glaring at him.

Scruffy held his pose for a few seconds, and then under that withering gaze he melted. He finally said to himself, *I guess I'd better confess.* He ran over to the children's plot, right to the spot where Sarah had taken the three shoots of collard greens. He stood there chattering.

And what did Sarah find? Two of her half-eaten cucumbers were in the exact same spot where she had taken the children's collard greens. But one was missing. So she looked at Scruffy, and Scruffy looked at her.

He may have shrugged, then he ran off to Sarah's garden plot, right into the far corner, back where it was hard to see. He stood there. Sarah and her friend came to look, and there was the third cucumber, half-eaten.

LOVE AND RESPECT YOUR NEIGHBOR

At this point, Sarah began to laugh because she could see the divine justice in this. She had no reason to take someone else's property even though she had taken care of the garden.

Sarah began to laugh because she could see the divine justice in this.

This was God's loving way of telling her in a gentle manner, "Sarah, you've got to respect other people's property or you stand to lose your own."

Richard Maybury is an economist and a political analyst. He studied all the different religions and the ethics systems, and he came to the conclusion that there are two basic laws. If people would follow these two basic laws, this would be a much better world. The two laws are: Do all that you have agreed to do, and do not encroach on other persons or their property. Sarah remembered the second of Maybury's two laws. That's the one that Sarah broke.

Sarah realized she had encroached upon the property of the children. And divine love sent a message to her through the squirrel, Scruffy, to teach her this Law of Balance, this Law of Karma. It's what the Bible refers to when it says "Whatsoever a man soweth, that shall he also reap."

By the way, Sarah said, "Scruffy had earned his peanuts."

The lesson from Scruffy was to learn to love and respect our neighbor as much as our self.

The lesson from Scruffy was to learn to love and respect our neighbor as much as our self.

I find it interesting today that in the political world, people looking for more power are so often using the politics of class envy—setting one class against another. Usually it comes out in soaking the rich, taxing the rich as one class. It doesn't bring people together if you say and do this sort of thing. It breaks them apart.

What I find interesting is that so many of the people in Congress who always say, "Tax the rich" are multimillionaires. But they have tax attorneys who can figure out how to make the best use of the laws that they create to befuddle the rest of the taxpayers. And when the rest of the people catch up to it, then there's a tax reform.

Often the motives of such people are not pure. This sort of thinking is a spiritual fallacy. This is why I'm bringing it up.

THE COMMODITY TRADER'S CRITIC

Over the years, a certain commodity trader had become very wealthy. It had cost him five nervous breakdowns.

Once he was talking to a younger man who had

been a trader only five or six years. The young man came to the elder and said he thought he was going to just sell financial information. He wasn't going to trade commodities anymore.

The older man asked, "This is because of losses?"

The younger said, "No, I was doing OK, but I've had a nervous breakdown."

The elder man said, "Just one? In my career I've had five."

So you look at the tremendous price that these particular Souls were willing to pay for certain lessons.

Every occupation, from TV technician to firefighter to consultant of any sort to homemaker to school-teacher—all exist for a certain Soul to get a certain experience about the spiritual laws of life. That's what these occupations are about.

Every occupation, from technician to firefighter to consultant to homemaker to teacher—all exist for a certain Soul to get a certain experience about the spiritual laws of life.

An occupation is neither good nor bad in itself. Whether one is a politician or cleric makes no difference. Some people will find a way to abuse their position no matter what profession they're in. On the other hand, in every profession there are the shining lights. It even holds true in religions. There are always the black sheep, and there are always the others who are good examples for their fellow creatures.

One day this commodity trader was coming home. He had plenty of wealth, so he had built himself a mansion. As he came home that day, returning from an errand, he was dressed in a T-shirt and blue jeans. He walked up to the front of his home, past a man standing on the sidewalk. The man was looking at the big house with a frown on his face.

This man was one of the townspeople. He did not recognize the owner in his scruffy clothes.

He said, "Nobody should be allowed to have a

place that big. One person doesn't need all that room."

The homeowner said, "I understand there's not just one person in there; there are four."

The critic on the sidewalk said, "Well, it's the same thing. Four people don't need that much room."

The commodity trader said, "What if the people in this home hired four or five people to help maintain the place, and these people were from town? Would that be OK?"

The critic said, "No, that wouldn't be OK."

The commodity trader said, "Well, what if they hired ten or twelve people from town to help maintain the place? Would that be OK?"

The critic said, "Well, yes. In that case, it would be OK."

The homeowner didn't tell him that they were employing between twenty and twenty-five people to help maintain that mansion. It was a huge place.

The owner of the home, the commodity trader, excused himself and continued home. But he went around to the back door because this man on the sidewalk was in a furious mood. The homeowner wasn't going to take a chance. He had learned something in the trading business, so he used caution.

The trader then thought this whole thing over. *What is the fallacy here?* he wondered.

He realized what the critic on the sidewalk was really saying was this: Because you built that home, I can't. And this is the great lie: Soak the rich, tax the rich. It's the great lie. It belies the spiritual powers of Soul.

This is the great lie: Soak the rich, tax the rich. It belies the spiritual powers of Soul.

A World of Abundance

You and I are Soul. As such, we have this spark of creativity within ourselves, which has no limits. In the power of divine creativity, there is no limitation whatsoever.

This world is a world of abundance. It's not to say that there is no need to carefully use the resources of this world and not gum it up, befoul the air and the ground. No, we do have to learn to become good stewards.

But to say that someone has too much of anything in this world of boundless gifts and opportunity— who's to say what's too much?

Those of you who are able to visit the higher worlds of God know that there are places which beggar the largest mansion on earth. Some of the buildings and homes in the other worlds are of such beauty and size and light that anyone who gets there is in awe of the wonders that exist in creation. These things exist. Anything that any human being can create here is a paltry, shabby, thatched-roof shack in comparison to the buildings in heaven.

If you have the ability to go to these other worlds— either in the dream state or through Soul Travel— you can have the experience and learn these realities for yourself.

You'll find that the bounties of God are much greater than the four corners of this little earth. This earth is just a tiny little pebble in God's worlds. It's a surprising thing, sometimes, that God even knows where this pebble is located in Its worlds. It'd be like trying to find a certain grain of sand on the beach.

But that's the language of love. God's love is so great that It created every kind of abundance for

You and I are Soul. As such, we have this spark of creativity within ourselves, which has no limits.

those people who would make an effort to look for it and find it. And you'll often find that people who spew this class-envy rhetoric either want power for themselves or are too lazy to use their creative powers and earn whatever they desire for themselves.

I am never completely disappointed in human nature. That would be hard to do because human nature can always lead you to new horizons of disappointment.

So if you don't expect much from human nature, you won't be disappointed.

But I look past human nature in a person. And when someone does an unkind act or deed, I realize it's because that person at that moment is not working with divine insight.

The language of love is the love God has for us and that we have for each other.

The language of love is the love God has for us and that we have for each other. We try to show this to those we love in some small way that gives this love back to God.

MAKING THE MOST OUT OF LIFE

About fifteen years ago, "Nancy" joined Eckankar. But the big problem was, How was she going to tell her mom? What would her mother think?

Nancy was a rational person. She thought out the situation and decided the best approach would be the direct approach. So she went to her mother and said, "Mom, I've joined Eckankar. It's a spiritual path."

Without a moment's hesitation, her mother said, "I've had Paul Twitchell's books up in the attic since the late 1960s. I kept them hidden from you kids so you wouldn't think your mom was crazy." Paul Twitchell was the modern-day founder of Eckankar.

A year later, the mother finally became a member of Eckankar too. Now Nancy and her mother are Fourth

Initiates. This is a level of advanced spiritual unfoldment. It takes a little while for people to get to.

One day, Nancy's mom asked her, "Am I living the
life of ECK correctly? I'm so happy. I just enjoy life."

Nancy, the very rational one, thought about it for
some time. Based on her observation of so many
people who seem to be unhappy, she said, "What
better goal in life could one have than happiness?"

She said her mother knew how to make the most
out of life.

This is how it should be. Life is a precious gift.
It's like the rain that falls on the good and on the
evil alike. The gift of life, human life, is given to the
good and evil. Making the most of life shows appreciation for the gift.

The language of love.

*Life is a
precious gift.
It's like the rain
that falls on the
good and on
the evil alike.*

GOD IS TRYING TO SPEAK TO ME

"Roy" came to the Temple of ECK for a forum
called Stories from the Heart. In Stories from the
Heart, anyone who has had an experience with the
Holy Spirit, the ECK, may speak about it if he or she
wishes.

Roy is a Mormon, and he's separated from his
wife. She's from another religious faith.

After the group sang *HU*—this is the love song
to God—the leader of the group, Sharmaine, said, "If
any of you have a story that you would like to tell
about an experience with the Light and Sound of
God, please feel free to share it with us. But only if
you feel comfortable doing it."

Roy said, "I don't know if I should say this." Then,
in a very quiet, reserved manner, he told the following story.

When he was about twenty years old, life was

very hard for him. He'd fallen into a state of despondency. His girlfriend loved him very much. One day when he said to her, "I think God is trying to speak to me," his girlfriend said, "Roy, I think you should see a doctor."

Because when people become despondent and then feel God wants to speak to them, it's time—a lot of times—to go see a doctor.

His girlfriend drove him to the hospital, and he saw a doctor. But inside, Roy still had this feeling of a lack of love.

Life went on. But he kept having this nudge, this intuition, that God was still trying to give him a message.

Odd things began to happen. One night he was out for a walk. Ahead of him was a house with the porch light on. As he approached this house, the light began to blink. When he walked past, he looked back, and it stopped blinking. He turned around and walked down the sidewalk toward the house, and the light started to blink again.

At first he wondered if it was some very clever, long-range security light. Maybe every time someone approached, the light blinked. Such a thing was possible, but it would have been working at an extreme range.

He was out walking, very lonely. He had this feeling God loved him, but he could not reach God's love. What could he do?

The next night he was out walking again, and he was very lonely. He had this feeling that God loved him, but he felt hollow; he could not reach God's love. What could he do?

As he walked, Roy looked up at the sky and saw the stars. They were so beautiful. One seemed to shine more brightly than the others. As Roy watched this star, it became bigger and bigger. And it came toward him, faster and faster. *Boy, this is very odd,* he thought.

The next thing he knew, the star exploded. He was inside the star. And a knowingness impressed itself upon him. The knowingness was this: God is light.

Even as Roy was inside the star, he was aware of himself as a unit of some sort, like a drop of light. He was so aware of this envelope around him, protecting him, that he could even tell where its surface had gone.

It was like the cohesion that occurs at the surface of water, the very thing that holds a drop of water together as it falls to the ground. Roy had that cohesion. In a number of different ways over the next hour this same message came through. Roy experienced a variety of variations on this theme. The message was always the same: God is light.

At this point, an ocean of love came down and wrapped itself around him. The envelope of love stayed with him for three days.

An ocean of love came down and wrapped itself around him. The envelope of love stayed with him for three days.

After he told his story, the group leader, Sharmaine, said, "You mentioned in your experience this ocean of love. In Eckankar we believe we are Soul, and what we want to do is go back into the Ocean of Love and Mercy."

Roy became animated. "Me too," he said. "I want to go back, but I don't know how to get there."

One of the other ECKists in the group said, "Well, you've come to the right place, Roy."

This is the whole point of the ECK teachings. It's to help those people who are ready to find God's love in the most direct way. These teachings are to help these people find that love.

As Roy was leaving, he said, "Sometimes I feel so lonely because of this separation from my wife." But then he added, "But maybe it's more than chance that brought me here tonight." He was very new to Eckankar. He'd been in a bookstore and happened to see my autobiography. He bought it, thinking, *Maybe this guy has something that he can tell me—something like my experience of the star.*

Roy had gone to an ECK Worship Service the day before this class at the Temple of ECK. He'd also seen some of the videos of my talks that members of Eckankar are getting aired on local stations around the country. Roy had seen these, and so he was familiar with the ECK teachings. He was familiar with what we stand for.

"Maybe there was a reason for my being here tonight," he said. He had looked in the book and realized that the Temple of ECK was right here in the neighborhood where he lived. That's what made him come to the ECK Worship Service, and his first contact with other ECKists was at the Stories from the Heart forum.

As Roy went out the door, he said, "Even though all human love may fail me, God's love will always be with me, won't it?" The rest of the class members said, "You've got it."

THREE REALIZATIONS

From this experience, Sharmaine had three realizations. From just the fact of Roy having come to this forum, Sharmaine said, "You never know what a heart may hold. But if you listen to others tell of their love for God and of their experiences with the Holy Spirit, their stories will open your heart."

Then she said, "Newcomers will inspire you to reach your highest spiritual goals."

When new people come into Eckankar, they re-

Sharmaine said, "If you listen to others tell of their experiences with the Holy Spirit, their stories will open your heart."

light the fires of love in the rest of the ECK members. By the presence of new people, the lives of the ECKists are enriched. In this way we are a living teaching. We are a living religion.

As the ECKist observed in the story about Russian Easter celebrations I referred to earlier, ECKists live every day what other people practice once a week. That's because the ECK, or Holy Spirit, begins to work very directly with ECKists. It raises their awareness of how the divine laws work, and the ECK does not give an ECKist a lot of room to make mistakes without bringing it to the ECKist's attention.

Like anyone else, an ECKist can ignore this gentle reminder from the Holy Spirit. But most of us, in our spiritual unfoldment, have learned about this. After the first few lessons—where our heads were a little thick—we realized we wanted to learn as quickly as we could. Because the Holy Spirit will get that lesson through the thickest skull. It simply will.

The sooner we learn about God's laws of love, the easier our life is for us. And the quicker we make our way home to God.

The third thing that Sharmaine realized from Roy's visit was that ECKists often ask, "What am I going to do as an ECK member? How do I serve God? What do I do?" They don't know. Some people just can't figure it out. Sharmaine realized there are people out there who want to find their way back home to God, and we, Eckankar, have a whole program to help them get there.

We teach Soul Travel, dream study, and the ECK-Vidya. This is the ancient science of prophecy, one of the methods by which the Holy Spirit gives people insights into their personal universe—not as a consistent thing, because it gets to be too much. We are

The sooner we learn about God's laws of love, the quicker we make our way home to God.

here to learn the lessons of everyday living.

If we've got our heads off in the clouds all the time, listening to this and that, we finally become unable to live among other people. That means we've gone too far. We're out of balance. Not to worry; the Holy Spirit will bring you back in line.

When I say the Holy Spirit, I include the entire line of the ECK Masters, and at the forefront of them stands the Mahanta, the Living ECK Master. He is given the spiritual responsibility to guide Souls back home to God. To learn the language of love.

We are here to learn the lessons of everyday living.

PAMELA'S TRAFFIC VIOLATION

"Pamela" is a new member of Eckankar who lives in Colorado. A business meeting once brought her to Denver. While she was in town at this business meeting, she heard that the author of an ECK book was going to be giving a talk about his experiences in the Light and Sound of God. So Pamela and a few of the other people at the business meeting, who were ECKists too, decided to take time off and go listen to the talk.

The talk went fine. On the way back to their hotel, Pamela was at the wheel. She knew this part of Denver like the back of her hand, she said.

Apparently, she didn't know the back of her hand as well as she thought. She got lost. Pretty soon she was driving in the opposite direction of where she wanted to go, and she became so confused that she drove right through a red light.

A patrol car was parked at the intersection to catch people who run red lights. The next thing Pamela knew, she was pulled over to the side of the road, the traffic officer was coming up to her, and she was crying. Tears were just gushing out.

To Pamela, the worst thing that could ever happen was to be stopped by a policeman for a traffic violation. She was a very law-abiding citizen.

Pamela sat there, gushing tears, assuring the patrolman that she didn't make a practice of running red lights.

The officer listened, and he reached for the ticket book, then Pamela began crying harder.

He said, "Let me see your driver's license."

After much groping around in her purse, she finally dug out her driver's license. She gave it to the patrolman with trembling hands.

"Stay here," he said. "I'm going to go back and check on this."

While the patrolman was checking her license, her friends began trying to console her. "Hey, it'll be OK," they said. "Sing *HU*. Everything will work out the way it should." I don't think any one of them thought she had a prayer.

The officer came back. "Everything checks out," he said, "and I'm not going to give you a ticket."

He was about to say more, but then the ECK friend seated in the passenger's seat interrupted. "It's obvious that you practice love in your duties, considering how you're handling her situation," the ECKist said.

Now I'm looking at it from the outside, but if I were a patrol officer and heard this, I'd say, "Buddy, that's pushing it. This one gets a ticket, and if you keep popping off, we're all going in to check things out."

But the officer said, "Every day."

One of the ECKists asked the officer what religion he was. He said he had been Catholic, but it wasn't working for him right now. He was looking.

While the patrolman was checking her license, her friends said, "Sing HU. Everything will work out the way it should."

After this the officer gave them directions back to the hotel. Pamela didn't get a ticket, or even a warning.

Later, she looked at the spiritual principle in this experience. She saw the guiding hand of the Mahanta, the Living ECK Master. It's a hand of love. It was guiding her, telling her, "Pamela, no matter where you are, no matter how confused you get on the roads of life, there will always be someone near you to help. Sometimes they will be ECK Masters." Her mind then flashed to the image of the experience she'd had with her ECK friends in the car. "And sometimes the help will come through the Mahanta." Now it flashed in her mind how the officer had been playing that role.

Pamela realized the Master had guided her gently through all the different religions she had been in and beliefs she had held before Eckankar.

Pamela realized that no matter where she was, how many times she'd taken wrong turns in her spiritual life, the Master was with her. He was showing her truth. He had guided her gently through all the different religions she had been in and beliefs she had held before Eckankar. Because each religion and each path had taught her something that was necessary for her spiritual unfoldment. We recognize the value of every true religion.

My definition of a true religion is one that does good in the world. It tries to find ways to help people be themselves. It does not try to shape people to be what we think they should be, then break spiritual or man-made laws to accomplish that. The sign of a good religion is that it helps the people grow to become more godlike, to be capable of more love and mercy— for themselves as well as for others.

How much can you love yourself in the right way? Because you must. You must love yourself before you can love another. And if you don't love yourself, whatever it is you're passing off as love for another is not the real thing. It's a shadow of it.

When Pamela got back home after leaving Denver, one of her friends who heard the story said to her, "This is unheard of. Running a red light with a patrol car sitting there, and you don't get a traffic ticket, you don't even get a warning." She said, "This is unheard of."

Yes, it is unheard of, unless you're in Eckankar.

BECOMING A CHAMPION FOR ECK

How best to share the Light and Sound of God?

Carol works at the Temple of ECK. She has been holding a series of classes to develop a leadership training program for Higher Initiates. These classes are a pilot—a step to developing a program.

In the third class, the discussion was on how to become a champion for the mission of telling others about the Light and Sound of God. The way that was spoken of—the way to be the best messenger of the Light and Sound—was not to discourage others who had their own way of telling others about Eckankar and the ECK teachings.

Sometimes it's human nature that if someone has a lot of enthusiasm for something, another person will come up and pour water on that fire. Human nature is very much a part of the human makeup of ECKists too.

Carol encourages such open discussion. She feels if there's any disagreement, it should come to the surface in the class so that it's possible to address the problem.

As the class was talking about the best approach to be a missionary for ECK, she found there was a

The way to be the best messenger was not to discourage others who had their own way of telling others about Eckankar and the ECK teachings.

strong split in the group.

Some of the old-timers, the ones who had been longtime members of Eckankar, liked the laid-back way: Leave a book out, put posters up, and then people who are ready can take the initiative and contact Eckankar at their leisure. That was one approach.

The other half of the class said, "That's fine, but sometimes as we go about our business in daily life, we come across people who have lost someone through death or some other thing. Or someone they love dearly is very ill. And at this point we tell them about HU, or we give them an ECK book or something." It's with the understanding that the person who is in spiritual need may use this information if they wish. You leave it up to them.

To some, this might sound as if it's the same sort of missionary program as the other; either way, you're providing your teachings to the world. Yes, but one approach does it indirectly through public methods. The other approach is more direct, person-to-person.

There was this tension in the class. Carol realized that it was a microcosm reflecting the macrocosm. They were seeing, on a small scale, what was happening out there in the world among the ECK initiates. What was happening in this class was happening everywhere.

Some people in class were on fire with ECK because of something that happened to them. They were full of enthusiasm. They wanted to tell others about this wonderful approach to the Light and Sound of God. They wanted to share it—just spill their hearts and say, "Here's what happened. Maybe this can help you."

The others were more aloof. They stood back at arm's length. This was the sort of tension that was going on in the ECK membership. Carol wanted to address it.

TWO APPROACHES TO SHARING ECK

When the class was over, Carol wondered, *Which of these is the better way to tell others about the Light and Sound of God?* In her experience, she has used both. And indeed, so have I.

Sometimes you give something directly to a person because there's a spiritual need. The Holy Spirit opens a door. It's wide open, and you can tell, and you just walk right in. The person is crying for help, and you give them something.

Other times I leave out posters and bookmarks. This way, people who are drawn to ECK information will take it of their own accord. Sometimes just putting up a poster introduces people to the word *Eckankar*. It becomes familiar to them.

I put up a poster that I had designed years ago. It's rather a plain poster. I put it up in this one place quite often, with three little cards in it. I'd come back a week later to see how many were left. The board was outside, and sometimes the rain had washed over it and no posters were up. Or very often, within a day or so, my poster would be plastered over with other posters.

After a time, I realized all the people who wanted to see this poster here had now seen it, so I decided to use another poster. I would be kind—let them see some other kind of presentation or image of Eckankar. We have to use such courtesies for each other.

When an old poster becomes so familiar that no

Sometimes you give something directly to a person because there's a spiritual need. The Holy Spirit opens a door.

one sees it, it's time to change it. So I put these old posters in my little postering box, and I will bring them out again a year from now. I do not throw these things away.

At the next meeting of Carol's pilot program, two High Initiates were chatting. They believed in opposite approaches to sharing ECK. They were chatting about where they'd been before. It turned out both had been in the San Francisco Bay area at the same time some years ago.

The younger, on-fire ECKist realized that it was the other one who had given an introductory class on Eckankar years ago. The younger ECKist had gone to it before he became a member of Eckankar. The longtime ECKist had given a dream technique that actually worked. This had impressed the newcomer. So that newcomer became an ECKist, and over the years, a Higher Initiate.

As Carol observed their sharing notes, she realized that there is a time and a place for each of the two methods of presenting ECK to others. Every person goes through cycles. There are times we go into the outgoing cycle, and there are times we are into the inward cycle. Because that's how life is.

THE WAVE OF GOD

This ocean wave that flows from the heart of God is a two-way wave. It flows out to the ends of creation. Out here on the end of creation somewhere, we find ourselves.

We can learn how to ride this wave, this Sound Current, back home to God. We can jump aboard this wave the way a surfer does. We can ride it back to the heart of God.

This is what the teachings of Eckankar are about.

This ocean wave from the heart of God flows out to the ends of creation. We can learn how to ride this wave, this Sound Current, back home to God.

This is the great mystery about dream study and Soul Travel. It's learning how to ride, in a metaphorical and a very literal sense, this wave of God, which is the Voice of God. This wave is the creative force that came from God and created all worlds.

God created the worlds through this Word, and this Word is the Holy Spirit. This Word issues forth, and the echo comes back. We want to ride the wave back.

LOVE IS THE CONDUIT

Carol shared one more insight that had been passed on to her by a dear friend. This friend had three meetings with the Mahanta—the inner side of myself, the Inner Master. These three meetings came during contemplation. Each time, her boyfriend was present too.

Finally, at the third meeting, the woman said to the Inner Master, "My boyfriend's not even an ECKist." The unspoken question was, "So why do you allow him to be here?"

The Mahanta said, "He loves you." This caught Carol's friend off guard.

When Carol heard the story, she realized that love is the conduit that carries the ECK and the Mahanta to others. Because in this spiritual position as the Mahanta, the Living ECK Master, I am just a channel. I'm an instrument. I don't try to convince you of something against your will, because to do so would take from my freedom. I am for spiritual freedom for everyone.

Carol realized love is the conduit that carries the ECK and the Mahanta to others.

But spiritual freedom comes with the recognition that our freedom ends where our neighbor's begins. And this line is called responsibility. When a person crosses it one way or another, this line then becomes the Law of Karma—cause and effect. Whatsoever a man sows, that also shall he reap.

Love is the bond between God and you.

But love is the bond between God and you.

For us, the ECK teachings are precious. The teachings are those of every good and great religion. They're always based on love. Love—our love for God and God's love for us.

ECK Springtime Seminar, Tampa, Florida, Saturday, April 14, 2001

Keep only such things around you as are in harmony with you. On a spiritual level, your beliefs need to be in harmony with the real you.

5
THANKS FOR THE HELP AND LOVE

*I*was reading a book recently that talked about how important it is to clean things out around you that you don't want. They weigh on you, and they're a reflection of who you are. If we want to clean up our lives or make life go more smoothly, we can change something in our home, office, drawers, or dresser. If there's a mess somewhere, just pick it up and clean it out.

If we want to make life go more smoothly, we can change something in our home, office, drawers, or dresser.

The same thing applies to clothes. My wife, Joan, and I don't often go shopping, except for groceries. Most of our clothes shopping is done through the mail. The post office loves us.

I got a shirt through mail order. I picked it out from a catalog. Joan said she wanted to get it for me, so she did. When the box came, I took the shirt out and looked at it.

"Hmm," I said, "very nice shirt." I'd picked it out, you know.

Joan looked at it the way a woman will who has any sense of clothing and style at all. "If you want to send it back, no problem," she said. She does it all the time. "That's how you do it with mail order," she told me.

Usually, if I buy
something, I
keep it. "I'll
keep the shirt,"
I said.

This was an education for me. Usually, if I buy something, I keep it. My mind labors on the repacking, driving to the post office, and how the company would have to pay somebody to open the package, look over the shirt, wash it, then move it to the resale shop and offer it at a discount.

So I was thinking about all this. "I'll keep the shirt," I said.

In the catalog, the shirt had been beautiful—a sort of plaid with crossed double blue stripes. Right down the middle of each blue square ran a very light golden stripe. In the catalog it looked golden. But when I put the shirt on, too much yellow came through. It didn't look good on me.

I never used to notice these things. All I wore was a certain shade of blue, and I was particular about it. But here I had a shirt with blue stripes and yellow. I let it sit three, four, five days. Then I tried it on again and looked in the mirror. I said, "Nice-looking shirt."

I don't look at myself too much in the mirror. So when I was trying on the shirt, I happened to look up at my face. It didn't seem to be all there. It seemed to fade away.

"Why," I said, "this is the strangest shirt I've ever seen."

Joan has often told me about clothes that overpower the wearer. She says clothes should enhance the wearer. "I don't even enhance the shirt," I said.

Because I write, I began thinking of titles. The Man with the Invisible Head was one.

"I could never wear this shirt to a talk because people wouldn't see my head," I said. "It wouldn't be there."

I wore that shirt one time. Finally I told my wife, "This thing is just too strong."

"I'll send it back for you," she said.

What's in Harmony with You?

Repackaging a shirt takes a lot of thought. You've got to decide when to do it—this week or next. So you read the receipt and find out how long they give you to return it. I put it off, because I don't like to send things back.

But Joan said she'd take care of it. And she did. And I'm so glad.

Having the wrong clothing in the closet is just awful. Even worse is wearing something that doesn't suit you, as I did with my golden-yellow pants last winter. They were awful. When I tried to hang them up, the pressed creases weren't even in accord with the seams. I like to hang pants straight. The creases on the front and back should be right where they belong. These drifted off to the side. And when I put the pants on, it looked like one leg was going here and the other leg was going over there.

Out of these experiences, I came up with a saying: Keep only such things around you as are in harmony with you.

On a spiritual level, your beliefs need to be in harmony with the real you. I'm talking about Soul.

We'll Be All Right

Sometimes parents think their children are going to go to rot if they do this particular thing or that. When I was young, it was listening to too much radio or reading comic books. Then it was TV, and now it's computers.

On a spiritual level, your beliefs need to be in harmony with the real you. I'm talking about Soul.

I look on the positive side. By the time these kids are twenty-five or thirty, they'll have a mortgage and a family, and they'll be scrambling like the rest of us.

Don't worry, most of them will turn out all right. This society will limp along the way it has for two thousand years. Two thousand years ago, the wise men of ancient Greece were worried about the future of their own society. Maybe they were right; Greece isn't a big power anymore. But Greece is still there.

WISDOM FROM THE *SHARIYAT,* PART 1

I'd like to read three paragraphs from *The Shariyat-Ki-Sugmad*, Book Two, but just one paragraph at a time. This is from Book Two:

> What the Mahanta, the Living ECK Master teaches in words is only a fraction of what he teaches by his mere presence, his personality, and his living example. The Mahanta is always conscious of his own worldly shortcomings and limitations of words and speech, which cause him to hesitate to teach the works of ECK by putting into words something that is too profound and subtle to be grasped by mere logic and ordinary reasoning.

I rely on you to talk to people at home, in your hometown, and listen to the concerns they have about their own life. Because you are there. You can tell them about the Light and Sound of ECK.

Sometime further on, they can make the connection to the inner part of myself, the Inner Master. The outer side is the Living ECK Master, the physical presence that I am right here. The inner part of myself is the Mahanta, the Inner Master, the Dream Master.

The whole title is the Mahanta, the Living ECK Master, which is a mouthful. But so it is.

I rely on you to talk to people at home, in your hometown, and listen to the concerns they have about their own life.

THE MAHANTA'S BLUE SUIT

"Mary Ann" had friends in the Minneapolis area. They knew she was in Eckankar. But what she didn't know was that they were watching the videos of some of my talks on local TV. They never told her in the three years they lived in the Twin Cities.

The group of friends moved to Florida. Mary Ann went down to visit them. Out of the blue, one of her friends said, "Is the Mahanta still wearing the same suit—the light-blue one?"

Mary Ann wondered, *How do they know the term Mahanta?*

"He got a new suit," she said. "His wife is working with him."

Upon reading this, I felt somewhat like a basket case.

"He even has two new ties," she added.

Until her friend mentioned the Mahanta, Mary Ann had no idea that they had been watching the videos of these talks on local TV. Mary Ann realized she was the connection for them to at least know about the teachings of ECK.

We are not rabid missionaries in ECK. We tell people about the teachings, but we don't go around pounding on doors. Because some people may have many other things to learn first before they are ready for the teachings of ECK. Other people just need to hear about ECK. And for them it's enough to just say, "We've watched it on TV a couple of times. Is the Mahanta still wearing the same suit?"

That satisfies them. That's all they need.

The ECK teachings say that everything is in its rightful place here and now. What's to worry?

We worry a lot, we change things, and we work

We tell people about the teachings, but we don't go around pounding on doors.

for good. But the Law of Karma has everything in balance, even during the states of great imbalance. It's just a matter of time before things switch back and regain a balance.

So thanks for the help and love.

CRAIG'S BOSS MAKES THE CONNECTION

Craig works in the Minneapolis area too, and he has a part-time job delivering newspapers. He began this seven years ago. At the time he started the job, he mentioned to his boss that he was a member of Eckankar. They had a short discussion at the time, but it never came up again.

For Craig, it hasn't always been easy working with his boss. There have been rough times. But all in all it's gone well, and after seven years Craig was still there. But the topic of Eckankar never came up again.

Then one day Craig was sorting his newspapers. His boss came over.

"Eckankar?" he asked.

Craig said, "Yes."

"Harold?"

"Yes."

"I've been watching him on TV," said Craig's boss. "I like what he says."

Again, here was this brief touching in with Eckankar. It took seven years to come to the next step.

So Craig invited his boss to the Temple of ECK for the next ECK Worship Service.

It's just a question of how ready and how much ECK does a person need at this time. If not so much, that's OK. Life goes on and on.

Again, it's just a question of how ready and how much ECK does a person need at this time. If not so much, that's OK. Life goes on and on. For those of you who believe in reincarnation and understand the principles of karma, you realize that God has set up this whole structure for Soul's purification.

PURIFICATION OF SOUL

This afternoon I went down to the kitchen, and Joan was there. She'll often hear something on the news, some atrocity committed by one nation against another. Or someone will have made a personal attack in the political arena. She asked me, "Why? Why do they fight?"

I said the thing that we both know: "It's part of the purification system that God set up."

The lower worlds have the elements of the positive and negative forces. The process of spiritual perfection is finding the neutral force, the balance between the two. When this balance is found, it marks a certain stage of enlightenment.

When that occurs, Soul will never again need to come back to earth.

I say "never again" with this exception: Soul may come back to serve others here as a Co-worker with God. The option is open—to serve as a Co-worker with God, either here or in one of the other worlds.

This is the whole point of life—to find the purification of Soul.

This is the whole point of life—to find the purification of Soul.

WISDOM FROM THE SHARIYAT, PART 2

The second paragraph from *The Shariyat-Ki-Sugmad*, Book Two, says this:

Despite this, the Mahanta does disclose the truth, out of compassion, to the few whose eyes have hardly been covered by the illusion. However, he strictly avoids speaking about the ultimate things and refuses to answer any question concerning the supramundane state of realization or similar problems which go beyond the capacity of the human intellect. He confines himself to show the practical way which leads to the solution of the problems of man in his spiritual capacity. He always explains the essential teachings of ECK in a form which corresponds to the capacity of his listeners.

This is one reason that spiritual masters have often used parables and stories to teach. People are used to hearing stories. They grow up with them. They like good stories.

HELP FOR JENNIFER'S FRIEND

"Jennifer" was in a class where the ECKists were sharing stories. Jennifer had a non-ECKist friend who was in a difficult marriage. For two years, Jennifer would pick up the phone when her friend called to complain about her husband. With much patience, Jennifer listened to these problems.

But from time to time she'd ask, "Have you considered seeing a counselor?"

The friend said, "I haven't gotten to it yet, but I will sometime."

After two years, Jennifer decided that there wasn't any more she could do. Listening to her friend's complaining wasn't changing the situation. So Jennifer decided not to answer the phone.

When it rang that day, she didn't answer. The next night it rang again. Jennifer let it ring.

Then for a couple of weeks there was no call at all from her friend. Jennifer wondered what had happened. She wondered if she had been too harsh. She wondered if she had done the right thing. She was trying to listen to the promptings of the Inner Master.

Jennifer wondered if she had done the right thing. She was trying to listen to the promptings of the Inner Master.

The Inner Master had said, "Don't pick up the phone for a while." So Jennifer didn't.

A couple of weeks later, she got a call from her friend. Her friend had taken Jennifer's advice and gone to a counselor. And it turned out, to her friend's surprise, the counselor was an ECKist too.

Jennifer looked at the whole picture. She said she could see the help and the love and guidance that the Mahanta was giving to her friend. Her friend may or may not be aware of it yet, because she's not a member of Eckankar. But she's getting help anyway.

This is how the ECK, Divine Spirit, works.

Jennifer could see the help and the love and guidance the Mahanta was giving her friend.

TWO ELEMENTS OF DIVINE SPIRIT

ECK is just our way of saying the Holy Spirit, Divine Spirit, Comforter. The ECK, or the Holy Spirit, is actually of two elements—the Sound and the Light of God. These two elements together are the Voice of God.

They are the creative force—when God spoke and the worlds were made, the speech was through the Sound and Light, and the Spirit moved upon the waters.

Sometimes people like to think of the Holy Ghost as a personage, but It's really a divine force. It's beyond words. It is pure love. It is of God—of Sugmad, as we call God.

In ECK we look to or listen for the Light and the Sound. These are very important.

The Quakers look for the Inner Light. In Eckankar we look for the Light—which may come in any color, any form. Usually it comes during contemplation or the dream state, and sometimes it comes in daily life. This is a sign that God is speaking to you, that divine love and guidance are yours. Because God's love is so great for Soul. God's love is all for you.

So, thanks for the help and love.

ROBERT'S FINANCE LESSON

The Mahanta often teaches not the esoteric teachings, but practical solutions to the problems of man.

"Robert" lives in Nigeria. His wife came back from her hometown and brought a chicken with her. In a year's time they would have another chicken. And these two chickens taught Robert two very important practical lessons.

The first was a very small hen, but she laid eggs like crazy. She laid twelve eggs and sat on them. The hen was barely able to keep all twelve under her, but soon twelve chicks hatched from these eggs. Robert was astounded.

He and his wife live in a large city, in a compound. A compound is a fenced or walled-in area with a group of buildings.

They decided to let the hen run loose, though they thought she should also have some of the formulated chicken feed. That way, she'd grow up good and strong, and stay strong. So Robert put out a chicken feeder.

But the chicken had a bad habit. She would go in the feeder and scratch around, scattering the seed all over the ground. To make matters worse, she'd scratch at it until she covered it up.

"This hen doesn't know how to feed her chicks," Robert said to his wife. "She doesn't know how to serve a meal." He didn't know what to do. But then he looked at her claws. They were worn down 30 percent more than normal. *This chicken is going*

The Mahanta often teaches not the esoteric teachings, but practical solutions to the problems of man.

through a lot of work to make it hard for her chicks to survive, he thought. But as soon as he noticed the worn-down claws, he began to wonder if there was a message in this for him.

Around this time, Robert had run into financial difficulties. He had asked the Mahanta to help him. "Mahanta, help me," he said. "I can't live within my means."

Once he noticed the hen's claws, it occurred to him to do some financial planning. He looked at all his debts, and he looked at his income.

"Now, where is my money leaking out?" he asked.

He found the places, and he stopped spending the money here, there, and everywhere. And after six months, even though he had the same amount of income, he could now live on what he made.

Then he realized that, like the hen scattering the seed, he had been scattering the gifts of the Holy Spirit.

KEEP IT CALM, KEEP IT BALANCED

Hen number two was entirely different from hen number one. She had only one chick. She was a rather talkative hen; she made a lot of noise.

One day, Robert decided to help out this hen and her chick by feeding them some bread from the table. The family used to feed the chickens fruit and other table scraps. The chickens loved these treats.

There was now a flock of hens and roosters, so Robert led the new hen away from the flock and fed her the little piece of bread. He thought it would help keep her strong and also help her little chick. So at the far end of the yard, Robert gave the piece of bread to the chicken.

Robert realized that, like the hen scattering the seed, he had been scattering the gifts of the Holy Spirit.

The chicken picked up one of the bread chunks and started running around, squawking and bragging.

Soon the other chickens heard. They knew what she was saying. They said, "Feast!" And they all came running. They ate all the bread that Robert had put out for the second hen.

To make matters worse, they even took the bread chunk from her beak.

Robert looked at this. Soon he got the picture. Now that he'd been doing better with his finances, he felt so good he wanted to dance. He wanted to shout and tell people—to act very much like that hen, running around, flapping his wings, and cackling loud.

Robert said, "The lesson here from hen number two was: settle down, keep it calm, stay in balance."

Three forces affect humankind: the positive, the negative, and the all-important neutral force.

Three forces affect humankind: the positive, the negative, and the all-important neutral force. The neutral force is the middle path. Or staying balanced, staying calm.

WISDOM FROM THE *SHARIYAT*, PART 3

The third section I'd like to read from *The Shariyat*, Book Two, is this:

The advanced teachings of ECK have been described as esoteric, or secret, doctrines. However, their purpose is not to exclude anyone from the attainment of higher realization or knowledge, but to avoid the empty talk and speculation of those who try to anticipate, intellectually, these exalted states of consciousness, without trying to attain theirs through the Spiritual Exercises of ECK.

The ECK Masters know no great spiritual unfoldment is ever made through the mind. It's not done
through reason, nor through understanding of the
mental sort. It's done through spiritual practice. A
practice of loving God and your fellow man.

Soul is a star of God. Soul, me and you, is made
in the image of God, which is something more than
a star. It is the origin of the universe. And maybe the
origin of the universe is something other than a big
bang. Maybe it's something from another, higher
plane.

It has its inception here as the big bang or
whatever people want to believe. It really doesn't
matter. What matters is, what are you doing with
your life right here and now?

Rose Dreams of
a Life between Lives

Dreams play an important role in the ECK teachings. We put a lot of emphasis on dreams because
they are a wonderful way the Holy Spirit speaks to
people—a way people can learn to understand. It's
a matter of dream interpretation.

"Rose," a woman from Germany, came to the 2000
ECK Worldwide Seminar. When she went home, she
practiced the spiritual exercise I'd given in that talk.
(See chapter 3, "The Secret Path to God.")

Rose had a dream where she was at a great dance,
but everything looked like it was from the early 1950s.
The clothes, the people, the music, the decorations,
even the very structure of the room—it was all from
the early 1950s. It occurred to Rose that that was
when she was born.

In the dream, Rose looked around for a partner.

Dreams are a wonderful way the Holy Spirit speaks to people—a way people can learn to understand.

She was going to dance with her aunt. But her aunt was dancing with someone else, and she looked happy. So Rose looked for another partner. But everybody was already dancing.

In this lifetime, Rose has had a very difficult time with her mother. It's been a rough road. They haven't always seen eye-to-eye. Her mother would give very definite rules, and Rose would have to follow them. Rose didn't like it, and this caused hard feelings.

In her dream, Rose looked along the wall. There, sitting on a chair all by herself, was her mother.

"I'll go dance with her," Rose decided. "She looks unhappy."

She went over to her mother and asked if she'd like to dance. The mother said she'd love to. So they started dancing and, true to form, her mother said, "Straighten your shoulders. Put that arm up higher." And other rules that a German mama might have for her child.

But Rose noticed that they danced together extremely well. In fact, it was the best she had ever danced. Rose admitted to not being a very great dancer out here in the physical world. But there, even with her mother, it was just wonderful.

Rose thought to herself, *No one's ever led me through a dance like this before.*

When Rose awoke, she knew the meaning of the dream. Between lives, before this one, Rose had chosen that particular Soul to be her mother. Rose had said, "This is a onetime deal only, OK?" Rose knew she needed certain spiritual disciplines so that she could lead a safe and happy life and eventually find Eckankar.

In a very special way, her mother led her to a very secure future and a good life. Rose is a happy woman

Rose knew the meaning of the dream. Between lives, before this one, Rose had chosen that Soul to be her mother.

now. She has a lot of zest for living. She feels the blessings of the Holy Spirit.

So Rose sent thanks. And again to her too, I say, "Thanks for your help and love."

Divine love is a mutual thing. We must give it to get it, and when we get it we must give it.

The problem occurs when people hold it in or shut it out. If they hold it in, no more comes. If they shut it out, they lead unhappy, miserable lives.

Some people can't accept gifts of love from other people. They can't do it. Their pride keeps them from it.

Divine love is a mutual thing. We must give it to get it, and when we get it we must give it.

JOHN'S FIRST SATSANG CLASS

"John" is a new member of Eckankar in the Minneapolis area. He had gone to his first ECK Satsang class. These are spiritual classes which are open for members. It's a small group of people—three, twelve, fifteen, twenty or more who get together and hold a class on one of the ECK discourses. These discourses come with membership.

After John's first Satsang class, he had a dream. In the dream, he awoke to find himself in a huge house. There were many rooms in the house. Around him, John found a new group of people. He recognized some of them from his Satsang class.

Soon this group of people split up—some went in pairs, some alone—to explore the many rooms in this beautiful mansion.

John sensed there was purpose to this mansion. He couldn't put his finger on it. But he said, "You know, that fits my personal metaphor: Life doesn't come with an instruction manual."

John figured there was a purpose there, and he

couldn't find it, but that was normal. That's how
things are. That's all he expects.

Some of the class went off, singly or in pairs, to
look for their purpose. Maybe they could find a clue
in one of the rooms. After a while, John found the
Mahanta.

"What are we supposed to do here?" John asked.

The Dream Master said, "Look around. Explore
the rooms. Each individual in class is looking for
something personal." All would later share in class
what they'd found. And when the class members
shared this information, they would learn about all
the rooms in the mansion. They would learn through
their own explorations and through the reports of
those who had seen other rooms.

A NEW LEVEL OF CONSCIOUSNESS

John realized the dream meant he was in a new state of consciousness. He had never seen anything of such beauty before.

John realized the dream meant he was in a new
state of consciousness. It was a very exciting place.
He had never seen anything of such beauty before.

Christ once said, "In my Father's house are many
mansions." It sounds backward, in a way. You'd think
he'd say, "In my Father's mansion there are many
rooms." But there are many different levels of consciousness in the other worlds. And each person's
state of consciousness will draw him to the level
where he belongs. And why to the one where he
belongs? Because that's where the individual is comfortable.

For this reason, John listens to the stories of the
other people in the ECK Satsang class. He realizes
that their stories are teaching him about some of
the rooms of the heavenly worlds that he has not
explored himself.

We're all here to help others find their way to the love of God. We're helping those who want to find another area of God's love they haven't known before.

My love and blessings are with you.

*ECK Summer Festival, Las Vegas, Nevada,
Saturday, July 7, 2001*

Such is the power of love. Love on both sides—Ann's love for her husband and the husband's love for her.

6
THE POWER
OF LOVE

hings have changed a lot since September 11. It's a new time, a time for compassion, understanding, and giving of aid. It's certainly not a time for pointing fingers and saying, "It happened because of this and that." Everything on earth happens because of this or that.

As Christ said some two thousand years ago, "He that is without sin among you, let him first cast a stone." And so it is. It's a time for compassion and a time for love.

IN TIMES OF LOSS

There was a great loss. Though for many the loss is of a national sort, it's just as personal even at that level as a loss of a family member. For some of us, the family includes even our pets.

After a loss of any sort—whether of someone in our family or a national loss—things won't ever be the same. But things do go on. They always have, and they always will.

When my grandmother passed on, and my dad, things weren't the same. Things were different.

But other things come into our lives to fill the emptiness and to refill our cup so that it overflows with other experiences, other people.

If we give love, we get love. Even in the most serious and most difficult of times, there is always a way to get through. The Holy Spirit, the ECK, will always have a way to get through to the next stage in life.

Things will never be the same as they were before, they never are. But we will go on. We will do well individually and as a people. And I speak here not just as an American citizen, but as a citizen of the world.

Even in the most serious and most difficult of times, there is always a way to get through.

SPARTA AND THE FOREIGN AMBASSADOR

One of my correspondents sent a little excerpt from a story about the Spartans. They had no use for rhetoric, the art of public speaking. They mistrusted it, and they went to the other extreme. They would use very plain, simple speech.

One time a battle was going poorly for a Spartan general. He was hopelessly outnumbered, and he said, "Breakfast here, supper in Hades." That pretty much spelled out how the day was going for him.

A foreign ambassador came to Sparta, and he was going to ask for aid. He went before the counselors and gave a long speech. When he finished, he asked for a response from the counselors. "We can't remember the first half," they said, "and we don't understand the second."

The ambassador went home and thought about it.

The next day, he came back. He brought a bag with him. He held the bag in front of him and said,

"Sack wants flour."

The Spartans talked among themselves, and their spokesman said, "You could have left off 'sack.' "

When it comes to words, I'm more like the foreign ambassador. At heart, I'm a Spartan, but there's something between where my heart is and where my tongue is. The heart is simple, but the tongue can't say it that way.

EVERYBODY NEEDS LOVE

Paul Twitchell, the modern-day founder of Eckankar, gave a talk at the 1971 Los Angeles Regional Seminar. The title is "Love, a Powerful Force."

Paul had just come from a meeting with the ECK youth. One little boy of eight or nine asked him what he knew about past lives. Paul looked at him. "At your age, you should worry about such a thing?" he said. Like the boy had better things to do. He had this full life out in front of him.

But then Paul began speaking of his own childhood when he was about that age—a young chap. He had a candy-striped suit, and every Sunday his stepmother made him wear it and took him off to church and Sunday school. At Sunday school, Paul had a gang, and there was another gang. One gang would sit on one side of the room; the other gang would sit as far from them as they could get. There they'd sit, eyeing each other, throwing threatening looks.

The young Sunday-school teacher was very wise in the psychology of little boys. At some point, he said, "All right, we'll all go outside. But these are the rules: No hitting, no tearing clothes; don't touch, just shout."

The two little gangs of boys went outside, and

The young Sunday-school teacher was very wise in the psychology of little boys.

they stood opposite each other and said every vile thing they could. They didn't worry about being on the Sunday-school grounds. After a few minutes, the teacher said, "All right, back inside." They all came in, and he had them sing "Jesus Loves Me."

Paul said he went home then with this feeling that somebody loved him. He said little boys need this because at that age they sometimes feel their parents don't love them.

WHEN PEOPLE COMPLAIN

Paul then went on to the subject of love. He said even adults—not all, but some—put themselves into two camps. One is for something; the other is against it. And they'll do everything they can to argue about it, fight about it.

But when Paul used to walk more among the people, before his health became very poor, what used to surprise and distress him was the complaints that some people would make about others. Finally, Paul wouldn't listen to any sort of complaints at all.

He knew what was going on, but he didn't do anything himself. But when it was brought to his attention through a complaint, he had to act. As soon as he had to act, he had to enforce some sort of discipline. And he didn't want to do that.

Paul preferred to be a neutral factor.

He preferred to keep himself open to the Holy Spirit, the ECK. He preferred to be a neutral factor. So when there were contesting sides to an issue, he would be a neutral party. And so he did nothing.

He said he found himself in this position where he could do nothing, because as the Master, he found he had to stand aside. People were simply working out their karma, even by the mere fact of making a complaint. And it was not for him to interfere. He was to let it run its course until people would give it up themselves.

STAYING IN BALANCE

Recently, a Higher Initiate said to me, "What is there I can do to keep from going out of balance?"

Because this initiate had seen so many others go out of balance, and she didn't want to ever be in that situation. She did not want to be one of the problem people, or a propeep, as Paul termed it once.

I looked at her and said, "Well, when that time comes, I would do nothing. I *could* do nothing. Because you're doing whatever it is you're doing because you need to do it. And the sooner you do it, the better for you."

But, of course, I also said, "Are you willing to take the consequences?"

Because in ECK, everything has a consequence. This is the cause and effect, and every action has an equal and opposite reaction.

Someone once said that a screen actor is simply a reactor. Someone sets something in motion, or a circumstance sets something in motion, and from that point onward the actor reacts to that initial cause. In that sense, everyone on earth is an actor. Everyone is responding to the Law of Cause and Effect—karma, if you will.

Paul finally realized that if he couldn't get involved in any disputes, that left him with only one thing. That was pure divine love for life.

That was it. It left him simply with love. There was no place else to go, nothing else to do.

Everyone on earth is responding to the Law of Cause and Effect—karma, if you will.

WOULD MARTHA DANCE?

"Martha" had a fourteen-year-old daughter who had been interested in ballet for a couple of years. The ballet company decided to put on *The Nutcracker* one Christmas.

At the first rehearsal, the director asked for parent volunteers. "We'd like some parents in the big party scene," he said.

Martha's daughter begged her. "Mom, would you please be one of the volunteers? You'd be great as the party mom."

Martha had seen *The Nutcracker* enough times to know that if she were going to play a party mom, she would have to dance. She didn't dance. Martha did not like to dance. Furthermore, Martha would not dance. So she said no, and she was firm. No.

About a month went by. Her daughter was at an all-day Saturday practice, and she called home. "Mom," she said, "the director asked if you would be willing to take the role of the grandmother."

Martha said, "I can't dance."

Her daughter said, "Don't worry about it. She's supposed to be just a little bit confused and forgetful, so that won't matter."

The director had actually asked the daughter two questions. First, "Would your mother do the part?" The daughter very confidently said yes. Then he asked, "Can she act?" Of course, the daughter knew her mother had never acted, but she said yes anyway. Pure faith in the power of the parent.

So Martha said yes, she'd do it.

She went to the first rehearsal, and the director explained that it would just be a lot of fun. But Martha hadn't ever been in a play before. She wanted to know

Martha did not like to dance. Furthermore, Martha would not dance. She was firm. No.

exactly what her dance would be. So she took home a video of the previous year's performance, and she studied the dance, breaking it down into different parts to understand it. Then she went to the rehearsals to see how her home study would work out in real practice.

The part of the grandfather was performed by an actor who had played that role for many years. This is where Martha began to see a spiritual parallel. The grandfather was like the Mahanta, the Living ECK Master. He'd been through this role many times before. He knew the part, the dance of life. But Martha also knew that it was up to her to do her part, not to expect the grandfather to lead her through the dance.

She studied hard. She missed a rehearsal when she came to the ECK Worldwide Seminar, but she studied the lines and watched the video. Her part required her to wear a wig, and even though she was supposed to wear it only for the performance, she decided to wear it to rehearsal just to practice. She is of the philosophy that it's better to make your mistakes right away—the sooner to correct them.

The wig kept slipping during rehearsal. Finally it just fell off. So Martha was glad she had thought to try wearing the wig during rehearsal and not waited for opening night.

The big night finally came. Martha was nervous at first, but when she went onstage, she turned everything over to the ECK, the Holy Spirit. *I don't know what earthly good my presence in this play will do anyone or anything*, she thought, *but I will support the others to the best of my ability.*

Martha had a good time. She had a lot of fun. There were nine performances, and after the first one she felt very confident. Originally she had been

Martha was nervous but turned everything over to the ECK. She thought, I will support the others to the best of my ability.

confused; she didn't know the steps. But everything went very well.

In one of the final scenes, the old grandfather danced. He did a little jig because, in the play, he had too much to drink. Martha was supposed to grab him by the ear and haul him off the stage, scolding him all the way. But she had decided to play the role of a loving wife. So she took him very gently by the ear and put her other arm around him for support, guiding him slowly offstage. When the uncle came up to give grandpa one more drink, Martha dumped it when no one was looking. These were all little touches she did herself because she was having fun.

Parents who had come to pick up their children after rehearsal had been very impressed by Martha's acting ability. Many people told her she was very good. But Martha had accepted help every step of the way. When it was time to learn makeup, she had gone to the library and taken out books on makeup. She ordered supplies and tried putting it on. At the first rehearsal, the woman who had played the grandmother the year before looked at her and said, "Oh, dear. I'm going to need to have someone help me with my makeup." So grandmother helped grandmother.

Everything turned out well, because Martha left herself open to help from anyone who knew more than she did.

Everything turned out well, because Martha left herself open to help from anyone who knew more than she did.

Through it all, she saw the spiritual lesson. She couldn't expect the Master to do it all for her. She had to do things herself. But she also had to listen to those people around her who could help. And then, above all, have fun.

ANN'S HUSBAND AND THE FIVE-DOLLAR CD

"Ann" was having a difficult time with her husband. He was Jewish and did not like the fact that she did the Spiritual Exercises of ECK. Anytime she tried to do a spiritual exercise, he would disturb her.

Ann would go into a far corner of their home, and she tried doing the spiritual exercises at different times of the day, but he would always interrupt her.

But she was the patient one. She never said anything, but she often wondered, *What can I do to make him understand the beauty and the treasure that I have found in the teachings of ECK?* How could she ever get him to understand this?

One year Ann went to the ECK Worldwide Seminar, and she asked the Mahanta, the Inner Master, "What can I do to help my husband understand why I love the ECK?" While she was there attending different workshops and all, she went to a certain workshop titled "Seeking God Consciousness in Everyday Life."

She hadn't really meant to go to the workshop; she was just passing by. When she looked in, the room was full. There wasn't a chair left over. But someone saw her looking in and said to her, "If you don't mind, you could sit on the floor against the back wall." So she agreed. She just sat there very quietly.

During the workshop, the group broke up into little discussion circles. Since Ann was seated on the floor, others nearby turned their chairs and faced her. So she automatically became a group leader. She had no idea this would happen; she hadn't been at a workshop before. But while the group members told stories about how they recognized God's presence in their everyday lives, Ann took notes.

Ann asked the Mahanta, the Inner Master, "What can I do to help my husband understand why I love the ECK?"

But suddenly, she realized something. The group leaders were supposed to report back to the rest of the people in the room what their group had talked about—to give a condensed version of the experiences that the group members had mentioned.

Ann was very afraid to speak in public. This is one of the great fears that people have—speaking in public. They fear it even more than translation or passing over to the other side. I can understand. I had that too.

When her turn came, she stood up and began to share some of the experiences from her own life. And apparently the audience enjoyed it because they were laughing. The laughter was warm, encouraging, and supportive. Ann felt like she belonged—like she was among people who understood her.

As she walked out of the workshop, Ann saw that somehow, in this experience, there was a message for her. It answered the question of how she could talk to her husband and tell him about ECK. She realized that she could talk about the coincidences that occurred in her life. That she could do.

The whole weekend, Ann had looked for a gift to bring home for her husband. She loved him very dearly. But she couldn't find anything. She'd looked in the ECK bookroom, and she couldn't find anything that he would like. And she'd looked in the shops, but she found nothing. By the time she had to leave the hotel to catch her flight, she still hadn't found a gift.

An inner nudge had told her to go there, and now she wondered why. Then she saw a light coming from around the corner.

She stopped in to the lobby of a hotel near her own. An inner nudge had told her to go there, and now she wondered why. Then she saw a light coming from around the corner. She found a little shop. It was open, so she went inside, but there were mostly trinkets and souvenirs, stuff her husband called junk.

Not knowing what else to do, Ann bought a few things. She was about to leave, when up on a shelf she saw some CDs. She looked through them. There was one CD of The Platters, a group from the 1950s, very popular back then. Ann only had five dollars and some change. And guess what? The CD was five dollars and, with tax, some change. She bought it, put it in her luggage, and flew home.

Her husband picked her up at the airport. On the way home, he started telling her about something that had happened to him. It was something very important and heartwarming. He performs in a club, and during one of his acts, there was a surprise guest. It turned out to be someone he had performed with many years ago. The man had come to the club to enjoy dinner and the show, but he recognized Ann's husband, and they talked awhile.

It turned out this man had gone on to become part of the singing group The Platters.

When they got home, Ann reached in her bag and brought out the CD. Her husband just stood there, his eyes and mouth wide open. Ann began to laugh.

"It's this thing between us," he said.

Ann said, "It's what I call the work of the Holy Spirit, the ECK."

And suddenly her husband had an insight into what this path is all about.

She said, "This is more than a coincidence. You can see that. The ECK did this for a reason."

After that, Ann's husband was much more open about her practicing the Spiritual Exercises of ECK. At last report, he disturbed her much less than he had before. Such is the power of love. Love on both

Ann said, "It's what I call the work of the Holy Spirit, the ECK." And suddenly her husband had an insight into what this path is all about.

sides—Ann's love for her husband and the husband's love for her.

IS YOUR HEART IN IT?

Nurse "Gladys" had looked for what she called "the path" her whole life. Her father was a Baptist minister, and even when she was a child in church, she would daydream. She knew her body was there, but she felt this essential part that she was, was someplace else, in a beautiful place.

Gladys often wondered about it. What was that wonderful state of being? She said she always had this gut feeling about it.

Research has lately found evidence that the body has at least three mind centers. There's the one in the head, the one we all have known about. But there's another one in the heart area. And a third in the intestines, or the gut.

The gut feeling is saying, "I don't like this at all."

The heart says, "My heart's not in this."

The head says, "But it makes sense."

If people would just listen to their body and its reaction to a certain situation or person, often they would read the circumstance more correctly. Because the body, through the gut feeling, is saying, "I don't like this at all."

The heart says, "My heart's not in this."

The head says, "But it makes sense. See? Look here. Black and white."

We've been taught to pay attention only to the mind center in the head, which says, Everything is right here in black and white. Two sides: this side, that side. Pluses, minuses, and so on.

I think research is going to find that there are other centers too—lesser ones. Little magnetic centers throughout the entire body. Some larger ones—like in the intestines, heart, and head—but also smaller ones. Worlds within this world of a physical body you have.

LOVE IS A TWO-WAY STREET

You are Soul. You are the eternal being, and you wear this body. At the time of passing over, you shed this body, and it turns to dust, but Soul lives on, because Soul is eternal.

Soul exists because God loves It. God loves us. And this love must be a two-way street.

Some people ask, How can I find love? And the answer, of course, is that to find love, you must first give love. People who can't find love need to take an honest look at themselves, because that's where the answer is.

That's where the problem is. It's all there inside each of us.

AN EXPERIENCE WITH THE MASTER

Nurse Gladys worked with the power of love. As I mentioned, her dad was a Baptist minister, she daydreamed in church, and for years she wondered, *Where will I find the path? There must be something more.*

She looked for many years. At a certain low spot in her life—the lowest spot she'd ever been in—she cried. She did not know how to face tomorrow. This was during the early 1980s.

That night when she was in a very light sleep, she suddenly noticed a man standing by her bedside. He was a white man in a blue shirt. Gladys wondered, *Who is this?* The man gave her such a look of compassion, love, and understanding that her heart was filled with goodness.

Gladys wondered, Who is this? The man gave her such a look of compassion, love, and understanding that her heart was filled with goodness.

When Gladys awoke, her depression had been lifted.

LOOK FOR GOODNESS

Going back to Paul Twitchell's talk for a moment, he said that he could not take sides in people's conflicts and he did not accept any more complaints. After that, he said, all that was left to do was to love.

He said that what you do now is look for the goodness in each other.

Charles Lamb, the English poet, hated someone in the club they both belonged to. Lamb would not speak to the man. A friend said, "You know, Charles, he's not really such a bad fellow if you get to know him." Charles Lamb said, "Well, that's the trouble. If I got to know him, then I might like him."

That's the mind talking. It's the ego saying, "I will never back down. I am always right, and nothing anyone else can ever say will get me to find favor with such a person." Myself, I wonder why they'd even try.

Life offers so many other good people to choose for company. Choose the good ones. Like the salesman going into a new territory—he looks for the easy sales.

Find the good people; find the ones with goodness. And those you need to associate with who do not have that goodness, look for it in them anyway.

Find the people with goodness. And those you need to associate with who do not have that goodness, look for it in them anyway.

GIFT OF A GOOD TEACHER

Joan, my wife, was an instructor for many years before she came to work at Eckankar. She always looked for the best in each student. She had high expectations.

I've found, in the ECK Spiritual Center and elsewhere, that whenever a former teacher comes to work for ECK, they bring a special quality. They make people go beyond themselves. They will always try harder.

I'm talking about a good teacher, a real teacher. They will get others to try their own wings, to realize their creative potential as a spiritual being. People will do anything to please a teacher who expects more from them than anyone had expected from them before. Joan has worked with so many people, and it's wonderful to see how they have blossomed over the years as they developed their skills and self-confidence.

I am in awe of these good teachers who have the ability to inspire others to be all they can be.

A good teacher, a real teacher, will get others to try their own wings, to realize their creative potential as a spiritual being.

FINDING THE HU

Now back to the story of Gladys. After she had this experience of this man appearing by her bedside, she called an old woman who was knowledgeable in things of this sort. The old woman said, "Just watch. See what comes of this."

Years passed, and nothing came of it, but Gladys always remembered. Still she wondered, *Where is the path? Where is love?*

In time, she found a husband, and they built a home. She had a set of chandeliers—an heirloom gift from her mother. She called an electrician to install this special chandelier. The man was Hispanic. He looked at the chandelier and said, "The wiring looks bad in here. I'll put it up if you want to, but there is a potential hazard here, and I would not recommend it."

Then he asked, "What religion are you?"

Gladys said, "Baptist Pentecostal."

"I have a tape I'd like to leave with you," he said. And it was the *HU: A Love Song to God* audio recording.

HU is an ancient name for God. It is the name of all names for God. It's been known to the East for a long time, and also in Africa.

The electrician said, "I'd like to leave this tape with you. Anytime you're in danger or in any sort of trouble—depressed, sick, whenever you need help of any sort—remember to sing *HU*." Then he sang *HU* three times to be sure she knew and would remember that name of God.

Before he left, the man said, "If I could, I would like to leave a book for you. I'll leave it on your doorstep." He didn't have it with him.

The next morning, Gladys looked outside. On the step was a blue book, *The Spiritual Notebook*, by Paul Twitchell.

Gladys had sung this word, HU, during a time of trouble in the family and was grateful that it had lifted the sorrow from her heart.

As the months passed, she wanted to look through the book and find out more about this word, *HU*. She had sung it during a time of trouble in the family, and it had helped. She was grateful that it had lifted the sorrow from her heart. So she wanted to know more about HU. But every time she'd pick up *The Spiritual Notebook*, she couldn't read it. Once she even carried it out to the garbage, put it in, and went back inside. But an inner nudge said, *Get the book. You might want it later.* So she got the book out of the garbage and put it on the shelf with her nursing books.

Gladys forgot about the book, except for the fact that it was there to pack every time they moved. They moved to several different states, but it always went along.

FINDING THE TRUE TEACHINGS

In 1995, her mother had an operation for breast cancer. Gladys was in the waiting room with her sister and brother-in-law. While they sat there, Gladys said to them, "I feel I've been here before." Her sister said, "You do?" Her eyes were smiling. She was smiling too—a very open, warm smile.

Gladys said, "Yes, I do."

Her sister said, "If you don't mind, I'd like to send you some books."

Gladys remembered the blue book. She said to her sister, "I have this blue book—*The Spiritual Notebook*, by Paul Twitchell." Then her sister said, "I'm a member of Eckankar." Gladys hadn't known that. And this was how Gladys came in contact with Eckankar.

Gladys went to an ECK center. Her sister had said, "Just look in the yellow pages under Eckankar, and you'll find that most cities have an Eckankar center." And hers did.

There happened to be a Soul Travel workshop that evening, and the people there were very warm, supportive, and inviting. Gladys and her husband felt right at home. So Gladys went to an ECK seminar some time later.

Gladys worked in a forty-bed hospital unit taking care of heart patients before and after their operations, so she sees a lot. She sees the patient, she sees the family, she sees everything. But after she went to the ECK seminar, her staff noticed something different about her. "There's a quietness, peace, and glow in your face," they said. "Tell us about this seminar you went to." So she was able to tell them about the ECK teachings.

"There's a quietness, peace, and glow in your face," her staff noticed. "Tell us about this seminar you went to."

Gladys, like all the others mentioned, loves God, loves life, and does the best she can. Such is the power of love.

JEWELS OF WISDOM

In *Stranger by the River*, by Paul Twitchell, Rebazar Tarzs speaks to the seeker on love. This is in the chapter "Jewels of Wisdom." Rebazar is talking to the seeker, Peddar Zaskq, by the banks of the Jhelum. Peddar Zaskq is the spiritual name for Paul Twitchell.

Rebazar said, "If you try to live in this world without cultivating love for God, you will be entangled more and more. You will be overwhelmed with its dangers, its griefs, and its sorrows. And the more you think of worldly things, the more you will be in need of them. Secure the oil of divine love, and then put thyself to the task of thine own duties of this world."

All the people mentioned in this talk did that. They secured for themselves the oil of divine love, and then they went about their tasks in this world.

Those are the words I'd like to say to you if I could put myself in the role of a teacher. If I were half as good as teachers who encourage students who do not know the first thing about reading, writing, or arithmetic—teachers who have the patience to bring their students to a higher level so that other teachers can take over.

If you have love, you have all.

Other teachers have brought you through the early stage of reading, writing, and arithmetic in the spiritual works.

Now you've come here to the path of ECK to learn how to find God's love for yourself. Because if you have love, you have all.

The power of love.

ECK's Helping Hand

How to Survive Spiritually in Our Times, Mahanta Transcripts, Book 16, is one of our new books. The ECK arranges things to be there as aid and comfort to those who need it, and this book is very helpful.

Some people who are in need of care or comfort, or just need someone to listen to, may not be ready for this book. But if you take the message in that book to heart, you don't need to carry the book with you as you go out doing your tasks in this world.

As agents for love, your task is to love, to understand, to give aid to others in time of need.

The most important thing you can do, as you go about the tasks in your daily life, is to show each other love, compassion, and understanding.

Whatever happens up here onstage is in the hands of Divine Spirit. I do the best I can. I've nothing to gain, nothing to lose, and I haven't since the experience related in my autobiography, about the stranger on the bridge. You just love God. Love God, love God's creation, and do the best you can.

Love God, love God's creation, and do the best you can.

It's a privilege to be here with all of you. Heart-to-heart, I say my love is always with you.

May the blessings be.

ECK Worldwide Seminar, Minneapolis, Minnesota, Saturday, October 13, 2001

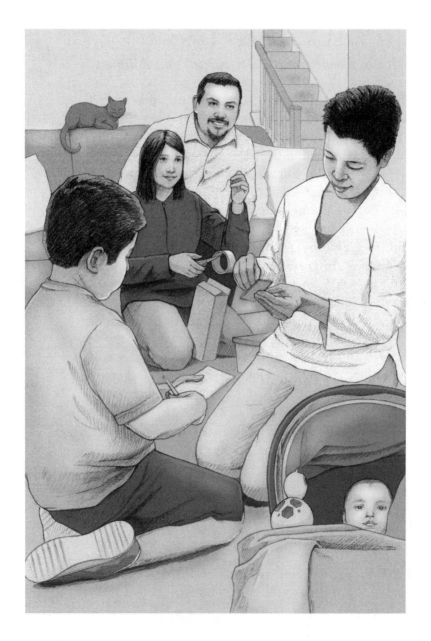

All each Soul, embodied in a human form is trying to achieve and realize is the love of God. The pure love of God.

7

THE QUEST
FOR LOVE

✳

*L*in Yutang was a very popular philosopher in America during the 1930s and 1940s. He said, in effect, "Let one thing go." You'll find this very helpful. Because karma has speeded up in these times. It's part of the purification of earth. This is all on a spiritual track. Even though we look around and see the many wars that have flared up recently, they've always been there. At any given time, there are always forty or more wars going on between nations or tribes.

We have all these things pulling on us today.

If at some point you just say, "I'm going to let one thing go," that helps.

DON'T STORE STRESS

The second saying I'd like to pass on is "Don't store stress." This came from the oldest woman in the world. She lives in Japan. Someone asked her, "How do you live to such a nice age, as you have?" The woman answered, "Don't store stress."

I like the phrase "don't *store* stress." It gives the

If at some point you just say, "I'm going to let one thing go," that helps.

125

image of something very much like a battery. A battery
that is fully charged, but then has a charger hooked
up to it, will overcharge and ruin itself.

You don't want that to happen to you.

So let one thing go, and don't store stress. Let it go.

THE QUEST FOR LOVE

This is Easter weekend, and I think it is the
greatest example of love. Christianity's history
shows that Christ laid down his life for the people
who needed help spiritually. What greater love than
this?

The quest for love is a quest all people have. It
drives them on in a search for God. But most people
don't know it's a search for God.

This is a quest for divine love.

People will experiment with all the manifestations of human love—all the aberrations and all the
pure, good kinds of love that one can think of. But
all each Soul embodied in a human form, or human
frame, is trying to achieve and realize is the love of
God. The pure love of God.

In *The Shariyat-Ki-Sugmad*, Book One, it says,
"If one begins to look for love, he will find it. If he
puts any conditions on love, there will be obstacles."

NO GREATER LOVE

You may know the story in *Stranger by the River*
in the chapter "No Greater Love." It's the story of the
ECK Master Rebazar Tarzs and his student Peddar
Zaskq.

On this particular day, they are in a graveyard
above the city. Nearby stands a small church. The
ECK Master, Rebazar Tarzs, is walking among the

The quest for love is a quest all people have. It drives them on in a search for God.

rows of white crosses, reading the inscriptions.

The seeker notices that he stops at one and is reading the inscription. So he goes over to Rebazar Tarzs.

It is the grave of a low-caste Indian, the seeker says, who gave his life to save a drowning white child in the river. Rebazar Tarzs had been reading the inscription that read "No Greater Love Hath Man Than To Lay Down His Life For Another."

The Tibetan says, "It is true that when man gives his life for another, he will be saved. That Soul touched the unseen power which we call the sea of life. By doing so he gained God's mercy and grace for himself!"

"It is strange to me," says the seeker, "that the beauty of life cannot be measured by mere attitudes and opinions. Because love is the greatest of all things, man is ever seeking it."

"Love is God," replies Rebazar Tarzs. "When you wish to bathe in the river, you go to the edge where the water is shallow and say that you have bathed in the river. Thus to love and receive the real benefit of God's love, we must give up that finite self within us and do deeds for the sake of our fellow man. That is the reason why this Soul is honored by his fellow man and enjoys bliss in heaven with God. He gave without hesitation."

So in the quest for love, we look at things we can understand. Something more down to earth.

"Love is God," replies Rebazar Tarzs. "Thus to love and receive the real benefit of God's love, we must do deeds for the sake of our fellow man."

A LITTLE HEN SAVES HER CHICKS

A farmer had a runt chick. It was always behind the other chickens. As the others grew big and strong, this little runty chicken fell to the bottom of the pecking order.

But in time, the little chicken grew up and wanted to have her own brood. Right on the henhouse floor, she tried to make a little nest and lay her eggs. But the other chickens would break the eggs when she was off eating. No matter how hard this little hen tried, she could never hatch any chicks.

The farmer had taken a liking to this underdog of a chicken. So he decided to build her a special coop away from the other chickens so she could have privacy and space.

In time, the little hen hatched a brood of chicks. Before long they were up and running around. It was warm, so she let them go outside in the yard. The little hen showed her chicks all the good places to find seed.

One day, they were out in the yard, eating with the rest of the chickens, when suddenly the flock scattered.

The farmer, watching from the house, saw a hawk in the sky above the chicken yard. The hawk was seeing a meal down below, and he was going to have some chicks.

The farmer started to go outside. All the chickens had scattered, including the little hen, hiding under tractors and wagons. But the little hen saw that her chicks were still out in the middle of the yard. They hadn't come to safety.

So the little hen ran out into the yard, calling to her brood. She spread her wings, and the chicks all ran under them. Then the hen sat down in the yard, and the hawk hit her hard. But before the hawk could do any more damage, the farmer arrived. And the hawk flew off.

The farmer stood looking at his pet hen. *Looks like she's gone,* he thought. *What am I going to do*

> The little hen ran out, spread her wings, and the chicks all ran under them. The hawk hit her hard.

with all these chicks?

Suddenly the little hen hopped up off the ground, shook herself, and strutted off, as if nothing had happened.

The farmer saw this as an example of the love that such a parent has for its own.

We humans have this vanity that tells us we are a special creation of God. Mark Twain had a lot to say about man and his high opinion of himself. But animals also have divine love pouring through them. And they also give this love to others of their own kind, and to others who are not of their own kind.

The quest for love.

Animals also have divine love pouring through them.

ALLOWING OTHERS THEIR SPACE

When I got here tonight, I realized I had forgotten my watch. A woman offered to let me use hers. But I didn't want to show up onstage with a woman's watch on my wrist—even though this is San Francisco and it's OK.

When I was a kid in high school, hitchhiking on the lonely highways, sometimes I would get a ride with people who were gay. This just wasn't my thing. So I asked one of my friends what to do. He was a runty little guy, but he was tough as nails. We called him Beef because he was always complaining about something, making a beef about something.

I said, "Beef, what do you do?" He said, "I just tell them it's not my game."

I thought that was a pretty good line. Whenever I needed it after that, I just said, "It's not my game, thank you." They were OK with it. So life went on.

That's how life is here. Some people go this way,

some people go that way, and it's all the same to me.

The only time I get agitated is when people, whether heterosexual or homosexual, get into my space. And since there are more heterosexual people around, they get in my space more sometimes.

It's all a wash as far as I'm concerned. We like our space, we like our freedom.

THE WINDUP WATCH

Anyway, I was looking for a watch when I got here, and I didn't want to take the woman's watch. Besides, it had a battery, and being sensitive to electromagnetic things, I don't like to get too much exposure to things like watch batteries. Then the woman said, "But wait! I have another watch in my office." I'm thinking, *It's still a woman's watch.* But then she said, "It's a man's watch."

I was impressed. No matter what happens, the ECK provides us with what we need. "And," she said, "it's a windup watch." Great! No electromagnetic radiation problems.

As I was dressing at home earlier, I put on my tie, and I noticed I'd lost weight. Some people worry about being overweight. Some people, like me, worry about being underweight. The last time I wore this shirt was six months ago. When I put my shirt on tonight, I said, "There's lots of room in here for all of us." I told my wife, "I think I threw out all the other shirts." But I didn't have time to change anyway. What you see is what you get.

When the woman gave me the windup man's watch, I thought, *Good, good. The ECK's providing well.* So I said, "Do you happen to have a shirt with a smaller neck?" She didn't. I figure I didn't need it though. It's very comfortable, having all this room.

> *No matter what happens, the ECK provides us with what we need.*

How We Learn and Grow

Some time ago a woman I'll call Mary was channel surfing while making dinner at home. On public TV she saw a program about Toni Morrison, the award-winning novelist, editor, and professor. Toni Morrison had once said, "There's got to be more to life than just getting by."

On the program, she was speaking at a dinner, and the speech was about public education. A black woman in the audience, a teacher, said, "So often black people who've made it, who've become successful, will tell black children, 'You can't learn that stuff. It's just too hard for you. You don't have the background.'" The black teacher asked Morrison, "Do you find this is so?"

Instead of giving a direct answer, Toni Morrison told a story. One time she had been visiting a classroom. Near the end of the class, the teacher had invited the children to ask questions. If they wanted to settle something in their minds they could do so.

So the teacher said, "Does anyone have a question?"

A young boy raised his hand. He came up to the front near the teacher and said, "I need to ax a question, Miss."

The teacher said, "Yes, but you do not say *ax*; you say *ask*."

The boy nodded. The educator, Toni Morrison, was sitting in the back of the room, and she could see that the boy wanted to ask his question. He was so full of enthusiasm.

But the teacher said, "No, before you ask your question, first repeat after me, 'I need to *ask* a question.'"

The boy nodded and said, "I need to *ax* a question."

The boy, so full of enthusiasm, said, "I need to ax a question." "No," the teacher said, "ask."

"No," she said, *"ask."*

This went on for some time. And Toni Morrison could see that the boy had a problem with his tongue and that it would never say the word right. Then came the end of the class, and the boy never got to ask his question. He'd been very enthusiastic about something, but the teacher had been so full of her own agenda that she never gave him a chance to ask a question that would have helped him grow.

The teacher never gave the boy a chance to ask a question that would have helped him grow.

LESSONS OF A TEMPLE TOUR GUIDE

Mary, the woman watching this program, had been having a hard time at work—a lot of uncertainty, a lot of broken promises on the part of her new employer. So she had a lot of worries. Mary prayed to God to help her, but she was getting bitter. She didn't want to be, but she was torn inside.

She realized that an ECKist does not pray to God for material blessings. If that's the case, the ECKist is in ECK for the wrong reason. But human nature was pushing at her, and she was getting into this thing against God. Her mind was saying to her, "Who wants to serve God if God is not helping out?"

In the middle of this TV program, the phone rang. A friend was calling. "We need a Temple of ECK tour guide tomorrow. Would you help out?" the friend asked.

Mary said, "I don't know. I'll have to think about it."

Mary was feeling kind of sore at God, kind of sore at the ECK teachings, at the Mahanta, at pretty much everybody—simply because she was hurting. When we hurt, we strike out, sometimes in anger, at whatever is near and dear.

She thought of all the reasons to say no. First she

had just been a tour guide last week; she needed a break. Secondly, she was very busy; she had stuff to do at home. Third (but she didn't dare say this one), God wasn't doing his part for her.

But God had sent a very particular friend to make this request of her. This friend had done Mary a big favor in the past when Mary first moved to town. Mary said, "I owe her big-time, because when I needed her help she gave it with complete love and without hesitation. The least I can do is do the same."

So Mary called back and said, "Yes, I'll do it."

The next day, Mary arrived at the Temple of ECK. "Where's the other tour guide?" she asked. There were three tour guides just leaving for the day. "We don't know," they said. And they left.

Mary was all by herself. *Maybe it'll be a slow day*, she thought. *Maybe I'll just get to read this new ECK book.*

After about fifteen minutes, the other tour guide came out to the lobby and sat down. It turned out she had been in a roundtable discussion. Now there were two of them.

They sat out front for a while, waiting for visitors. So far only one visitor had stopped by, a student from the University of Minnesota. It was quiet at the tour-guide table. So Mary excused herself. "If anyone comes, just call me," she said. "I'll be in the sanctuary. I'll be reading my book." She wanted some peace and quiet.

She got comfortable and started reading. Just as she was feeling really cozy, settling into the seat the way you would in front of your favorite TV program, the other tour guide came in. "We have two visitors," she said.

Oh, great, Mary thought. She had been thinking of going home early, at four instead of four thirty.

God had sent a very particular friend to make this request of her.

But she said to herself, *Probably two ECKists. I'll go out there, and this will go really quick. They just want to look around.*

Mary came out of the sanctuary and saw two young men in black slacks with name tags on. Two Mormon missionaries.

Just what I need today, she thought. *I don't know if I can handle this.*

EXPLAINING ECK TO OTHERS

Mary's fears and frustrations from work were right there. She just wanted peace and quiet, to finish her shift sitting in the sanctuary reading her book, but here came two Mormon missionaries. It wasn't like she was at home and could ignore them or turn them away. This was different. She was on duty.

She said inwardly, "I'm not ready for this."

But the Mahanta said, "Well, ready or not, here they come."

She introduced herself. "And what's your name?" she asked one.

"Elder," he said. She looked at the name tag. It said Elder. She looked at the other person's name tag. It said Elder too. Later she learned that *elder* meant "teacher." But at that time she didn't know. "Well, you don't look like brothers," she said. She thought *elder* must be a title of some sort. Mary then wondered, *How do I present the ECK teachings to two closed minds?*

Of course, she didn't realize her own mind was closed to them. She realized that later too, but not at the time. She was so closed up with her own concerns.

The Mahanta said, "Keep it simple. Give them the truth as you know it. And that's it—no more, no less."

The Mahanta said, "Keep it simple. Give them the truth as you know it. And that's it—no more, no less."

She thought she could handle that.

The tour started. She talked about the physical Temple. The two young men were very cool, giving her icy smiles—at least she saw them as icy smiles. She mentioned that the same contractor who built the Temple also built the Mall of America. That sparked a mild interest, but no fireworks, no clapping.

The next big challenge was explaining the Light and Sound of God. How was she going to go about this? She tried to tell them about the Light, that It was the same thing seen by Saul of Tarsus, who became St. Paul after his conversion. With frozen smiles, the missionaries said, "Hmmm."

Mary then realized she didn't want to pit Eckankar against another religion. That was not right. So she tried to show what ECK had done for her spiritually, how she had grown spiritually. She tried to explain the Sound of God, saying, "It's many different sounds, a lot of them in everyday life. Those are on the outer, and there are some on the inner, like ocean waves and the sounds of birds."

So she tried to show what ECK had done for her spiritually.

Her explanation about the Light seen by Saul on the road to Damascus—that went nowhere. And now her explanation about the Sound of God—big splat. Her mind chided her about this: "Your speech missed the mark badly," it said. "You just weren't up to it." She began feeling really down on herself.

Just about that time, the University of Minnesota student, the other guest, came out of the sanctuary. He came over to the tour group. "All right! Church of Latter Day Saints!" he said. "Hey, do you happen to know Elder so-and-so at the U?"

They'd never heard of him.

The student, who was an ECKist, said, "Well, have you heard of Elder so-and-so?"

As a matter of fact, they had.

The next thing Mary knew, lively chatting had broken out, and she noticed the two missionaries had lost a bit of their icy coldness. They seemed to be melting. Of course, Mary didn't realize that *she* was melting. She saw the change around her, and she thought it was some lucky coincidence that that ECKist student showed up and was friends with Mormon elders at the university. Mary was completely baffled by this.

The ECK provides. The Holy Spirit provides. In this case, It happened to provide the ECK student. He waltzed right in, right on cue. He didn't know it. And Mary didn't know this was going to happen. And of course, the two Mormons didn't know it either.

Soon the student left. Mary was alone again with the two Mormons.

They all went into the sanctuary. "There's the Blue Star of ECK," she pointed out. "I haven't seen it myself (she was being totally honest now), "but sometimes people see it as a blue star in contemplation or as a blue light." She said, "It's a manifestation of God's love."

Frozen smiles. She saw fixed, frozen smiles, polite nods. Then Mary showed them some ECK paintings. Previous visitors had oohed and aahed about these paintings. These two said, "Nice." With frozen smiles.

Next on the tour was the groom's room; the Temple is sometimes used for weddings, and there's a groom's room and a bride's room. They are just little rooms, and Mary knew the missionaries wouldn't be wildly impressed. They smiled their cool smiles.

Finally they arrived at the chapel. This was Mary's favorite room. She gushed about what this room meant to her. But the two men didn't seem impressed. One

The Holy Spirit provides. In this case, It happened to provide the ECK student. He waltzed right in, right on cue.

pointed to the pictures of the ECK Masters, then to the one of the Living ECK Master.

"How is he appointed?" he asked.

Mary looked at the ceiling for inspiration, but it wasn't coming. Then she got the gentle nudge: keep it simple. She said, "He's appointed by God." That got thin smiles. Then followed endless questions about how the ECK Masters are appointed. She did her best to answer them.

DIVINE INSPIRATION

In the middle of all this, Mary had an inspiration. She had become curious about their religion. "What about your religion?" she asked. "Tell me about it." Their faces lit right up. One of them said, "Our prophet is also appointed like yours." They told her the process. She asked about their prayers. She told them about the HU and how ECKists usually just say thank you to God. That's pretty much it: Thank you, and I love you, God.

The Mormons said, "That's basically what we do too." But they might throw in a few extra requests. That was OK with Mary.

Then one of the elders said, "The Light of God is part of our religion too."

Mary was getting an education. She was softening up. Their smiles seemed warmer. She realized she'd gone into a panic for nothing. She realized that the ECK teachings and the Mormon religion had a lot in common. The icy faces she had seen were only a facade.

All during the tour, she had noticed the two men kept asking the same question: "What is Eckankar about?" She began to wonder, *Am I like the teacher*

Mary had an inspiration. "What about your religion?" Their faces lit right up.

in that TV program? So full of my own agenda that I can't even listen to what the child's question is?

How do I answer this question? she wondered. She did her best and let it go.

When they got to the bookroom, one of the missionaries asked, "What's Eckankar's definition of God?"

When they got to the bookroom, one of the missionaries asked, "What's Eckankar's definition of God?"

Mary said, "God is impossible to explain in human language, but ECKists often define It as love, wisdom, and power."

The two elders said, "So true."

Mary said, "People experience God in their own way."

"Yes, so true. So beautiful." And it is.

Their faces were like lamps. Then the tour was over. Before it had started, she'd asked them, "How long do you have for this tour?" They'd said, "Thirty minutes." She looked at the time. It had been an hour. Then she wondered, Should she offer them ECK literature? Would it be the right thing to do? But when she offered, they said, "We'd love some, whatever you can give us."

This took her aback again. So each got a book and an information packet. And she gave them an audiocassette set that maybe they could share.

SIX SPIRITUAL LESSONS

From this Temple tour, Mary learned six lessons.
1. The tour had lifted her worries about her own job.
2. She knows the ECK needs her services.
3. Serving ECK is a gift.
4. You can't always guess people's spiritual needs;

and the ECK, the Holy Spirit, is big enough to take care of Itself. Her mind flashed to the University of Minnesota student, who just happened to arrive on the scene at exactly the right time. Of course, the Holy Spirit sent him.

5. Don't ever compromise your religion. She hadn't. She kept it simple. She kept it to the doctrine without trying to play up to the visitors. And they were honest with her; they did the same.

6. All true religions have a common bond. And, of course, this bond is love.

The quest for love.

THE MAHANTA'S MIRACLES

This is from *The Shariyat-Ki-Sugmad*, the Eckankar bible, the Way of the Eternal:

The Mahanta does not desire that worldly people in large numbers flock after him. He prefers only those who are eager for the realization of God to them. He does not perform miracles for people to see, but moves in the mysterious ways of the Lord. The true disciple does not believe in the miracles which the Mahanta may perform at varied times but instead believes in the teachings he imparts to give each a lift into the heavenly worlds.

Yet these miracles happen all the time. When the Mahanta, the Living ECK Master says, "I am always with you," it *means* I am always with you. Often the ECKist is unaware of it, even though other people who are not ECKists do see the ECK Master with the ECKist.

But the other people don't know that they're seeing

These miracles happen all the time. When the Mahanta, the Living ECK Master says, "I am always with you," it means I am always with you.

someone who is invisible to anyone else but themselves, and even to the ECKist. And the ECKist doesn't know that the ECK Master is there.

MEL'S MYSTERY FRIEND

This story is about "Mel". His father had had open-heart surgery. He and his wife later came to visit Mel in the southwestern United States. During dinner, Mel's daughter came running into the dining room. She said there were bugs covering their mimosa tree.

Two years earlier there had been an infestation of bugs. They had just about stripped the tree of its foliage. In no time at all, they had done a lot of damage in the area.

Mel ran outside. He stood about twenty feet from the tree, trying to decide what to do. In the meantime, his dad came out on the porch. He stood there, watching from the porch, for quite a while. Then, without saying anything, he went back inside.

By that evening, the problem with the bugs had been taken care of, and the family was sitting around talking about the events of the day.

The father said, "I saw you were talking with your friend, or neighbor, about the tree. So I went back inside."

This stunned Mel and his wife. Mel's father was not an ECKist. They were itching to ask him, "What did the neighbor look like?" Because as far as Mel knew, it had just been him and the tree out there.

Then his dad said more. He had seen someone dressed in blue standing with Mel, discussing the tree. But Mel thought he was by himself, making a decision on his own.

Whatever happened, the bug problem was handled by that evening.

His dad had seen someone dressed in blue standing with Mel, discussing the tree.

"I AM ALWAYS WITH YOU"

On the East Coast, an ECKist was waiting at a bus stop. She noticed what looked like a family dispute between a man and woman. The man took a child who looked about five years old, and moved away from the woman.

The woman then came up to "Vi," who was a Higher Initiate in ECK. "Do you have a pen?" the woman asked. Then the man came up close, and the woman said to him, "I'm getting job info. I need some information about a job." He moved back but looked suspicious, as if he wasn't quite sure what kind of information she might be getting from this person at the bus stop.

Very quietly, this woman said to Vi, "Lady, can you please help me? I'm being kidnapped."

Then, louder, she asked if she could sit by Vi on the bus and go over the job info.

They sat together on the bus, supposedly talking over some job prospects, and the man was in the seat right behind them. The bus was otherwise empty except for one passenger, way in the back, and the bus driver. The woman wanted Vi to give a note to the bus driver. The note said the man was an escaped criminal and was going to harm her children.

Vi knew if she just passed the note to the bus driver, it wouldn't resolve the situation. She needed to get ahold of the police.

So she got off at the next stop and called 911, the emergency number.

The woman on the bus thought she'd been abandoned, left to her own devices. Another citizen, faced with danger and worried about getting involved, has bowed out of the situation and wants nothing to do with it.

Very quietly, this woman said to Vi, "Lady, can you please help me? I'm being kidnapped."

Not the case. Vi told the police. Police from two towns came out, five squad cars and a SWAT team. They were all waiting at the next bus stop. When the criminal got off the bus, they took him without incident.

When it was all over, the woman was talking to Vi. She said when she first came over to ask for the pen, she'd seen Vi with a man in blue. Of course, there was no one there with Vi. She was alone.

SEARCH FOR THE HOLY GRAIL

Again, someone who was not an ECKist was seeing an ECK Master. She didn't know it was someone in the spiritual body, in the Soul body. The ECKist wasn't seeing this because the ECKist wasn't to see this.

I'd like to repeat the quote from *The Shariyat*:

"If one begins to look for love, he will find it. If he puts any conditions on love, there will be obstacles."

The quest for love has run in all of us throughout our many lives. For many people, it's the driving force, and yet they haven't a clue as to what's driving them. They think it's money. They think it's power. They think it's the accolades of men. And they think it's a good home. They think it's the solitude of their church, the comfort of their friends.

But it's really this desire for the love of God. Because you see, Soul is of God.

God is love, and love is God. What is God? God is love. So simple. Love is God. So simple.

This is what mankind is looking for.

GOD'S TEACHERS

This is what drives people at the frenzied pace of today's life in the mainstream. It's what drives life

Again, someone not an ECKist was seeing an ECK Master.

in the backwaters. It exists in spite of the prejudices and the closed hearts and minds of people.

This love of God is always there. And God always sends someone to show the way.

God's teachers are many. There is a teacher for every classroom, for every grade, for every school. There are the teachers in advanced education, there are teachers in the graduate area, and on and on. There are just teachers and teachers.

The teacher of the Light and Sound of God—there are several of those. And there's the teacher of the Light and Sound and the love of God, and of the many other things that go with the true spiritual path.

The quest for love. On the path of ECK you will have found this holy grail.

HOW TO GET LOVE

There's such a search for this holy grail. People are looking for it in the markets. There must be a magic way to make the bucks. They're looking for the holy grail of health. There must be one final answer, one final way.

But life has a funny way of receding like the horizon, keeping just ahead of our feet. We can move forward, stand still, or move backward, and the horizon is always there, always around us.

The way to get to the love of God is to open our hearts. The true Master can give the key to open the heart. And this key, of course, is love. It works through the Light and Sound.

Now, what are the Light and Sound? The Holy Spirit, the ECK. The Light and Sound of God are the manifestations of God speaking, in action. This wave is both coming and going. It comes from the heart of

The quest for love. On the path of ECK you will have found this holy grail.

God and returns to the heart of God, all at one and
the same time. Soul's mission is to catch the wave
home.

I would like to leave you with this. Remember
that on your journeys I am always with you.

ECK Springtime Seminar, San Francisco, California,
Saturday, March 30, 2002

In a dream, Lawson felt the happiness and joy in that place. Because this yellow light was the Light of God.

8
ALL HAS MEANING

Joan and I go grocery shopping at a store where there's a very good checker named Al. Al is very careful. Other checkers are lightning fast. Sometimes I'll get greens of some sort and squeeze all the air out of the plastic bag so it lasts longer in the refrigerator, and these checkers can still tell at a glance what kind of greens are in that bag.

Al tells stories while he checks us out, but he is very careful. While he's talking and checking, we have a very good time.

A couple of weeks ago, Al's end-of-day tally was off by an average of only fifty cents. He was very proud of that.

One day Joan and I were going through checkout. Joan was ahead of me. She put some items on the belt, and Al tallied them up.

LIVING THROUGH OUR MISTAKES

Suddenly Al froze. He didn't say another thing. He just stared at the screen. When we looked at the screen, we saw a four with all these little zeros. Joan interpreted it first.

"The computer owes me four hundred thousand dollars," Joan said. Al stood there; he couldn't believe

Suddenly Al froze. He just stared at the screen. He couldn't be off four hundred thousand dollars.

it. He couldn't be off four hundred thousand dollars.

I teased Al. I said, "It's going to take a long time to get your average discrepancy back down to only fifty cents a day." But Al had no sense of humor just then, poor man. He reached into his cash drawer, pulled out a little form, and wrote "four hundred thousand dollars" on it. This was going to be a very hard thing to explain to the boss at day's end.

He hardly looked up at us. "I haven't seen so many zeros since Moby Dick was a minnow," he said. The poor man looked totally crushed.

Al is also an actor. He does checkout at grocery stores to keep body and soul together in between gigs. He is trying to do two things at once, and it's easy to make a four-hundred-thousand-dollar mistake once in a while. Nobody should hold it against him. I didn't. Joan didn't.

I got to thinking about Al's mistake. Saint Paul said, "Let him that thinketh he standeth take heed lest he fall." Al was so proud of his fifty-cent average discrepancy, and I think he made himself hard to live with among the other checkers. But they're going to coast for a long time now. They'll never hear another word from Al.

Al probably won't want to check us out next time we go to the store. That's OK. He's a good guy, and we won't hold it against him. We'll go to his checkout anyway.

SHARING THE CHALLENGES
OF SAINT PAUL

I was thinking about what Saint Paul had said: "Let him that thinketh he standeth take heed lest he fall."

> I got to thinking about Al's mistake.

It sounds like Saint Paul was well versed in King James English as well as Hebrew and Greek.

I feel the King James language is some of the most beautiful there is. I sincerely enjoy it, because all these people got together and put words together very poetically to express something from another language.

Any of you who speak two languages know that the idioms of one language do not translate exactly over to another. Word-for-word translation doesn't work. You've got to take the idiom from one language, find an idiom from the other language, and match them up. Once you do that, the translation has some sort of meaning.

We're having the same challenges today that Saint Paul had way back then.

We're having the same challenges today that Saint Paul had way back then.

Saint Paul found out very early that his mission would be to the Gentiles. The Jews were well taken care of by Saint Peter and some of the others. Paul had a special talent, plus he had special credentials. He was a Roman citizen. That meant he could go anywhere throughout the Roman Empire. Rome was the ruling power with extensive influence, much as the United States, and its English language, are all over the place today.

The United States is putting its fingers in everybody else's pie, and the Romans were doing very much the same thing. The Roman language, Latin, was the language of commerce. But the elite spoke Greek. This means the government officials, the intellectuals; they had their children educated according to Greek thought and Greek philosophy.

The Greek philosophers at that time included the Stoics and the Epicureans.

OUR PAST AS ECKISTS

Now you're wondering, *What has all this to do with me?*

A lot of ECKists had past lives during these early formative years of Christianity.

In one life you may have been a follower of Judaism. Then times changed, and all of a sudden friends of yours were going over to Christianity. Now there was a problem. You each had different beliefs.

You wondered, *What shall I do? Is my friend very important or not? Is my belief important or not?*

When Saint Paul was wandering around on his missionary journeys, and the other apostles were out there too, some of you were in the congregations, listening to these early speakers. You heard the dynamic sermons of Saint Paul, and maybe you were convinced. But there were problems.

TYING IT ALL TOGETHER

Saint Paul's Jewish name was Saul. When he became a Christian, he converted and took the name of Paul. That was his Gentile name.

He traveled to the island of Cyprus, then up to Greece, and throughout much of what is Turkey today. Then he went to Italy. It was all different kingdoms and principalities and powers in those days, yet the Romans were the world rulers. They had long since displaced the Greeks.

Saint Paul saw a need to tie together Judaism, this new teaching of Christianity, and Hellenistic thought. Hellenistic thought included that of the Stoics. They called the creative or divine principle the Logos. In the Bible it's called the Logos too, but it's referred to as the Word: "In the beginning was the Word. . . . And the Word was made flesh."

A lot of ECKists had past lives during these early formative years of Christianity.

Saint Paul was straddling two worlds, the worlds of Judaism and Hellenistic thought, trying to match things up to give an intellectual foundation, something that would satisfy the Christians too. Because it was a belief.

This belief was founded on the unmanifested God coming down to earth and manifesting. Somebody had to make sure that this message of the divine law of love would continue to be carried forward.

SAME SPIRITUAL CHALLENGES

Where does ECK fit into all this?

We're having the same challenges today. We were once an itinerant teaching. We were the nomads moving here and there. We had no place to call our home. Home was wherever Paul Twitchell was at the time. He lived in San Diego, then he established an office in Las Vegas. But eventually his advisers said, "Paul, this isn't going to work. Everything rests on your shoulders. Everything's incorporated under your name, or it's under you as a person. And if you're gone, then the teachings of ECK are done. Under our laws and under our structure in society today, we recommend that you set up a board that oversees a nonprofit structure."

Paul Twitchell saw the wisdom of this. He said yes, we'll do it.

ESTABLISHING A SEAT OF POWER

Paul was also looking for a seat of power.

The Roman Catholic Church has had its seat of power in Rome for a long time. Another was established in Constantinople, which is Istanbul today. There are also political seats of power such as Washington, DC, for the United States; Mexico City for

Somebody had to make sure that this message of the law of love would continue.

Mexico; and London for the United Kingdom.

Paul Twitchell saw that he would have to establish a seat of power for Eckankar. Until that happened, wherever he was, was the seat of power. First he looked in Nevada, but then he passed on.

VIEWPOINTS ON LIFE

Saint Paul tried to blend all the ancient Judaic teachings into the new teachings of Christianity. Today, Eckankar comes into a society that's predominantly Christian. And we run into the same thing. People will come to ECK with all their education and doctrine. I almost said indoctrination, because of course it is; a religion is a view of life. If you are Hindu, you're going to have one view of life; if you're a Christian, you'll have another. The same is true in Eckankar.

We find many similarities to other religions that already exist here. We believe in one God, for instance, and responsibility for personal actions. We see that as a necessity.

The ancient Stoics were the tough guys; they wouldn't flinch no matter what happened. This was a philosophy that fit the Romans well.

The Christians picked this up. They have a Latin (originally Greek) word for it—*apathia*—which is indifference.

Professor Daniel Robinson of Oxford and Georgetown Universities has an excellent audio and video series on the Greek philosophers and others. Some of his lectures are very interesting.

WE'RE PART OF THE WORLD

These are the lower worlds. You can't go around saying, I'm above all this. We're not above all this.

A religion is a view of life. In Eckankar we find many similarities to other religions that already exist here.

If it rains and you go outside, if there isn't a sidewalk, you're going to get mud on you. You can't be above all this unless you can fly through the air like Superman. Otherwise you can't get above it.

In Eckankar, we don't try to get above it in the physical sense. We try to get above it spiritually. This is our whole aim—getting above things spiritually— moving above the human state of consciousness into a higher state of consciousness.

We do this through the Spiritual Exercises of ECK, through dreams, through Soul Travel. Soul Travel simply means shifting the state of consciousness from a lower state to a higher one. Yet some of the ways Soul Travel occurs may be very dynamic.

BUILDING A FOUNDATION

So those were tough times for Saint Paul. But he was up to it. He had the talent for it. He was a Roman citizen, which gave him a passport to a lot of countries. It gave him a lot of political freedom to move about, to do everything an ordinary Roman citizen could do.

Against this backdrop, Saint Paul was trying to find an intellectually satisfying basis for the teachings of Christianity, one that would link back to things that had preceded it. He found a lot of connections— like the concepts of one God and taking responsibility for oneself.

So this foundation was laid down. We in ECK share many of these same values. Plus we offer ways to go to states of consciousness that people maybe have forgotten how to get to today.

In ECK we offer ways to go to states of consciousness that people maybe have forgotten how to get to today.

Sometimes the old teachings get tired. Then people want something fancier; they want to bring out the guitar and enhance things. Pretty soon people don't come to the services anymore. Or you get a bunch of people who come to the services, but as soon as something goes against the grain a little bit—somebody says something untoward—they're out the door, and they don't come back. Soon the congregation shrinks.

Why? Because the basic tenets of the religion are important to people. They spoke to the heart at one time in centuries past. And there must be that memory, that message, still existent today.

This is what every religion—every minister, pastor, priest, and spiritual leader—is working to stay in the center of: How can I best serve the people who are searching for truth? We have to recognize that God has established all religions—*all* religions—so that there will be something there for every state of consciousness.

God has established all religions so that there will be something for every state of consciousness.

WE'RE ALL UNIQUE

We can kid ourselves and say everybody's alike, we are all free, we're all equal, we're a brotherhood of mankind. But it isn't so, because states of consciousness are unique. As each one of us is made from a mold, the mold is thrown away.

What is the mold? The mold is our experiences. And where do these experiences start? In past lives. And do these experiences just come from the past lives? No, they start up again as soon as you're born.

You come into this world, you cry, and starting from your conditions at birth, you go one way or another. From this moment on, your experiences are all different from anyone else's. Each person's experiences are totally different.

The more hours, days, and weeks you add to your life, the more experiences and the more variety come to you. This tends to make you even more of a unique being than you have ever been in the past. You are more a unique being, for better or worse, than you ever were in the past.

HOW DO PEOPLE FIND ECK?

How do people find ECK? One way is via the good-neighbor policy.

An ECKist will have a friend who is not an ECKist. This non-ECKist friend will look at the ECKist and say to himself, "I don't know much about his or her personal life, but I like the person's values."

Friends see that ECKists stand for something. They're solid. You can count on them. Or they're able to come up with ideas when everybody else is sitting down, looking at each other, wondering what to do.

They may not be overly talented, but they have this goodness about them. People just like to be near them. Why is it? Because they have this aura.

THE SPIRITUAL SELF

Kirlian photography can take pictures of this aura. Some people have a big aura with clear colors, others have a solid-type aura with murky colors. This affects the personality of the individual. This aura is often the thing that people feel before they even get within hand-shaking or hugging distance. You either like someone or you don't.

Why? You don't know, but it's a sense, an intuition. It picks up this cloud around a person—a sort of radioactive dust or something that emanates from the spiritual being that is truly inside the physical body.

How do people find ECK? One way is via the good-neighbor policy.

That's why we say you are not the physical body. It would be better to say "I am Soul, and I have a physical body." Because to say "I have a soul" indicates a false possession. It puts the divine being that you are at the mercy of, subjugated to, the human consciousness—the part which lies, cheats, gets tired, gets crabby, snaps at people, and becomes impatient.

This spiritual unit, Soul, gives life to the human body. Saying "I have a soul" makes the human body the taskmaster of Soul, and that's backward.

SEEING THE ESSENCE OF GOD IN OURSELVES AND OTHERS

It shouldn't be that way. But most people don't know the difference. If somebody asks them, "Do you believe you have a soul?" they say, "Yes, I believe I have a soul." They're all speaking backward. They don't really know they're subjugating the divine part of themselves to the fallible and imperfect human nature.

This is one of those crimes of ignorance, not malice. It's just something people don't know they're doing. But it's a very important point to bring out. Because if people were more aware of what this meant, they would be very proud to say, "I am Soul." And they'd also say, "I know that you are Soul too."

See the essence of God in yourself, then take the next step and see it in someone else.

As soon as you can see the essence of God in yourself, then take the next step and see it in someone else, this certainly would be the beginning of the brotherhood of the spiritual order. Something much higher than the brotherhood of man.

Man is in the human consciousness. The brotherhood of man is generally made up of people who blunder about, having problems just barely making their own lives run and yet trying to tell others how to run the world. That's the human consciousness.

Coming to ECK

The new person comes to ECK, and he finds this belief system, this way to come to a higher stage in ECK. A good neighbor may tell him about it. The non-ECKist goes to the ECKist and says, "There's something special about you. What is it?" They talk a little, and gradually the information comes out that this person is an ECKist, a follower of the Light and Sound of God.

Then the new person will listen and say, "Hmmm, that sounds interesting." Or they won't care much—it'll be like they are hearing a weather report from some far distant place on the other side of the earth, where you don't really care that much what's going on. The new person may think, *It's good information, maybe I'll look into this some other time.* But he'll still respect the ECKist—the values, or the character, or this indefinable something about this individual.

The non-ECKist goes to the ECKist and says, "There's something special about you. What is it?"

Lawson Follows the Yellow Light

"Lawson" was from Ghana. His favorite uncle lived in a neighboring town, and Lawson went to visit him.

A little while after he got back home, he heard his uncle had come down with an illness. Very shortly after that, his uncle died, or translated, as we say in ECK. He was gone.

The day before the burial, Lawson had a dream. The first thing he saw in the dream was this pure, rushing yellow light. He wondered about this light. And he followed it, because he was in the other worlds, in full consciousness, and it was beautiful.

In the middle of these beautiful rays of shining yellow light, Lawson saw his uncle.

His uncle came up to him and took him by the hand. They went down through these yellow rays until they came to a white temple. On the side of this temple, in big yellow letters, was the word *Eckankar.*

Lawson woke up, very curious about this word. He'd never heard the word before. Whatever could this mean?

He tried to put it out of his mind, but it still bothered him, so he said, "I'm going to see my cousins and ask if they know what this word means."

So he asked his uncle's children. They said, "Dad was a member of Eckankar."

Lawson knew that his uncle had been an artist. Whenever there was an ECK seminar in a nearby or distant town, his uncle would finance a troupe of ECKists from his village to travel there. They would share their creative talents—singing and art—with people at the seminar.

So finally Lawson understood these seminars were about Eckankar. The inner place he had visited in the dream was so beautiful that he said to his cousins, "Show me the place where they teach about Eckankar."

In that town there was an ECK center, and they took Lawson there. It wasn't long before he became a member of Eckankar.

Lawson found the teachings of ECK through a dream because his uncle had come and talked to him. "This is the head office of Eckankar in this region of heaven. So don't worry," he said, "I'm fine. Don't worry about my death. I'm absolutely fine, and it's wonderful here."

Lawson felt the happiness and joy in that place. Because this yellow light was the Light of God, one of the twin aspects we talk about so much in ECK—the twin aspects of Light and Sound. These together are the Holy Spirit, which was referred to by the ancient Greeks as Logos, the Word.

Marian's Near-Death Experience

When "Marian," a girl from Germany, was fourteen years old, she got meningitis. A bacterial infection turned serious, and in just a matter of hours she went into a coma.

Her parents called an ambulance, and Marian was rushed off to a hospital.

While the ambulance was driving along, Marian found herself out of the body for the first time. She was standing next to the stretcher in the ambulance. The paramedics couldn't stand up straight in the ambulance, but she could, because she was a viewpoint, in the Soul body.

Marian said, "Hey, this is pretty good. I'm there, but I'm here too." She realized that life didn't have to be just in that body, but life was here too.

When they got to the hospital, the doctors hooked Marian up to life support. She was mostly out of the body all this time, but one time she came back in. Just as she did, she heard the heart monitor going in a long, steady screech. That meant her heart had stopped. She was back in the other worlds again.

This time Marian saw a brilliant blue light, all around her. And with it came a humming sound.

The humming sounded like a high-powered generator. This is one of the sounds that an individual can hear in the other planes; it's one manifestation of the Sound of God. For Marian, it came with the Blue Light, which often refers to the Mahanta, the Living ECK Master, the spiritual leader of Eckankar.

While the ambulance was driving along, Marian saw a brilliant blue light. And with it came a humming sound.

The Master and the Seeker

This Blue Light is part of the Master's ability, part of his duties, to act as the Outer and the Inner

Master of the seeker.

The Master of Eckankar is only the Master of ECKists. He isn't the master of the whole world; he isn't the master for Christians or Muslims or Jews— just ECKists. And for all those who have been in Eckankar before.

So Marian saw the Blue Light and heard this humming sound. She looked at the doctors working frantically, trying to bring life back to her body. But Marian realized, "I'm Soul; that's my body."

Sometimes it takes spiritual experience to get it right, to get the horse before the cart again. She said, "I'm Soul. I live. I don't need that body to live. Everything's beautiful and happy."

Marian realized, "I'm Soul. I live. I don't need that body to live."

TRAVELING OUT OF THE BODY

Marian rose up and up, until she was looking down from high above at the hospital. Then she went up further, and she found herself in a broad, green meadow.

It's a little bit like on *Star Trek*. A couple of crew members on the starship get into the transporter. They stand very still, their bodies break down to atoms, and they're transported to a planet or another spaceship. They dematerialize here and re-form there.

This is what happens when Soul moves from place to place on the inner. This is the quick way. There can also be some preliminary stages, where there is a sense of movement, sometimes a rushing or roaring sound like a jet. But other times it's simply like dematerializing here and re-forming there. Suddenly you're there.

Time and space are collapsed. You don't have to go through the laborious, time-consuming process of moving through space. To go from one point in space to another takes time, and you can do away with all that.

MEETING GOPAL DAS

Marian found herself standing on a huge, beautiful lawn. There was dew on the grass, she was barefoot, and she had on some sort of light clothing. In the distance, coming down from a green hill, she saw a figure.

As the figure came closer, she saw it was a tall man in a white robe. As he got even closer, she saw he had long, blond hair to his shoulders and bright blue eyes. He came up to her, and she could see that his aura was full of harmony and energy. This aura engulfed her.

The man took her hand. "Welcome," he said. "Let me show you the Kingdom of God, and then you can return to the physical plane, with refreshed memory and knowledge, and wait until the time is ripe for you to begin your mission."

Marian didn't know this was the ECK Master Gopal Das.

Some people mistake him for Jesus Christ. But often it's Gopal Das, even though Jesus Christ does work on the inner planes and some of you have met him. Each of these masters has a place and works in the far worlds.

You might say no such a thing can be possible. For many people, heaven is this huge room with God the Father sitting there, and on his right hand or somewhere nearby is his son. And how big is he? What does he look like? Blond hair, white robe, maybe. And what do people do in eternity?

But these are issues that really have nothing to

"Welcome," he said. "Let me show you the Kingdom of God, and then you can return to the physical plane refreshed."

do with the spiritual advancement of anyone. That state of being is whatever it is. There are steps to it; there are different degrees of consciousness, even as there are manifestations of places where people express these states of consciousness. These different places are the different levels of heavens.

After Gopal Das gave Marian this greeting, she went back into the body. It took her a number of weeks to recover enough to leave the hospital. But after this out-of-body experience and meeting Gopal Das, she remembered. She also remembered other experiences she had had with this being. And then she started looking for him.

Marian had to look for eighteen years before she made her first contact with Eckankar.

She always thought of Gopal Das as her guardian angel—this blond-headed, tall man, very fair of face, with a good feeling about him because he had this good aura.

Years after her near-death experience, she met an ECKist who later became her husband. And she told him her story.

Her husband showed her some pictures of the ECK Masters. "Maybe your guardian angel is one of them," he said. Of course, there are a lot of other ECK Masters besides the handful shown in ECK pictures.

Marian saw the picture of Gopal Das. "That's him," she said.

She came into ECK because of this near-death experience, her first out-of-body experience, when she met an ECK Master.

Why did Gopal Das meet her, and not someone else, like Shamus-i-Tabriz? Sometimes the Mahanta, the Living ECK Master will send a certain ECK Master to a certain individual because they had a

Sometimes the Mahanta will send a certain ECK Master to a certain individual because they had a past-life connection, a bond of love.

past-life connection. Marian had been a spiritual student of Gopal Das in some past lifetime. They had a bond of love between them, a spiritual bond. This is what she knew and understood, and so he came.

Gopal Das was the Mahanta, the Living ECK Master in Egypt, about 3000 BC. He now teaches the Shariyat-Ki-Sugmad, which means Way of the Eternal. This is the ECK bible. He teaches on the Astral Plane, in the Temple of Golden Wisdom there.

All has meaning.

THE DOGGED CAT

An ECKist had a coworker whose name was "Brigitte." Brigitte had a cat. She and her husband had ten cats, in fact. But this one cat is the subject of our story.

The family moved to a new home about a mile and a half from their old one. It was a beautiful home, and everybody was happy except this cat.

Cats are lazy by nature. They will usually not exert themselves, especially in Florida, where it's hot. But this cat had an opinion, and it was stronger in its opinion than it was lazy. So every morning, the cat would get up when the family went off to work, and it would walk one and a half miles to their old home.

There it would sit. Because that was its home, and that's where it was going to stay.

When Brigitte came home from work the first night, one of her old neighbors called her. "Did you know your cat's here?"

Brigitte thought her cat must have a sense like a homing pigeon. "I'll come get it," she said. So she got in her car, drove over, and got the cat.

The next day, Brigitte got another call. Same

This cat had an opinion, and it was stronger in its opinion than it was lazy.

neighbor, same cat, same routine. After work, the last thing Brigitte needed was to jump in the car and chauffeur a cat around. But she did it, because the bond of love between parent and kitty was so strong. You will do anything for a child, whether it's got fur, feathers, or skin. This is divine love showing itself down here on earth. It's one of the finest and most noble things: human love expressing the divine love.

> It's one of the finest and most noble things: human love expressing the divine love.

This went on for eight and a half months. Every morning, this cat would get up and walk a mile and a half, then the mother would come pick it up at night.

It got to be an interesting thing. At first, Brigitte would drive up and call the cat. The cat would come running, Brigitte would open the car door, and the cat would jump in. Then it got so that the cat started looking forward to Mom coming at the end of the day. So the cat began waiting at the curbside, just like a child waiting for the school bus. Pretty soon Mom didn't even bother opening up the car door. She just rolled down the window, and the cat jumped right in. This was how it went—for eight and a half months.

The neighbors would come out to watch this. They thought the neighborhood cat was quite privileged. They would watch and say, "The cat's chauffeur will be along soon. Here she comes. Watch the cat, watch the window. There goes the window, there goes the cat." The neighbors had a good time with this.

It takes a long-suffering mom or dad to put up with this, but that's what love is about. It is long-suffering and patient, almost to the ends of the earth.

HOW WE LEARN

Brigitte told this story to an ECKist friend. The
ECKist saw a parallel to the teachings of ECK and
the roles of the Mahanta and the ECKist.

After eight and a half months, the cat had become
solid muscle. Walking every day, going through all
kinds of things, this cat got really strong and tough.

The cat's owners had gotten it a new home, like
a new state of consciousness, a new heaven. But the
cat was attached to the old; it did not want to move,
would not move, would not change. It was like it was
tied to the end of a big rubber band: as soon as the
door opened in the morning, there would be this big
snapping sound, and the cat would go clean out of
sight, landing back home at the old house. The cat
had a strong band of attachment. It would snap back
to its old home, even if that took a long, laborious
walk. Then mom would take it back to its new home
every evening.

When a cat's got its mind set on something, a cat
will carry through on it. Usually it's got its mind set
on napping and resting, and that's usually what it
carries through on.

We had fourteen cats on our farm. Each one had
a definite personality. We had the lazy, we had the
loving, we had the noble, we had just about everything. They were a lot of pleasure.

So the ECKist was looking at the story of Brigitte's
cat, and she said, "Sometimes Soul can't detach Itself
from Its old state of consciousness. So the Master, like
the cat owner, tries to move the individual to a new
place. But there's this resistance. And the person
keeps going back to the old state."

Sometimes a person is taken from poverty, maybe

The ECKist said, "Sometimes Soul can't detach Itself from Its old state of consciousness. So the Master tries to move the individual to a new place."

by winning the lottery. But what happens five years later? Maybe there are better money managers now, but it used to take about five years on average for the money to be gone. The winners had given it away to their friends. Now the lottery winners needed money and help, and the friends were gone. And so was the money.

INITIATION CHANGES

People always think the old way is better. Why? Because change is such a difficult thing to come to grips with. Nobody likes to change, because changing from one state to another is a spiritual process. Nobody likes to go through spiritual processes. It means having to do something unfamiliar. Everybody likes to do the familiar thing.

But at some point Soul, or the individual, like the cat, says, "OK, I can see the advantages of the new home. I'm finally used to it, and going back to that old state of consciousness is just not worth the trouble. There are lots of advantages in my new home. I like this place."

This also happens with an individual who resists a new state of consciousness. There is wear and tear, and all sorts of things go wrong.

When a person gets another ECK initiation—the Second, Third, Fourth, or whatever—right before and right after, there are all kinds of problems that occur. Why? Because the individual is starting to move to another state of consciousness, a higher one.

But he or she is unwilling to let go of the old habits and the old values, to accept the higher ones.

Because to accept the higher values is to accept more of God's love. Many people aren't ready to do

To accept the higher values is to accept more of God's love.

that. The more love you get, the more you must give, and that's a responsibility that requires growing into.

All has meaning.

SYLVIA'S THREE COINCIDENCES

A German ECKist named "Sylvia" has a family—a husband and two children, both teenagers. The son's away at school, out of the country. The daughter is fourteen.

Sylvia went to the ECK European Seminar, and when she got home, the three of them went out to a restaurant.

On the way to the restaurant, her daughter said, "Mom, did you remember to bring something home for me?"

Her mother smiled and said, "As a matter of fact, I brought you a story, a wonderful story."

At the seminar, Sylvia had gone to an ECK workshop titled "The Spiritual Tools We Have in Life." When she got to the door, one of the hosts gave her a sealed white envelope and said, "Don't open this until you're told to during the workshop." Sylvia said OK and sat down.

She had picked a seat next to an elderly man who was an ECKist.

When the time came, the ECK workshop leader said, "Open your envelopes." Sylvia opened hers. Inside was a postcard, and on it was a picture of a room in a building.

She recognized this room. It was in a museum, and her family had often gone there.

This museum featured experimental architecture and art—ways to blend it all into the landscape.

One of the hosts gave her a sealed white envelope and said, "Don't open this until you're told to during the workshop."

One of the rooms in this museum was entirely bare. It was painted white, and it had high windows looking out over a lush, green lawn. That was the room. But they also experimented with sound at this museum. They were looking into sound, in addition to architecture and art and landscape.

The ECKist would come here with her family, and they'd sometimes sing *HU*. Sometimes they'd sing Christian songs or other songs. Sylvia's an ECKist, and her family is Christian. They get along fine because they honor each other's beliefs and love each other.

They would sing, and then just stand and listen. Because they liked the acoustics—the resonance. It was just beautiful in there.

At the ECK seminar, Sylvia recognized the same room on her postcard. It was an odd chance that this picture would be of a room she recognized. This was the first of three coincidences.

The second coincidence was when she shared the picture with the elderly ECKist. She told him the story, and the man looked very closely at her. "I think we met a long time ago," he said, "in this very museum."

Sylvia thought about it. "About ten years ago?" she said. There had been an ECK event in this museum, with ECKists from a number of different regions.

Sylvia's an ECKist, and her family is Christian. They get along fine because they honor each other's beliefs and love each other.

HEAVEN IS OPENING FOR US ALL

Later, in the restaurant, Sylvia showed the picture to her daughter and husband. That's when they told her what had happened to them at the museum. While Sylvia was at the ECK seminar, her husband

and daughter and a friend of her daughter's had gone to this museum.

Sylvia's daughter looked at her. "We were there, and we had a wonderful time." She and her friend went into the room in the picture. The daughter said they sang Christian songs, and one they especially loved was "Der Himmel geht über allen auf." This means "heaven is opening above us all." The girls sang this, and they were so happy they cried.

While Sylvia was still at the seminar, her family had come home from the museum, and they went to a Christian service at a French church in a nearby town. Her husband had arranged the service. The theme addressed the deep longing that people have for a lively experience of God. A band played, and the congregation sang songs. And one of the songs was "Heaven Is Opening above Us All." It was an overwhelming experience for everyone. They sang that song over and over. They had started with other songs, but they finally settled into this one, and they just sang it and sang it.

At the end came a standing ovation. Probably for the spirit of divine love that had caught them all up and they had not felt such a wave of love before. All went home deeply moved.

This was the third coincidence. All these things that took place were connected—the service at the church, the visit to the museum, the ECK seminar. All has meaning.

HEAVENLY MUSIC

If you've ever heard the heavenly forms of music, you know that Soul just writhes in ecstasy because the sound is so beautiful. It's beyond anything you've ever heard.

All these things that took place were connected—the service at the church, the visit to the museum, the ECK seminar.

I listen to a fair amount of classical music in
addition to country and talk radio and everything
else. But this music, this heavenly music, is so far
above the others that they are just a faint echo. Yet
I keep looking for it.

I like Mozart especially. I'll be listening to a CD
while I'm working, and I'll hear a familiar piece, and
it's usually Mozart. I like Vivaldi, Beethoven, Ravel,
Bach. I got a lot of Bach back in religious school, so
maybe I have had enough.

NAN HEARS THE MUSIC OF GOD

"Nan" had a lifelong problem with feelings of
inadequacy and unworthiness, that negative state.

But one night Nan had a dream. In this dream,
a friend handed her a golden sword. The friend had
picked it up at a yard sale and thought it was a great
deal. It was beautiful, and it was exactly for Nan.

When the friend put this sword in Nan's hand,
there arose the most beautiful, rich music, as if from
nowhere. Nan was hearing the music of God. On the
golden sword in her hand, she saw the printed words
"Property of Eckankar." A warm, fluctuating, bright
light then came toward her, as if from around a corner.

She realized that this was the unconditional love
of God.

She also realized it was important for her to
remember how all this was taking place so that she
could help other people. Remember, Nan was trying
to overcome feelings of inadequacy, doubt, and unworthiness.

She asked, "What did the golden sword mean?"

It meant that Nan was to be an instrument for
divine grace and mercy. I'll repeat it. She was to be
an instrument for divine grace and mercy. These

What did the golden sword mean? It meant Nan was to be an instrument for divine grace and mercy.

are the counterpoints to the doubt and feelings of unworthiness.

ACTING AS IF

Now, just because Nan got the sword on the inner, it doesn't mean that these positive qualities are in her automatically, that she will thus be this. But you act as if.

It's like the Constitution of the United States: it guarantees certain rights. But they didn't even exist at the time the founders created the Constitution. Or by the time it was ratified. These rights weren't even in place then. But they were an ideal to strive for, something to aim for.

In those days, for example, some people still had slaves. It took many years before slavery was abolished in this country. In the same way, Nan must set the ideal and act as if.

Some of the Greek philosophers felt very strongly that virtues develop through habit. Indeed they do. You develop the right habits, and you can develop many virtues of character. Some people say we are victims of DNA. It's not true. The latest research is finding that even DNA can change. It depends upon how a person approaches things. Their habits.

You develop the right habits, and you can develop many virtues of character.

All these things have meaning in some sense. People have to figure out, What does it mean for me? Nan got her meaning in one way through the experience. It opened within her heart.

LUCY'S FIVE O'CLOCK BLESSING

"Lucy" was in a lonely desert when it came to matters of the heart. Every time she went out with someone, he turned out to be a loser.

One night, she went out to a restaurant with a

man. He looked promising. They ordered, and he started talking about past girlfriends. A big no-no. Then he started talking about all his problems, his thoughts, his feelings, his attitudes.

As he talked, his food grew cold. He hadn't even touched it. And as the food got cold, so did Lucy's ardor. *This guy is so full of himself there isn't even room for his food*, she thought. She finished eating and said, "Could you take me home, please? I don't feel well." That was it.

The next day was Sunday. Lucy went shopping for a gift for her mother's birthday. During the drive she was thinking, *Loser after loser. Won't I ever find love? Isn't there love in this life for me? Am I going to go through my whole life like this?*

As she was thinking these thoughts, there came a strange tugging at her chest. It was like something inside her burst out and flew into the universe. Something was set free, like a little bird from its cage. She looked at the car clock; it was five o'clock in the afternoon. That turned out to be a very significant time.

The next day, Lucy went to work as usual. She worked as a counselor in a five-hundred-bed men's prison. She gave self-help classes on how to take care of yourself, on relationships (of all things), parenting, and other subjects.

She was between classes, in her office doing paperwork, and she heard a very soft knock on the door. A huge, muscular man came in. He seemed awkward, like he didn't really want to be there, like he had something to say but didn't quite know how to get it out.

"Could I talk with you for a minute?" he asked.

Lucy said, "Sure." She was wondering, *What's this about?*

> *Something inside her burst out and flew into the universe. Something was set free, like a little bird from its cage.*

The man finally said, "May I ask you a question?"

Lucy said, "Sure" again.

"What were you doing at five o'clock yesterday, if I may ask?"

If he'd asked about any other time during the day, she wouldn't have had a clue. But five o'clock she knew. She'd been out shopping for a present for her mother's birthday. But what she didn't tell him was that she had also at that time been feeling all these feelings of loneliness and abandonment. She had felt cut off from God's love.

She told him about shopping for the birthday present. But the prisoner seemed a little bit nervous. He said, "Well, I was sitting in my cell, reading, and suddenly it seemed liked you were in the cell with me. Your presence was very strong. Then I heard a voice." Then he stopped talking and just sat there.

The prisoner seemed a little bit nervous, as if waiting for some sort of negative response.

Lucy said, "What did the voice say?" She was starting to feel strange and floaty.

The man said, in a quick, quiet, low voice, "The voice told me to tell you that you are loved." He sat there, as if nervously waiting for some sort of negative response, hoping that what he said wouldn't be misinterpreted. Then he added, "And it was five o'clock."

MESSAGE OF LOVE

In this moment, Lucy felt blessed and loved. Warmth washed over her, and tears came to her face, and she realized that Divine Spirit was responding to her cries for love. She was filled with gratitude for this man who had allowed himself to be a vehicle for Divine Spirit.

Three days later, Lucy heard another knock on the door. This time the knock wasn't quite so quiet.

It was the same big, muscular man, and he looked very happy. In his hands he had a sheaf of papers, and he waved them in the air. Beside himself with ecstasy, he said, "I just got my parole papers. I didn't tell you the other day, but the voice also told me that if I didn't give you the message that you are loved, I wouldn't be paroled."

The ECK has a sense of humor.

The ECK has a sense of humor.

The man was the perfect messenger. His name was a variation on the French word *l'amour.* This was the man to bring the message of love to Lucy.

May the blessings be.

ECK Summer Festival, Orlando, Florida,
Saturday, July 6, 2002

Kristy opens her eyes and realizes the love of God is all around her, as near and dear as Misha.

9

THE ROAD TO SPIRITUAL FREEDOM

*I*t's been unseasonably cold here in Minnesota. Some of you were at the dedication of the outdoor ECK Celebrations of Life Chapel, and I think you'll vouch for the temperatures being colder than they ever should be for this time of year.

But there's a good chance it'll get colder. If you live in Minnesota, you don't look ahead too far. You just steel yourself and hope your blood is getting thicker.

After a couple of months, you get used to the cold weather. Then spring comes. First time it gets twenty degrees above zero and the wind isn't blowing, you'll see somebody outside in a short-sleeved shirt. Somebody else will jog by in shorts. Once I would have shared their enthusiasm, but not in this lifetime.

In Minnesota, first time it gets twenty degrees above zero and the wind isn't blowing, you'll see somebody jog by in shorts.

STAND UP TO CHALLENGES

I go out shopping occasionally, but I am being very careful about the electromagnetic radiation. I'm learning to work with it better and getting some strength.

Our chiropractor, a very dear person, showed us how to work with a little magnet years ago. She told us that it's supposed to help. My wife and I have refined the process, and when we pick up a lot of electromagnetic radiation, this method helps balance things out a little quicker than if we just let it go the normal way. It has helped.

This is the way life is. Whenever a challenge comes up, you can either stand up to it or give up the field. It's your choice.

Sometimes people ask, Why do you bother? Why do you strive so hard? And you just say it's the nature of survival. That's what Soul does. It goes on and on, and It does the very best It can.

It's an exercise in working with the ECK, listening so carefully moment by moment by moment.

THE SPIRITUAL EXERCISE OF SURVIVAL

It's a spiritual exercise—this trial of survival in working with the ECK. It's an exercise in working with the ECK, listening so carefully moment by moment by moment. Sometimes, for me, it has been moment to moment, day after day, week after week, month after month, for four or five years. It's where you face a major crisis maybe four or five times a day. And you can never look back.

It's like when the Minnesota winter is over—you don't look back. Spring is coming. It may be wild and woolly, but you sure don't look back. You go forward.

You always go forward. And you keep your face to the ECK.

Because the ECK, the Holy Spirit, is the Voice of God. You keep your face to the Holy Spirit, to this Voice, this ancient, primordial Voice, because that's the direction of Sugmad. That's where God is. So you go there.

That's what the challenges of life are about. You learn to use them as a spiritual exercise to help you become stronger spiritually.

As you go through your challenges, sometimes you just want to cry. You want to say, "I can't do it. I can't do one more thing." We all do. It'd be a lot easier just to give up.

That's the whole game of it. The hard part is to not give up but know there is some way to make things better—even just a little bit. Finally things get the tiniest little bit better, you try to tell someone, but they don't have any idea what you're talking about. So you don't talk about it anymore, because they can't understand. They haven't had the experience. That's fair, because you haven't had theirs either.

Life is a very individual experience.

The whole game of it is to not give up but know there is some way to make things better—even just a little bit.

How Life Was Created

Before time began, God, or Sugmad, sent Soul into these lower worlds to get experience. And before that could happen, the Sugmad created the lower worlds, working through Its Voice, the Holy Spirit.

World upon world, plane upon plane, from the highest to the lowest, formed throughout eons of time—through the forgotten ages, It created mysteries for our scientists so they'll have something to do—so they can go to bed at night and say, "Ah, there's a reason to get up in the morning. I still haven't solved the riddle of creation. Was it really the big bang? Is there more to it that we can't see but we know is out there? Is there more to it than this physical universe?"

Since they're into hard science, they'd have to say

no. They'd say, "I can't see it, I can't pinch it, and it doesn't say ouch, so I can't believe in it."

But all this was created way back before time. Then time began, and eventually Souls began to come down from the spiritual worlds, the pure heavens. God sent Souls, us, down here to get experience. Why? Essentially, so that God could know more of Itself.

God sent Souls, us, down here to get experience. As Soul came down, Its memory of freedom in the high worlds was gone.

SOUL'S FIRST INCARNATIONS

As Soul came down, Its memory of freedom in the high worlds was gone. It forgot.

It was down here taking on the first human bodies in the worlds of time and space. The first human bodies were inhabited by Soul, but there were so many layers of materialism over this Soul—many layers and coverings of varying density, many layers inside the outer, physical shell.

They were the Mental, Causal, and Emotional bodies, and they felt like those tight sports bandages used to bind up a limb when it's sprained. There was a tight wrapping all around Soul, and It could hardly move. There was hardly any connection to Its spiritual nature. And almost no connection to the Sound and Light of God—this Voice of God.

Soul came into this cold, lonely, dark place with barely enough fire to warm It.

Here, I'll switch to speaking about Soul in the human form. "He" for convenience.

Early man came down, looked around, and said, "What can I make of this place?" He took to living in the trees because the animals on the ground were too fierce. Then came the trials—struggling with the animals, with the birds of the air, with hunger, with his fellow man.

Back in those earliest times, the first, unknown

ECK Master came to work with people and began to help them in their test of survival. He helped them learn which things that grew could be taken for food, which things were not good for food, which things were poisonous. This got complicated, because plants that were good at certain times of the year were not good at other times.

The ECK Masters showed early man things that could heal him when he damaged or hurt this covering that man took to be himself. Because way back then, we identified very closely with the human shell. We thought, *This is who we are.*

SOUL'S SEARCH FOR FREEDOM

Time went on. We'll skip through the ages here and come up closer to today. Soul began to look for freedom. Probably the first time that a group of people ever made an effort in the direction of freedom came during the time of the ancient Greeks, about 500 BC. This was political freedom, because even just a few thousand years ago, this was all man could conceive of.

Probably the first group effort in the direction of freedom came during the time of the ancient Greeks.

The ancient Greeks put it like this: they wanted to make their own laws to live under.

All the kingdoms of the world were run by monarchs. These monarchs had a different game plan in mind. The king was the ruler, and everybody in the kingdom was the slave of the king. It became a mental enslavement of a sort that people accepted. Why? Because they grew up in it.

They grew up in it as surely as a black child in the South before the Civil War in America grew up a slave. Why? He was born a slave. And what would a slave do? Whatever his folks told him to do and whatever the master told him to do. This was just a

carryover from the old monarchs. People were willing
to let someone else run their life for them.

Even if they weren't willing, the odds were against
them. The weight of opinion was against them. The
might of arms was against them. People who spoke
out too loudly for independence or freedom, who
wanted to make their own laws for themselves as
individuals, got put in prison. Or the king ended their
life. That was the end of any dissent.

But around the fifth century BC, the Persians
were a strong force. Darius was the king of the
Persians, and he had attacked some of the Greeks in
Asia Minor. But the Athenians—the Athenian
Greeks—decided to send a few of their own up there
to help their fellow Greeks in fighting against the
Persians. But the Persians had gotten very good at
fighting, so they beat the Greeks. It was always the
same—the Persians won, and the Greeks lost. And
everybody else lost too, because the Persians, way
back then, had an empire that was roughly as big as
the continental United States. A big place for those
primitive times. Nobody stood up to the Persians.

*The great
Persian king
got his forces
together and
came down to
subjugate and
enslave the
Athenians.*

Eight years after the Athenian Greeks had had
the cheek to send men to fight against the great Persian king, he got his forces together and came down
to subjugate and enslave the Athenians. This was an
old score to settle, and he was going to settle it.

The Persians had an enormous force for those
days—twenty-five thousand soldiers, including cav-
alry. They had excellent archers, and King Darius
sent his two top generals to wipe out the Athenians.

Greece's biggest city-state was the size of Rhode
Island. The country was made up of all these little
city-states because they couldn't get along with each
other. They were all pigheaded, bullheaded, indepen-

dent people. They all wanted to do it their way. Some of these city-states weren't much more than just little towns or villages.

This collection of people is what made up Greece. Hardly any of them wanted to go fight the Persians, because everybody knew the Athenians were going to lose. Why get into it?

The day of the fight came. What could the Athenians rustle up? They had nine thousand citizen-soldiers, their national guard. One thousand citizen-soldiers of another city-state said, "Yeah, we'll come along. We'll do the best we can." Ten thousand of these ragtag Greeks were going against twenty-five thousand of the best-trained troops in the world. The Athenians were outnumbered more than two to one.

WERE YOU THERE?

This was the battle at Marathon in 490 BC.
Some of you were there.

The Persians had a real strategy for battle. First of all, they had archers who were accurate up to a couple hundred yards, which might sound unbelievable today. But this was commonplace for the Persians. When any opposing army would come, the Persian archers would loose all these arrows, and it would cut down many of the enemy soldiers.

The Athenian citizen-soldiers were all infantry. They each had a helmet, some body armor, a heavy metal shield, a short sword, and a seven-foot spear. They were called hoplites. The general in charge of the Greeks said, "Hop to it, hoplites," and they came running. They came running so fast that the archers didn't have time to shoot many of them with arrows because the Greek soldiers weren't out there that

This was the battle at Marathon in 490 BC. Some of you were there.

long to be shot at. They were running.

They weren't all young men of twenty and thirty; the Greeks had soldiers ranging from their late teens to their fifties.

The Persians were experienced fighters. They liked to look right into their enemies' eyes. They had these huge wicker shields they'd plant in the ground in front of them. They'd take cover behind these shields, with both hands free, so they could use bows, spears, or swords. But here came the Greeks. They had metal shields, not wicker. The Greeks liked to see their enemy and look him in the eyes too.

The Greeks won against overwhelming odds.

To make a long story short, the Greeks won the battle against overwhelming odds. The Persian general said, "No problem. Athens is empty. We're going to send the ships around while the soldiers are still here. They can't get back home in a day's time. We're going to take the city because it will be unguarded."

As legend has it, that's when the famous runner ran twenty-six miles, all the way back to Athens. He arrived and said, "Athens has won the battle." And he fell over dead.

The Athenians shut their gates. And when the Persians arrived, they still had a force big enough to take the city if they could have convinced the Athenians at home that their soldiers had lost the battle. The Athenians would have given up in the city. But that marathon runner brought the news. He said, "We won." And the Persians were outside the gates trying to figure out what to do.

The next day, here came the Greeks! The Persians fled. The Greeks even tried to board their ships, but the Persians sailed away to bide their time. They didn't give up, though. The son of King Darius led them back again, and there was another huge battle.

HISTORICAL PERSPECTIVE OF FREEDOM

This was Soul trying to have political freedom. This is the first stage of spiritual freedom in this world. This is why there's such an interest in politics. People are looking to make freedom and a better life through politics. Essentially, they're going back to mental enslavement, where someone else does the thinking for you and everybody is a slave to that thinking. That is what it is.

When we find ourselves in a place where the conditions are tolerable enough to allow the freedom of belief that we would like to practice, then we agree. We let everything be, and we support a good government.

Xerxes, the son of King Darius, came back to beat the Greeks. The Greeks eventually beat the Persians again. Meanwhile, Xerxes said, "Hey, let's be friends. All I want to do is count you as friends and allies. Of course you will have to live under Persian law, but it's no big thing. Everybody likes to live under Persian law."

The Persians did have good administrators, a top-notch government, a lot of money—they were the imperial power of the day. But the Greeks said, "No. We're going to fight you every day until we die. We don't want this thing you're offering us. We want freedom."

I don't believe the ancient Egyptians and Persians really had a word for freedom. There was no such word because there was no such mental concept. Because there was no such physical condition.

This was history, and time marches forward. We'll next come to the nineteenth century. There were a lot of people who, in the meantime, worked to fine-tune this political freedom, and they're still working at it today. But other groups of people have come in

> *People are looking to make freedom and a better life through politics. They're going back to mental enslavement.*

to act as champions of societal change. This is a little
more diversified than political change.

MARK TWAIN'S UNCANNY VISION

Mark Twain knew he had a mission. Practically
no one else did, but he knew. His mission was to
release this bear trap that had a hold on people still
thinking in terms of slavery.

He was born about twenty-five years before the
Civil War, in 1835. Two weeks before his birth, Halley's
Comet arrived at its closest point to the sun, and it
was again visible at the time of his birth. His real
name was Samuel Clemens; Mark Twain was the pen
name, the pseudonym. He came across as a guy from
a small town in the Midwest. He was born in Florida,
Missouri. Then he moved to Hannibal, and from there
he went back east for a while. He ran away from home
because he had this itch to travel. He told his mother,
"I've got to travel, travel, travel. I can't wait to get
going."

*Mark Twain
had a destiny.
He came with
his specific
mission to free
people from
one level of
enslavement.*

But he had a destiny. He came with his specific
mission to free people from one level of enslavement.
As time went on, he went out west with his brother,
who was named the territorial secretary for Nevada.
This was when the Territory of Nevada was first
established.

Mark Twain had a bunch of experiences in the
West. He forgot to get up one morning, and so he
missed out on a fortune in the silver mines. I think
that happened a couple of times. He was just sick
about it afterward. Just one of those strange turns
of fate; he always got up, always checked his mail,
but on this particular day he didn't do it. That day
there was a very important message for him, and
so he lost out on untold wealth, and he had to live

with himself after this.

He then traveled to the Sandwich Islands, which today are called the Hawaiian Islands. He said they should have been called the Rainbow Islands, because he never saw rainbows like he saw there. The ones back on the mainland were colorless, shapeless things compared to the rainbows in the Hawaiian Islands.

He was working as a journalist by this time, and after his time in the Pacific, he went to Europe and the Holy Land.

When Mark Twain set out on these travels, the Civil War was over. Slavery was supposed to be over. The Civil War lasted from 1861 to 1865, and he left for Hawaii in 1866. When he got back from Europe and the Holy Land, he wrote a book, *The Innocents Abroad*. He had already written "The Celebrated Jumping Frog of Calaveras County" and other short stories; he'd already made a name for himself. But when he wrote *The Innocents Abroad*, consciously or unconsciously he was trying to show something to Americans. They were as scattered as the old Greeks had been in their city-states—headstrong, stubborn people, all for themselves and their little groups. Twain wanted to show them that America was a giant ready to stand on its own feet, that it had its own literary future, that it had its own men of letters. America already had writers like Walt Whitman, who wrote poetry that was more free-form than the very tight structure that had come from England—the very tight European structure with rhythm and rhyme. Longfellow was prominent too, and Emerson. These were some of the men of letters in America, but at this time, Mark Twain did not yet have a place among them.

Twain wanted to show that America was a giant ready to stand on its own feet, that it had its own men of letters.

BREAKING ILLUSIONS

Once Twain gave a talk about this. He made up a story, poking fun at these American authors, and it was not well received by his audience. Whenever Mark Twain spoke, the press would cover it, and there was a lot of cluck-clucking. After this lecture, they said no, no, he went too far this time.

Twain began to learn the limits of humans—how far he could go with humor. Because when you're breaking illusions, what are you doing it with? You're doing it with truth, and this is what Mark Twain did. He had this uncanny vision where he could see through all the illusions of mankind in society. One of his targets, of course, was the Bible, but he found he had to be careful poking fun there. Because people wanted to laugh, he could get away with just a little bit in his stories, a little bit in his talks, but not too much.

Mark Twain had this uncanny vision where he could see through all the illusions of mankind in society.

He came into his own in the years after the Civil War. The American nation had been torn and needed to heal from all its blood and wounds, and it was a nation that needed to laugh. Mark Twain came to let the people laugh. And that's all they wanted from him.

Sometimes he felt he wasn't able to give out real truths in the literary depth that he felt that he had in him. He tried. But every time he'd get a little serious, people would cluck at him. So he backed off.

The Innocents Abroad was a funny book. In some of Twain's writings, such as *Pudd'nhead Wilson*, he had a lot of little sayings. You've heard some of them. I'll give you three. "Truth is the most valuable thing we have. Let us economize it." "Truth is mighty and will prevail. There is nothing the matter with this, except that it ain't so." "One of the most striking differences between a cat and a lie is that a cat has only nine lives."

These are examples of Mark Twain at his finest, and this is what people wanted to hear. But at the same time, now that the Civil War was over, there was another issue. The Civil War had supposedly ended slavery, but it hadn't really ended it at all. Now there were black people who were the freedmen. But many of them didn't know any kind of life except the plantation. What to do with all these freed slaves?

There'd been different ideas tossed around. Should they have freedom all at once? Oh, no, said some. They feared that unleashing such a force on society, while stripping the plantations of the people who gather the cotton, would destroy the economy. No, we shouldn't do that. What if we just free a few of the Negroes at a time, work our way into this slowly— a few this generation, a few the next generation. How about that?

Other people said, "Let's send the black man back to Africa." There were plans for this. Lincoln supported that for the longest time. We think Lincoln was always for complete emancipation. But he didn't get to that until his second term.

When you're in politics, you've always got your finger up. You wet it and see where the wind is coming from. Lincoln was the same way.

THE MASTER-SLAVE RELATIONSHIP

Sometimes it's a little disillusioning, even for me, when we see how the so-called process of political freedom works. It's always in *someone*'s best interest—someone who's a lord up there, thinking and doing the best in *his* interest, supposedly for you. *Whatever political promise it takes to get into office,*

> The Civil War had supposedly ended slavery, but it hadn't really ended it at all.

so be it; but after that, I'll do as I please, thinks the candidate, *until my term is up. And no term limits as far as I'm concerned*. It's very hard to get people out of office, once they get in.

The honorable ones respect term limits. The others say, No, I'm too valuable now; I've put in so much time. Of course, they also get many benefits that the rest of us never see in terms of pay, retirement, and all this.

This is part of that master-slave relationship that's a carryover from way back.

Now, don't get me wrong. Without it society would crumble. It would fall in on itself. The best that Soul can hope for on earth is to live in a good society run by a good government. This is the best you can hope for. A place that allows you to have religious freedom—to worship God in your own way—and to live according to just laws and the dictates of your heart. Which, of course, then should be according to the divine will.

> The best Soul can hope for on earth is freedom—to worship God in your own way—and to live according to just laws and the dictates of your heart.

THE TRAP OF ARROGANCE

Mark Twain was trying to get Americans to see that we were a growing force in the world—not just a literary force, but also a political one. Someday the United States was going to become a great nation, and it should become a power for good. It should never, ever go the way of the ancient Persians. They fell into the trap of the misuse of power. Along came the Greeks, and they did the same thing. Aeschylus, the great Athenian dramatist, who wrote about the democratic founding of ancient Greece, warned the Greeks not to fall into the same trap as the Persians.

Mark Twain said that if America rises, it should use its power for good. Let it never fall into the trap of arrogance.

Of course, this is the big challenge for any country, because this is what generally happens anywhere a group of people come together and gain great power. They fall into this thing called hubris, which leads to the abuse of power. Why do they do it? Simply because they can. Then they say, "What we're doing is good." Why? Because it feels good.

Around 1898, Spain was still the ruler of Cuba, and the Spaniards were notorious for the cruelty with which they governed. The yellow press in America got everybody really worked up. "We cannot have this sort of thing going on in our hemisphere," they said. Then came the Spanish-American War. The United States went down there, easily beat the Spanish, and the war was over real soon.

Spain also had the Philippine Islands. So we sent our warships over there, and we defeated the Spanish navy in Manila Bay.

Mark Twain cheered, and many other people like him cheered. But then they saw that President McKinley and the rulers of America had no intention of giving the Filipinos their freedom. This is when Mark Twain changed his tune and criticized the imperialism of the United States.

Still people are saying, We want to make our own laws. And if we go into another country, we should allow them their own laws.

This had gone on in ancient Greece and all throughout history. It was going on in nineteenth-century America, and there are still these forces at work today. People are saying, even as the Greeks did, We want to make our own laws. And if we go into another country, we should allow them their own laws and not impose our will upon others.

PRINCIPLE OF FREEDOM

This is part of the principle of freedom. This is what we do. Your freedom ends where my nose begins. But a lot of times somebody ends up with a bruised nose, then the fighting starts. Nations or tribes go after each other. Someone overstepped, thought he was bigger than he actually was, and the other one says, "Get off my forty acres." The Greeks said to the Persians, "Get off my forty acres." This is what happens.

I find it ironic today that so many people say we shall work for peace. But until there's peace in every man's heart, there won't be peace in the world. It starts with each individual. And it begins with consciousness.

The general consciousness of the human race isn't there yet—where there is peace in every man's heart. It's not even in the leaders. That's how it is. Because this is earth.

WHY DOES GOD ALLOW EVIL?

Who set this place up? God set this place up. Who's running the place? The negative power. Why? Because God said so. Why? Because that's his job.

Challenges make Soul call forth Its creative powers.

It takes the most negative person to run this place. Why? To create challenges. And what does that do? It makes Soul call forth Its creative powers. It makes the individual look beyond his physical strength and mental powers to something that people don't really have a word for or an understanding of. There is a word: Soul. But people think this is some sort of a higher mind. They don't understand Soul. They don't understand that Soul is a chip off the old God.

I think one of the hardest questions that religion has to deal with is Why does God allow evil? If they could just accept the fact that Satan is one of the angels of God here to do a job—to throw up challenges, to throw the dirt in our face.

Johnny Cash sings a song that ties in with this, "A Boy Named Sue." A man names his son Sue. Much later, he tells him, "I knew I wouldn't be there to help ya along. So I give ya that name and I said good-bye; I knew you'd have to get tough or die. And it's the name that helped to make you strong." I just love that song, and Johnny Cash was one of my favorite singers. He was one of the country singers who sang from his heart, and he didn't just run the words.

So often today, people just run the words. And in the field of sports, people make so much money they don't want to go out there and get hurt. It would ruin their retirement. But the boy named Sue grows up to be a mean old son of a gun himself. He walks into a bar one day and sees this old man. From an old picture, he knows right away it's his dad. Sue says to himself, I'm going to put an end to him right here. So they go at it with fists and knives, thumbs and teeth. The old guy finally goes for his gun to administer the coup de grace, but the young one beats him to it. Then the father says, "I know you hate me, and you got the right to kill me now, and I wouldn't blame you if you do." But he says his son ought to thank him first for having made him so tough by naming him Sue.

They throw down their guns and call each other Pa and Son. They become good buddies, so the song ends happy, with a tongue-in-cheek twist. That was Johnny Cash, having a good time. There was a lot of fun in those times.

> Satan is one of the angels of God here to do a job—to throw up challenges, to throw the dirt in our face.

FREE WILL AND FATE

But Mark Twain never found the fun. He came to break up the illusions right after slavery was gone.

The South tried to figure a way out of this whole thing, and about a dozen years after the war, they started enacting the Jim Crow laws. This meant blacks were supposedly equal to whites, but separate. On streetcars (and, later, buses), blacks rode in back, the whites in front. Black schools, white schools—equal but separate. Mark Twain was very much against this.

He was one of the people who came to effect societal change. He was trying to find freedom, and he came here with a mission. Unfortunately for him, his mission did not have a second half—to fill life up with something spiritual. So he never knew about ECK.

Still, he had this sense that he had come with a mission. He was a child of fate. Determinism is what he felt ran the whole show. It held true for him, so he figured it held true for everybody else too. In a sense, yes. All humans are sent here by the Lords of Karma to balance out some fate, good or bad, from the past. But once they get into their circumstances, in their environment, they have free will to make choices. Mark Twain had less leeway, because he was on a mission.

By 1910, he was a very disillusioned, sour old man, down on what he called "the damned human race." So much so that even his friends got tired of hearing him say that. They said, "Come on, Sam, get off it. You don't have to do that all the time."

In public, during the last twelve years of his life, Mark Twain was the idol of America and the world. Because he showed only his happy side. This is what

All humans are sent here to balance out some fate, good or bad, from the past. But they have free will to make choices.

they needed. This is what he was to them. His family, except one of his daughters, had all died off. Some people claim they are offspring of Samuel Clemens, but it's not so. His line died out.

He died in 1910. Halley's Comet had reached its perihelion two weeks before his birth seventy-five years before, and the day before his passing it again came to its closest point to the sun and could be seen from earth. Twain had said, "It will be the greatest disappointment of my life if I don't go out with Halley's Comet."

Many of his writings refer to a comet. He dictated over a million words in the last decade of his life. Some of his stories were never published during his lifetime. *The Mysterious Stranger* and others were published later. People weren't ready for them.

THE FULL SPIRITUAL MESSAGE

Mark Twain didn't have the satisfaction of knowing the full message.

You in ECK today have the satisfaction of knowing the full message.

You in ECK today have it. You know about ECK. Many other people still don't. They think their salvation is in politics, or in societal change which works hand-in-hand with political change. That's got to be it, they think. There can be peace on earth if we just all get together and put our shoulder to the wheel.

I believe ours, in ECK, is a happier world.

THREE THINGS FOR SPIRITUAL FREEDOM

There are three things needed for spiritual freedom. The first is the Living ECK Master. Why? Because he can show the individual Soul the way to the Light of God and open his ears to the heavenly music. The first step is the Living ECK Master.

The second is the heavenly music, the Voice of God, the ECK.

Then Jivan Mukti—spiritual liberation in this lifetime. This comes at the Fifth Initiation. The Fifth Initiation comes after Self-Realization, which is the experience of the ECKshar. The experience comes first. When a person truly has it, it's an ecstasy of Soul.

Those of you among the initiates of ECK who've had the true spiritual experience of Self-Realization have known an ecstasy such as no other. Your ears have been opened to the music of God and your eyes to the Light of God. You see the Blue Light, the Light of the Mahanta, in other people. Then comes spiritual liberation, or spiritual freedom.

SOUL HAS COMPLETE FREEDOM

Spiritual freedom simply means that, at this point, one need never, ever come back to the lower worlds.

A Second Initiate need never come back to the physical world, to earth. He's broken that after the Second Initiation. Of course, there's always the free will and the freedom to give it up, to give it back. The individual can say, "No, I don't want to go any farther. I want to become an Episcopalian, or a Pentecostal, or a Baptist, or a Catholic, or a Muslim, or a Hindu, or something. I want to become something else."

The Mahanta, the Living ECK Master will never, ever stand in an individual's way. He will always let each Soul have the freedom to do as It will. Because that Soul is operating within the state of Its own consciousness. It must be where It's comfortable. It must do what It feels right doing.

There's no hurry. There is absolutely no hurry.

The Mahanta, the Living ECK Master will never, ever stand in an individual's way. He will always let each Soul have the freedom to do as It will.

LEARNING ABOUT ILLUSION

One of the young people in ECK, "Kelly," was on a long road trip to visit her family.

She came to Las Vegas, and she stopped to take in some of the sights. She also took in a magic show where the performer was very good.

As Kelly watched, she could see through the magician's illusions. Half the time, she could see just how the tricks were done. And when she couldn't exactly see how the magician had done a trick, Kelly still knew pretty much how she'd done them.

In the past, she said, she would have felt cheated; she'd have thought this was a waste of money and a waste of time. But now there was a difference. She found it very interesting and enjoyable trying to figure out the illusions. Each time she saw through one, she enjoyed it and said, "Wow, that was good. Let's see if I can catch another one."

DREAMS AND SOUL TRAVEL

Over time, Kelly also has learned to move from the dream state to direct Soul Travel. She finds this a very interesting experience. She lists a few points that she notices as the difference between dreams and Soul Travel.

First, she says, when Soul Travel begins, she's aware when the shift occurs. She knows the experience is real.

Secondly, she knows she really is somewhere in full consciousness. She knows it. She's there.

Third, she's in control of herself. When she moves from the dream to Soul Travel, it's such a dramatic shift that it's like the difference in being asleep and waking up. It's like waking up. You say, "Hey, I'm

When Soul Travel begins, Kelly knows she really is somewhere in full consciousness. She knows it. She's there.

awake." That's Soul Travel.

Fourth, in Soul Travel she knows that the physical body is asleep. So she has experiences on the inner planes and is able to work with the Mahanta, the Living ECK Master, who is the Inner Master, the Dream Master.

KELLY'S MISSION TO THE GANARIANS

One night Kelly met the Mahanta. At first she's talking about this or that and wants to know one thing or another. But she sees that the Mahanta has something in mind; he wants to say something. So finally she takes a moment to be quiet.

He says he has a mission for her. Would she go on a trip to another part of an alternate universe and help the Ganarians?

At this point, the person I've called Kelly will immediately know this is her story. I've changed her name to protect her privacy; it's up to her to go spilling the beans if she wants to.

Sometimes that holds things back because then people put you on a little pedestal. It feels good to be up there, but then you're off into politics full time. Nothing wrong with politics, though, as long as you don't think it is the beginning and end of freedom. There are people in the political field who are working in the spiritual side of things too. They know and they understand. They're doing something for spiritual reasons, and not for personal gain.

So, Kelly agrees to go help the Ganarians. Three other young, friendly people are to go with her, and it's going to be a good trip. She says to the Master, "What do the Ganarians look like?" The Master says, "They have triangular faces."

They go off traveling—Kelly and her companions—

One night Kelly met the Mahanta. He says he has a mission for her.

and they end up in this other place. The Ganarians they meet remind her of the Brady bunch. They're filming in their living room. They're doing this because that's how it is in their world. And it's really interesting—they are humanoid, but they do have these triangular faces. They are very good, happy people.

IT'S ALL ABOUT LOVE

When Kelly and her companions set off to visit the Ganarians, she called back to the Master, "I love you." But the Master didn't appear to hear her.

She called louder: "I love you!" Still he didn't seem to hear her. She said it a couple more times until he finally heard. Then he looked embarrassed or maybe even just a little irritated.

That's all Kelly remembers of the experience. She doesn't know what happened from that point on. But she does remember her reaction when she noticed that the Master looked embarrassed or irritated. She thought, *Wait a minute. That's just how I react sometimes.*

She used this inner experience to gain a very valuable insight into her own nature. Sometimes when love came too close, she would hold it away. And she'd be embarrassed or maybe a little irritated. It was like she wanted to say, "Don't bother me with that, because I've got things to do. This is a fast world, and I want to get on with it."

But when you get right down to it, it's all about love.

MAY I SEE THE FACE OF GOD?

Kristy has written many times about her cat Misha. Beautiful, beautiful Siamese cat. He's got this

Kelly thought, Wait a minute. That's just how I react sometimes.

quiet way of walking—like a ghost, he comes very quietly.

She'll be working at her desk, and next thing she knows, there's Misha on the sofa right next to her. She never heard him come. Or he'll appear when she's in the kitchen. Suddenly, there's Misha, just to be near her. Very dignified cat, very stately. He has these piercing, penetrating, loving eyes.

One day, Kristy goes to do a spiritual exercise. She sits down, and this one question comes up that has been through her mind a couple of times before. She had always forgotten about it, but now it comes up again. It is: May I see the face of God?

So, as she's doing the Spiritual Exercise of ECK, she dares ask the Inner Master, "May I see the face of God?" She hesitated at first but then thought, *Hey, go for it.* Once the question came out of her mouth, she thought, *Why not?* She had the courage to say it, so she'd see what would happen.

So she's sitting there real quiet, listening for anything, looking on her inner screen—looking, listening.

She hears this funny little sound. She listens, and it's not a sound from the inner planes. It's some sound out here. Strange, she's never heard that peculiar sound before. What could it be? It couldn't be Misha. Misha walks like a ghost. She never hears Misha walking anywhere. Misha just appears.

So Kristy focuses her attention and gets rid of all those little thoughts that try to take a person's attention away from the Third Eye—that seat of Soul back by the pineal gland in the middle of the head. She's looking there, her eyes shut, crowding out all outside noises and distractions. But then here's that sound again. She wonders, *Shall I peek?* She opens

As she's doing the Spiritual Exercise of ECK, Kristy dares ask the Inner Master, "May I see the face of God?"

her eyes, and seated right in front of her, looking right
into her eyes, is Misha.

Just looking at her—looking wise, eternal, and so
full of love.

Kristy looks at Misha. She thinks, *If ever there
was a huge symbol of love, it's Misha.*

And what is God? God is love.

So in answer to her question, May I see the face of
God? Kristy hears this little sound, and it's Sugmad
(God) and Misha in cahoots. Misha makes this little
sound he's never made before. Kristy opens her eyes,
and she realizes that the love of God is all around
her, as near and dear as Misha.

Kristy is laughing and laughing, because it's like
a divine joke to teach her the truth—to help her see
through the illusion of where the face of God might
be.

She saw truth that poor old Mark Twain never
saw. It's all around you. The Light of God is in every
person.

INSIDE THE GREATER WORLDS

Enjoy the good things in others. Overlook and
forgive the negative things where Soul still needs to
polish.

Eckankar is the entrance ramp for the road to
spiritual freedom. The road to spiritual freedom.

So often I get up in the morning and tell Joan,
"I see so many people. I work with them, I talk with
them—chelas of ECK and many others who haven't
heard of the ECK teachings yet. Many understand,
and I try to help them see even better. It's all inside
there in all the greater worlds. This is such a dark,
little world, and we make such a big thing of it. This

Eckankar is the entrance ramp for the road to spiritual freedom.

is our big illusion down here."

Joan is very patient because she's able to get around on the inner planes herself. So she's good for company, and she helps some of you too, even as the Higher Initiates of ECK work with the Mahanta, and even as the initiates of ECK work with the uninitiated Souls in this world.

So I would like to thank you. My love is always with you. I am always with you. May the blessings be.

ECK Worldwide Seminar, Minneapolis, Minnesota,
Saturday, October 26, 2002

Here was a woman who had to supplement her income,
but she was living to serve others.

10

TRUE WISDOM

ll of us today, with everything going so fast, find that our plate is full. Yet there's still food on the table, and we'd like more of it.

Then comes the trick of trying to figure out how to cut down. How can we avoid becoming gluttons and hurting ourselves with too much of something that's good for us?

I'd like to mention a book about health, Paul Pitchford's *Healing with Whole Foods*. It's rather expensive, but it has a good presentation of a number of different healing systems all folded into one book. It's a very good reference. And for those of you trying to take care of yourself, you'll find this good to have at hand.

WHAT IS TRUE WISDOM?

I think it's fair to say that true wisdom comes through the right kind of experience—experiences that lead us through life to a higher state of consciousness.

That is in contrast to much of the experience that Souls gather on earth—the kind where they do the same thing again and again and again.

True wisdom comes through the right kind of experience— experiences that lead us through life to a higher state of consciousness.

We are in a Judeo-Christian culture here in the
United States. As ECKists we never forget that there
are people with different beliefs from our own, and
we are grateful for the freedom of religion that we
enjoy in this country.

A CONVERSATION WITH THERESA

I was at a food store this past week, and as I was
checking out, one of the people came up and offered
to bag my groceries for me. I noticed her name tag
and said, "Thank you very much, Theresa."

With a name like Theresa, I figured she'd be
Christian. Just to pass the time of day a little bit, I
said, "Are you ready for Easter?" She looked at me
and said, "That's not my holiday."

I thought, *Nice going, Harold.* You put your foot
out to try the water, and you think it's going to be
pleasantly warm, but instead you're in ice water. Now
I'm standing there wondering what to say.

Then she asks, "Are *you* ready for Easter?"

Now I'm just a little bit at a loss for words, and
I say, "It's really not my holiday either."

Theresa had looked so tired and worn before she
started to bag the groceries. It's hard work, and she's
near retirement age, but she probably needs the income. I wanted to say something positive to make her
feel good.

I learned a long time ago that if you see someone
looking tired, you don't say, "Boy, do you look tired
and worn out!" I did something like that once, and
I saw the person wilt. Next time I saw him, I made
it a point to say, "Boy, you sure look good!" And actually he did. He looked very good. And he looked a
lot better after I said it.

I learned a long time ago if you see someone looking tired, you don't say, "Boy, do you look tired and worn out!"

Theresa finished bagging my groceries, and I was about to leave. She looked a little bit puzzled, like she didn't know what to say. "Well, enjoy the holidays," she said. Then she started to laugh. I said, "I will. And you too."

LOOKING FOR SOMETHING MORE

So we laughed, and it released the tension. In a way, we were both strangers in this Christian culture. But I'm sure she wasn't entirely so, and I sure wasn't either, because I grew up in the Christian church and studied in the preministerial area for a long time. But there comes a time that Soul finds It has learned everything in a certain arena that It wishes to learn. When that time comes, it's when you migrate toward another teaching.

That's when you become the seeker. You begin to ask, "Is this all there is to life?"

People around you will say, "Why aren't you satisfied? We are." But something inside you is saying there's something more, and you owe it to yourself to look for it.

There comes a time when you become the seeker. Something inside you is saying there's something more, and you owe it to yourself to look for it.

TALKING TO THE MAILBOX?

I'm still dealing with electromagnetic radiation. It likes to play havoc with the nerves. I've learned to control it better, and I can at least get out occasionally when I need to, if only for very short periods of time.

I went to the post office with my wife. Joan went into the next room where the clerks take packages at the windows. I was going to gather up our mail from our post-office box. This way we'd both finish about the same time and we could get going.

My post-office box is on the bottom row, right next to the floor.

I've noticed a pattern. Post-office boxes I've had in the past seem to be either the ones way at the top or way at the bottom. I don't know how they know I'm coming, but that's how it works out. The boxes on top are too high to see into unless I stand on my tiptoes. I've no idea how Joan finds out what's in the box; she's a little shorter than me.

One of the mail clerks, Don, is a very cordial, friendly man. He's usually at one of the windows and we chitchat a lot.

One day, he saw me opening the box, and from behind the wall he called out that we had packages and he'd take them up to the window. I looked around the lobby and saw there were people walking around. It isn't really good to be talking to yourself. But everybody's got cell phones now, and you can fake it. So I called back, "OK." When people in the lobby looked at me funny, I made out like I was putting my cell phone away and just continued getting my mail.

I opened the door to my little post-office box, and I heard this voice coming out of it. All I could see was a pair of feet. "Is that you, Don?" I called out.

But today it was a couple days after April 15, tax day, and it was raining very heavily. People had seen all of the post office that they wished to, so nobody was in the lobby.

I opened the door to my little box, and I heard this voice coming out of it. I bent down as low as I could get and peered through the box, but all I could see was a pair of feet. "Is that you, Don?" I called out.

No answer. If it wasn't Don back there, someone behind the wall is wondering about this person out in the lobby shouting through the hole.

In the meantime, I hadn't noticed that a woman had come into the lobby and was standing behind me.

But when I heard someone open a box, I looked around. I thought, *Oh, great! This woman thinks I'm talking to my mailbox.*

I didn't look up. I was wearing a cap that day, and I had the bill pulled way down over my face.

I didn't know what to do. But the woman knew what to do. I heard her footsteps going click, click, click and her heels went very fast out the door. I shut my little post-office box, got up, and went in to where the clerks were. I had to see if the mail clerk who was waiting on Joan was Don or someone else. If it was someone else, I was in trouble. If it was Don, he'd understand. It was Don.

When I told him about this, he began to laugh. He had a very good laugh—at my expense, I guess, even as Theresa did at the store. Sometimes during the seminar week, the ECK, the Holy Spirit, sets up situations to bring laughter into the lives of people, and into my own too.

The pace of life is so fast for you and for me that we sometimes forget to stop and laugh. But the ECK, or the Holy Spirit, remembers and gives us what we need.

MAKING A HAPPIER DAY

I was in one of the large grocery stores, in a hurry, looking for two things: baking soda and white vinegar. I wanted to do some cleaning at home, and these are useful for cleaning. They're not as good as commercial products, but commercial products give me problems because of chemical sensitivities.

I was standing in an aisle, looking at rows and rows of goods, wondering where the baking soda would be. Around the corner came a woman in her eighties. She had no special store uniform; she was

The pace of life is so fast we sometimes forget to stop and laugh. But the ECK remembers and gives us what we need.

dressed just like a customer. But she said, "Can I help you?"

I said, "Would you happen to know where the baking soda is?"

"Certainly," she said. "Come with me; I'll show you."

The woman took off at a very crisp pace and went all the way up the aisle. "It's right up there," she said, pointing.

Then she asked, "Is there anything else I could help you with?" I couldn't think of anything, because often I can't think of anything that quickly. I could have asked her for the white vinegar, but I didn't think of it until she had walked away. And she walked away very fast.

So then I started looking for the white vinegar. As I came around the end of the aisle, here came the same woman. She saw the big question mark hanging over my head. "Can I help you with something else?" she asked.

"Would you happen to know where the white vinegar is?"

"Sure. It's over in aisle . . . No, I'll show you."

I was thinking, *Here she's over eighty, and she can outwalk me.* My walking's come back pretty good. But she was outwalking me.

"There it is, right over there," she said. Then she gave me a coupon. She was doing a demonstration a little bit later on in the day, and she'd come in early just to look around and get things set up.

I thanked her very kindly.

Here was a woman who perhaps had to work to supplement her income, but she was living to serve others. Such a gracious, kind person. When I go out every day I say, "I hope I can make someone's day

When I go out I say, "I hope I can make someone's day a little happier too, the way the people I meet make my day happier."

a little happier too, the way the people I meet make my day happier."

THE CLOSED LOOP OF KARMA

There's an interesting anecdote about Winston Churchill, British prime minister during World War II. He was a special man, a statesman as opposed to an ordinary politician.

I think it's quite possible he was a reincarnation of one of his ancestors. Reincarnation is the resurrection that the Christian religion has a fragment of in its own doctrines. This is not to belittle another's belief, but just to try to expand the area of knowledge of what life is all about. Some will understand, others won't. If you understand, fine. If you don't, no offense meant.

It's quite possible Winston Churchill was a reincarnation of one of his ancestors.

Winston Churchill was born in 1874. He came from a noble line. His ancestor of some two hundred years earlier was John Churchill, who became the first Duke of Marlborough. And the careers of the first Duke of Marlborough and Winston Churchill ran on parallel courses. Both were brilliant speakers, both were soldiers in the field, both were politicians, both rose to the heights of power, and both fell from the heights of power.

The first Duke of Marlborough was a distinguished soldier. He fought in the battles of the day, he worked his way up through the ranks to top command, then he entered politics and was second in line to be the prime minister.

But at the very pinnacle of his power and influence, court intrigue and the jealousies of lesser men and lesser minds set out to destroy him. And they did destroy him and his career.

Everything he had—all positions of influence—was taken away. He ended up in a very nice home but with nothing to show for all the service that he had given to his country.

Pretty much the same happened with Winston Churchill. Even as a young man, he stirred controversy. He was a poor student, he didn't get along well in school, and his father had no use for Winston at all. He wouldn't even recommend him to go to the same public school as the father had gone to because he was afraid Winston would embarrass him. Public school in England is something more like a very exclusive private school.

Winston was sent to four other schools, and at the end of each year at graduation, the students would march to the closing ceremonies lined up according to their academic standing. Winston Churchill was always lumbering along, the very last in line. It became a joke with the other parents. They said, "Here comes Churchill's son again—last in line every year." This humiliated the father. He didn't want anything to do with Winston Churchill.

Not too much love on his father's side. And not too much love from his mother either. She turned him over to a nanny, and that's how he spent his youth.

Winston grew up in controversy, but he always wanted action.

Winston grew up in controversy, but he always wanted action, and he entered into a military career. He wanted to get into the field, and he did. He went to Cuba in 1895, and he liked what the rebels were doing there. He volunteered to go as a correspondent; he wrote news dispatches for a paper in England, and everybody loved them. Over the next several years, as both soldier and correspondent, he went with the British army to India, Egypt and the Sudan, and then to South Africa. He was in the Boer War, where descendants of the Dutch were rebelling against the British empire.

But he had the poor grace to criticize the army officers. He said at times they were cruel to the captives and the conditions under which they kept their prisoners were awful. So, of course, he made no friends.

Winston Churchill was following pretty much the path of his ancestor—himself in another lifetime, two hundred years before. Then along came Hitler.

Winston Churchill could smell Hitler back in the 1930s. Churchill was a great student of history, and he had seen tyrants before. He could see where this was going to end. He tried to warn his country. He said this would lead to the greatest war we have ever seen. But no one wanted to hear. No one, especially among the leadership in Britain, wanted to listen. They wanted good times. They wanted to be happy.

When Hitler came in, the political party in power decided to ignore and exclude Winston Churchill. They said, in effect, "There's only one thing to do. We're going to have to compromise with Hitler. We're going to have to say to him, 'OK, Adolf, you can have the continent, but in return we want to be left alone; we want Great Britain to keep its sovereignty.'"

This is what they said had to be done. This is what the leading politicians thought.

The difference between a statesman and a politician is that a statesman has a moral compass. There are very few statesmen. Winston Churchill was one of these rare individuals in politics who had a moral compass. He had a strong foundation of principles, a sense of what was right and what was wrong. So he inspired the nation to stand up to Hitler and to fight.

The difference between a statesman and a politician is that a statesman has a moral compass. There are very few statesmen.

In 1940, in a part of a famous speech he said: "We shall fight on the beaches, we shall fight on the landing grounds, we shall fight in the fields and in the streets, we shall fight in the hills; we shall never surrender."

The common people in England wanted to fight. It was just that the leadership in Great Britain had lost its backbone.

Winston Churchill was the backbone. So he inspired the nation to stand against the Nazis, and he inspired the British Empire to fight for its freedom. Then, when it was all over, it came time to stand for election, and you can guess what happened. The thankless public, the masses, they elected someone else. This devastated Winston Churchill again, as it had two hundred years before. He hadn't had a sense of what people were really doing behind his back. Again, court intrigue destroyed him.

This is an example of someone going through the lessons of karma in a closed loop, never quite having learned the lesson, having to come back and repeat the experience of the past to see if he can find a way out of the maze this time.

A TODDLER'S PAST-LIFE RECALL

There are so many youth in ECK. They make up roughly a quarter of all ECKists. The youth are the future, the ones who will carry on the works of ECK in their turn. In Africa, the youth make up two-thirds of all the members. So there is a lot of potential in Africa.

Sometimes children will refer to a past life. They'll just bring it up out of the blue.

Sometimes children will refer to a past life. They'll just bring it up out of the blue.

A mother wrote me. She babysits a number of toddlers during the day. Her own daughter is fifteen.

One day the woman found a little girl sitting on the couch with the fifteen-year-old. Usually this little child was chattering all the time. But today she was very quiet. She was thinking. Then suddenly, without any prompting, she said to the fifteen-year-old, "When I was big, I was driving down the street with my daddy. We'd eaten dinner out, and we were late picking up my sister. My daddy drove right through a stop sign, and he crashed the car. I went through the windshield and laid on the ground for a long time before anyone came to help me. I died. When I was big, though, my name was Amanda. And I was big like your mommy."

Now in her rebellious years, the fifteen-year-old sometimes had her questions about Eckankar and reincarnation. She looked at her mother and said, "Mom, did you hear what she said?"

The mother said, "Yes, I heard."

The teenager tried to get more information from the toddler, but it was as if the screen were pulled down. The child said no more.

The mother said that this experience pointed out for her, and for her daughter, that reincarnation is simply another day in the life of Soul.

TRUE WISDOM

This is part of the true wisdom. We celebrate the resurrection too, and we celebrate this life as the resurrection, because life always follows death. And it doesn't do it just one time.

In Eckankar, we believe and know that this progression and cycle occurs again and again.

Many people are not at the point where they can understand this. It's not the time. They have many

This experience pointed out for the mother, and for her daughter, that reincarnation is simply another day in the life of Soul.

other things to learn that are very important.

Not to say that the ECKists who've come further along the path have solved all the problems that people around them are still working on. They haven't. But at least they've come to an understanding that there's a way out. There's a way off the wheel of reincarnation.

THE BOY WHO LISTENED

Another woman was working with children in summer camp. One of the children was a five-year-old. He was very inquisitive and had a good imagination, but he was impatient. If there was something he couldn't do, he'd become very angry. Then he'd pick a fight. Then he'd say, "I'm hungry. I want to eat."

The woman knew the routine: He gets angry, he fights, he gets hungry. She was trying to figure out, *How can I help this child?* She thought about it quietly within herself.

Maybe there's a way, she thought. *Is there a way?*

As she became still, she heard this beautiful sound. This all occurred years before the woman became a member of ECK. There seemed to be colors around this sound. She couldn't explain it, but that's how it seemed.

The child came up, put his ear to her heart, and said, "I hear a flute, and I can see colors! Beautiful colors!"

The child noticed something. He came up, put his ear to her heart, and said, "I hear a flute." He began to shout. He said, "I hear a flute, and I can see colors! Beautiful colors!"

Neither of them knew they were hearing and seeing the Sound and Light of ECK, the Holy Spirit. The Holy Spirit is the Voice of God. The Creator speaks to his creation through the Light and Sound. At lower levels, this Light and Sound will manifest and come into a matrix—sometimes as a Master, sometimes as an angel. But in the highest, purest form of this communication between God and Soul, It will come as Light and Sound.

FRED AND THE LOST FILE

"Fred" wasn't an ECKist, but he married one. And he told of an experience that convinced him there was something to Eckankar, HU, Soul Travel, and the Spiritual Eye. He and his wife lived in Canada. His wife had come from Germany, and after they'd settled in Canada, they decided to go back to Germany and pack up her belongings.

So they made the trip. They packed everything in boxes, and his wife told Fred, "You take care of everything in the office and mark the boxes *Office*; take care of the files and whatever else you find."

Fred went to the office and put everything in boxes. In a front room, there were soon rows and rows of boxes stacked to the ceiling. After they'd been at this for most of the day, Fred's wife asked if he had happened to see a certain file. "I need that file," she said.

Fred said, "I don't know anything about the files. You just said to pack them; I didn't read them.

"We're just going to have to find that file," she said.

The office boxes were mixed with the rest of the boxes, so as they had time, Fred and his wife pulled boxes down and looked. But they couldn't find the file.

The night before the moving company was going to come, Fred's wife said, "I know how we can find it."

It was late and he was so tired. He said, "How?"

She said, "Come in here to the couch. We'll sit

The highest, purest form of this communication between God and Soul will come as Light and Sound.

down and do a contemplation."

He said, "What?" She hadn't talked to him too much about contemplation.

She said, "We'll sing *HU*."

Fred had heard about HU, the holy name for God, only once before. But he was too tired to argue. He sat down on the couch with his wife, and she said, "Put your attention at the Spiritual Eye, which is back in the center of your head right about here." She touched the place between her eyebrows.

They sang HU. Then they came out of contemplation, and Fred said to his wife, "I know where the box is."

As they sang *HU*, Fred felt a slight pressure there. Then suddenly, just as clearly as a slide projector throwing a picture up on a white screen, he saw the box. He saw the row, and he saw where it was in the row. They came out of contemplation, and he said to his wife, "I know where the box is."

They went into the room. The box was in the second row, third box back from the wall, at a certain height. They had to dig. Fred said, "And you'll find that the file is upside down in the box. That's why you couldn't find it."

They looked in the box, and Fred's wife pulled out a file that was upside down. It was the very file they had been looking for. And they were both astounded—even the wife, the ECKist who knew all about HU.

At first Fred thought, *Maybe this was just something in my subconscious mind.* "That's where it was, dear," he said. "It was in my subconscious mind."

His wife said, "But you didn't open the file. You didn't even know what it was."

Fred said, "That's right. You're right, dear." What's a husband to say?

But this experience got Fred thinking. His wife had told him about Soul Travel and Eckankar, and maybe there was something to it.

THE KISS THAT COULD NOT WAIT

The Master's love shows up in different ways.

"Harriet" is an ECKist from Ghana. She and her husband had six children: four were ECKists and two were Christian. Eckankar is making great inroads in Africa.

There is this split in the families even as occurred during the time of Christ. He said, "Think not that I am come to send peace on earth. . . . For I am come to set a man at variance against his father, and the daughter against her mother." He was trying to speak of the division that happens in families when truth of a higher nature comes into a culture that has become fixed or frozen in time. There will be sparks. It's like a cold front moving into an area and causing storms. There's going to be a storm. This is what Christ was talking about.

This happened in Harriet's family. At some point their eldest son came to his parents and said he would like to become a Christian minister.

They sent him to the school, and they gave him their blessings. When he came out, he was a pastor. He had some misgivings about Eckankar for a while; he was very tense about the whole situation. But after a while he got used to it, and he relaxed more. And then he recognized that his religion was for him and his parents' and siblings' religion was for them. He realized, with great understanding and wisdom, that each group needed the religion they belonged to. It was good for their spiritual unfoldment.

One night Harriet had a dream. She was in the United States at the time, and in the dream she was in the bathroom. Her son came to the door and said he had to talk to her. "Can you wait a minute?" she said.

Harriet's son, a Christian minister, realized that each group needed the religion they belonged to. It was good for their spiritual unfoldment.

He said, "No, now." He came in, and he wanted a kiss, and so she kissed him. Then the dream faded away.

Harriet was very curious about this. She called her family in Ghana and learned that her son had been bitten by a very poisonous snake at just about the time she had had this dream. The son knew enough about the ECK teachings, and he had come to say, "I want the Master's love and protection." Very quickly he found the remedy that was necessary. He got the treatment needed. He suffered no lasting ill effects.

Harriet was reading the third series of *The ECK Satsang Discourses*. These discourses come to members of Eckankar. A section title in lesson 5 is "How the Master Works." And Harriet recognized that the Master was working in her life and helping her son overcome a very serious problem.

SPIRITUAL AID FOR ALL

Harriet realized something more: the Mahanta, the Living ECK Master isn't there just for ECKists. He's there for all Souls.

Harriet realized something more: the Mahanta, the Living ECK Master isn't there just for ECKists.

He's there for all Souls. In fact, the greatest work of the Master is often among the people who are between paths.

When I say to you, "Go out and tell people about the teachings of ECK," the ground has been prepared. All you need to do is throw some seed on the ground, and nature will take care of the rest.

When Soul hears the music of God, It yearns, It longs for the return to Its heavenly home. And nothing will prevent it. Nothing will stand in Its way— no family connections, no dangers, no fears.

WORKING WITH THE
LAW OF MANIFESTATION

The Master's love works in everyday life.

"Tony" found himself out of work, as many have, after the crash of March 2000. He was trying to figure how to find another position.

He did all the right things, but every time he came close to getting a new position so he could replenish his bank account, the potential employer would call back and say, "Well, we've got to think about this. Something's come up. Don't call me, I'll call you."

Tony, who is a Higher Initiate in Eckankar, waited a long time for the call that never came. Then he began to work with the law of manifestation.

Basically the law is this: Visualize the goal accomplished. See what you want done. See what you would like to be. Imagine the office you would like to be in. All that.

So Tony did this, and soon he had three nibbles. He got three job offers, so he responded to them all. He wrote up proposals and sent them in. Then poof! All three job offers disappeared into thin air.

He wrote me about what he was doing as he tried to work with the law of manifestation. He did the daily spiritual exercises, and he put his trust in the Mahanta and the ECK, the Holy Spirit, to take care of everything that he needs in his everyday life.

He had taken care of the down-to-earth business; he had written his proposals in response to the job offers.

But people kept coming back to Tony, telling him everything was on hold.

"What am I doing wrong?" he asked me. "Am I missing the principle of detachment, of vairag? Is

The Master's love works in everyday life.

that it? Every time I turn around, there's the Kal, the negative power, throwing a wrench in the machine, and it all grinds to a stop."

And he said, "Is it fear? Is it my emotions? Is this what is doing it? Even though I visualize what I wish to be, I'm afraid that it won't really happen."

He wondered if maybe he ought to think of something else. "Maybe I ought to think of the reward at the end of this," he said. "First of all, visualize what I want to be, then picture how I am going to treat myself. How about a nice trip to Hawaii?"

Tony said that every time his bank account got down to zero, something finally opened up. Then he added, "I know this is the spiritual path, but there must be an easier way to go about it."

THY WILL BE DONE

I have to agree. I found the same thing. In the past, even when I said, "Not my will but Thine be done," I always had opinions about exactly how the Holy Spirit was to carry out my goal.

And the same thing was true for me as for Tony—as soon as my bank account was reading empty, something happened. I found my attitude changed. I think I was more willing to accept conditions that weren't exactly what I had visualized.

Divine Spirit, in Its wisdom, knows better what you need than you do yourself.

Because Divine Spirit, in Its wisdom, knows better what you need than you do yourself. You're facing a busted bank account, and you're thinking, *Now what? What will this do to my lifestyle? What am I going to do now?* It's at this point that you let go. You let go and let God.

It becomes truly not my will, but Thy will. Let it be done.

DOING YOUR BEST AND LETTING IT BE

In many countries, people do not have the same freedom of religion as you do, perhaps, in your country.

Some governments are suspicious of anything new and different, especially in religions or spiritual teachings. Something new could be a threat to the established power. They don't realize that we have no interest in doing anything but letting the powers that be move forward. They are moving under a different law.

Of course, as individuals we may want to do things to make things better. We may be involved in politics as private citizens. We can do all these things, but there is a sense of detachment about it. I will do my best and then let it be.

In a certain country—I won't name it—the government is suppressive, and there is an ECKist there. The ECKists are not in direct contact with Eckankar in the United States.

An ECKist, whom I'll call Sarah, is in her fifties, and is in very poor health. Twelve years ago, she contracted a very serious illness. It was thought that in just a matter of a few days or weeks she'd be gone. Her illness caused a lot of pain.

But she gave her life over to serve the Mahanta, the Inner Master.

So every two weeks she would hold a Satsang class, a class on ECK, very discreetly. She would always ask the Master, "Is it OK to do this class?" As long as she got an all clear, she would do it. But sometimes a warning came, and she would just stop the class. She would not hold it for a period of time. She told the other ECKists, "Wait until I call again, and then we shall have another class."

We may be involved in politics as private citizens, but there is detachment about it. I will do my best and then let it be.

Sarah's husband had died when she was very young. She had had a child, and the child died at the age of eighteen. It was two years after this that Sarah found out about her very serious illness. Now twelve years later, she is still alive, giving her life to ECK, listening to the Mahanta, hearing the true voice of what the divine will wished.

She didn't, and doesn't, superimpose her will upon the Holy Spirit. She listens and then very quietly does something. It heals people, holds them together.

She didn't, and doesn't, superimpose her will upon the Holy Spirit. She doesn't say, "We'll do it this way because the Holy Spirit told me to do it" or, "The Master told me to do it." Not at all. She listens and then very quietly does something. It's constructive. It heals people, holds them together.

KARMIC RESPONSIBILITY

On the other hand, some people will say, "Oh, I got this from the Mahanta. I was to do this and that." They tear people from their faith in ECK.

When someone does this, they become responsible for the karma that they create. They are responsible for the karma of the people they lead off the path of ECK. It may not show for a week, a year, a lifetime.

But that's what reincarnation is about. There's lots of time to pay, lots of time to learn. No hard feelings.

WISDOM IN A HARSH LAND

One night, Sarah was having a hard time. The pain was so bad that she said, "I don't want any ECK or Mahanta; I just want to die and be released from this hard pain." She was ready to go.

During the night, the Mahanta came to her. He said, "If you can tolerate this night, you'll see success." Then, a day later, the pain subsided greatly. It didn't go away completely, but at least she was able to enjoy life.

She enjoys serving life, other people, as she's serving the Mahanta.

But she says she's also seen what happens to those who rise against the Mahanta. The Law of Karma catches up to them. She told of a member of the country's ministry of information. Of course, this usually means the ministry of propaganda, or disinformation, where you give some truth but the rest is all lies. It's the idea that if someone tells the big lie, people will believe it even if they don't believe the little ones. That's what Hitler did, and it's one of the common practices of a tyrannical government to tell the big lie.

The man Sarah mentioned had written an article against the Mahanta, and it appeared in the newspaper. Within a year, the government put him in prison. Sarah said he then committed suicide in a most unfortunate way. She realized that every chela who intends to misuse ECK will lose everything he has.

Sarah is a wise woman in a harsh land.

The New Member's Survey Card

Carol Morimitsu is on the ECK staff at the Eckankar Spiritual Center in Minneapolis. She sent me one of the new-member surveys someone had sent in.

The card says, *Please check your choices.*

The first question is: How did you first learn about Eckankar?

The person had checked two things—"Friends and family" and "Book."

Carol on the ECK staff sent me one of the new-member surveys someone had sent in.

Second question: What other contacts with Eckankar did you have before becoming a member? Again, two checkmarks—"Book" and "ECK seminar."

Third question: How much time passed between first learning about ECK and your becoming a member? There are a whole bunch of choices: "Joined immediately," "One to two months," "Three to five months," and so on, all the way up to two and three years. Then "Other" with a blank to fill in.

This person had written, "Approximately twenty-five years."

The fourth question also had a blank to fill in: Why did you decide to become a member of Eckankar? This question becomes very important after twenty-five years.

This new person said, "Only a Master can take you to the heavenly worlds."

This new person had written, "Only a Master can take you to the heavenly worlds."

CLAUDIA'S JOURNEY TO ECK

"Claudia" was raised in an orphanage in another country, came to America, and didn't know how to speak English. She grew up in southern Alabama. The 1960s were very troublesome years for anyone who was different. Since she didn't speak English, Claudia took an awful beating from her classmates. People there weren't tolerant of foreigners.

Finally she learned English and made some friends.

Then her family moved to Hawaii, and it started all over again. She was white, and most of the two thousand kids in the school were Hawaiian, Tahitian, Samoan, Filipino, Japanese, or Chinese. There were only a hundred *haoles*, or white kids. A hundred against nearly two thousand; Claudia said it wasn't a ratio she ever wanted to be on the low end of again. There were gangs, the kids carried weapons, and it was a terrifying place for a twelve-year-old.

Her family then moved again.

Claudia was a troubled youth. She was always running away. At the age of fifteen, she ran away one time too many. Her father got tired of it and turned her over to the state. She went to the worst juvenile detention center in the history of Tennessee.

Many of the kids were there for minor infractions like running away from home. But others were there for major crimes: assault, armed robbery, murder. It was a horrendous place. The conditions were horrible, and Claudia became very sick. So they transferred her to a hospital.

After her health stabilized, they sent her off to a girls' home, and after a while, they let her go.

Claudia moved two thousand miles away to work, and she supported herself while she was earning a high-school diploma. She was a bright youth, and she got her diploma at the age of seventeen. But she was a very old seventeen.

Over the next thirteen years, until she was thirty, she held some good jobs. But at the same time she was often under the influence of drugs—anything that would numb the pain. In spite of the good jobs, the drugs landed her in a county jail for three months. When she came out, she realized that she had lost everything.

Most of all, she'd lost her self-esteem.

Then came one of these switches that occur in life. Cinderella became the princess. Claudia met a multimillionaire. As Cinderella, she did well. She got a taste of the other side of life. Now it was a life of Cadillacs, country clubs, and a very affluent lifestyle.

Then came one of these switches that occur in life. Cinderella became the princess.

But Claudia saw that her life was pretty much gone. She had lost it herself, and she realized it was up to her.

Then she found Eckankar. It could offer her a lot more than the material goods that she had with the multimillionaire. A person who comes to the path of ECK—not always, but sometimes—has run along a very rocky road.

Now what Claudia didn't realize at the time is that often when a person is about to come into Eckankar, there will be a quick replay of the very lowest parts of one's experience—like rebellion or use of drugs—and also the very highest, a time of complete happiness. Like Winston Churchill, the person may rise to the pinnacle, then fall.

So she gave up her boyfriend. She gave it all up, and she had barely enough money to get by. But every day she did the spiritual exercises, and morning and night she focused on the five virtues: detachment, contentment, humility, discrimination, and forgiveness/tolerance.

Claudia also sang *HU*. It helped her stay open; it kept her heart open to the Light and Sound of God.

She likened herself to a butterfly coming out of a cocoon—a creature who had lost its liberty and was now set free.

It's the same with Soul in Its prison. When Soul finally finds the teachings of ECK, It is freed of the body and its consciousness.

It can rise through the planes to the high worlds where God dwells.

She likened herself to a butterfly coming out of a cocoon—a creature who was now set free.

ECK Spiritual Skills Seminar, Washington, DC, Saturday, April 19, 2003

How important it is to imbue yourself with the living essence of the Light and Sound of God.

11

THE HEART AND
HAND OF GOD

I was coming out from backstage, perfectly fine, when I heard you singing *HU*. The sound of HU—what a beautiful, beautiful sound. I'd better get started before I cry.

As I told my wife this evening, I have absolutely no idea what direction this talk is going to go. In the two weeks preceding this seminar, the ECK has run through a number of different streams as to where this talk might go. Maybe it's to just get it out of my system so it doesn't perplex you. It'll help some of you, uplift others, frustrate more, and probably anger a great many.

The sound of HU—what a beautiful, beautiful sound.

DUTIES OF THE LIVING ECK MASTER

Not long ago, I went to the drugstore. I put on my anti-electromagnetic shirt and I went in and out of the store fast. I like to swing through the children's books area. I love all kinds of books—children's books, youth books, books on history, literature. I've been flat on my back for three months, and what are you going to do? You're going to write; you're going to read; you're going to sleep; and you're going to heal. What a slow, slow time.

Someone very close to me, a Christian, said, "You've been into alternative health care for a long time, long before other people ever thought about it."

I said, "That's true."

"Well then," he asked, "how come you are so sick all the time?"

I said, "Let me explain—but I don't think you'll understand." Because people don't understand how the ECK works with the Mahanta, the Living ECK Master. The Living ECK Master has duties, and he signed on to them before he took the job.

Before I took this job, I got to look at what the future held. After the preview had been running awhile, and I had seen some of the future, I said, "You'd better stop it, or you're going to have to find someone else."

BURNING OFF KARMA

These past two and a half months leading up to the seminar have been rough for many of you, as you've been burning off bundles and bundles of karma. This means debts made in past lives, debts made in this lifetime. You've been working them off.

The normal way to dissolve this is through the ECK Life Stream. It depends upon your state of consciousness. The higher it is, the faster the dissolving goes. But in many cases the Living ECK Master becomes the holding tank. Rather than let you go through the long, drawn-out period of burn-off and the suffering that it entails, guess who gets the karma? The holding tank. And guess what happens to him? Just anything that you can imagine.

When this person asked me, "Why are you sick all the time?" I said, "I don't think you'd understand." And he wouldn't, because he doesn't accept my po-

Many of you've been burning off bundles and bundles of karma. This means debts made in past lives, debts made in this lifetime.

TTH

sition. Nor do I expect him to. He's of a different faith, and I love him dearly. I don't expect him to sign on to what we believe. But whether he believes it or not, the fact is the fact—someone takes a beating.

PRICE OF SPIRITUAL LIBERATION

There is real power in the path of ECK, real power in the teachings. There is real power to help people find spiritual liberation. But that comes at a price.

You pay part of the price. This comes with taking responsibility for yourself. This means that if you have the ability to work, and the youth to work, you will work. You will not let other workers carry your load for you. I tell you this is a lie of socialism. And many people buy into it.

Many of those who work for the government as givers are out beating the bushes trying to find more people who are "poor." This insures a job for the government workers themselves.

Meanwhile there are many people who've put in a lifetime of work—the elderly. They earned a dollar when it was still worth a dollar. They have no understanding about the power of inflation to kill the dollar—to take what was once worth a dollar and make it worth only a nickel today. In terms of buying power, they've seen their dollars turn into nickels. And if someone else is handling the money, they might never know. All they know is that if they're living on their savings, the savings aren't making ends meet in their retirement.

So where do they have to go? Right into the divine hands of the government which will save them. And who created this mess? The government, by inflating the money supply.

> *There is real power in the path of ECK to help people find spiritual liberation.*

These forces are at play all the time. Our fore-fathers, the founders of the United States, knew about these forces that could tear down the republic—the republic that was to stand. Our founders were highly educated men. They stood head and shoulders above most educators of today—those who pretend to be the educators of our children, preparing them for to-morrow.

EDUCATION OF OUR YOUTH

Today's educators give youth this pabulum. They say, "Go out in the world; do what feels good." But when these youth get out in the world, their new employer asks, "What can you do? Can you read, write, add?"

"Let me get out my calculator," says the person.

"What happens if it breaks or your batteries go dead?"

"I'll buy another battery or get a new calculator."

"What if the whole society melts down?"

"I'll get on my cell phone."

"Your cell phone won't work."

Those of you who were on the East Coast during the power blackout, you experienced that. When the power goes out everywhere, the cell phones go out. What works? The old faithful landline.

A grocery store I used to go to had a terrible problem with its cash registers. They've since been bought out by a profitable chain and now seem to be on the way back to making money. I went in there once and talked with a new employee. "How's it going with the new management?" I asked.

"Fine," she said.

I said, "There seems to be a lot more room in the store. What happened? Did they move the aisles apart?"

She said, "The new owners came in and moved the junk that was crowding the aisles."

The aisles used to be dark, and you couldn't find anything. Now suddenly there was light. I said, "This is a nice place now."

And she said, "Thank you."

I noticed the big, numbered signs above the checkout stations. They were no longer held together with tape. I looked at the cash registers; they actually worked. I said, "Looks like the new owners put in some new equipment."

She said, "Yes, and it's a good thing." Before that, the employees were counting on their fingers. They hadn't learned to count in school. It was a very sad thing having to help the cashier figure out your change. It took so long, and the registers would break so often, they always had to open another checkout lane. Somebody would run up and down and see which of the checkouts had a cash register that worked. You'd run over there, get at the back of the line, and think, *Why do I do this?* After a while I started going to another store.

Anyway, as I started to say, I went to the drugstore a short time ago. I looked around and came to a section with children's books.

Recently one of the youth wrote and asked a question: "Harold, if you could recommend some books, what books would you recommend for the youth?"

That was hard! Young readers run anywhere from age six all the way up to age eighteen and beyond. Each age-group has its own interests, its own books. And I couldn't begin to give you any idea of all the books that are available for each age-group. Since I knew this particular youth's age, I gave her some ideas.

One of the youth wrote and asked: "Harold, what books would you recommend for the youth?"

I'd like to give a few more that I ran across in the drugstore. You may not be able to find the editions I did. They were illustrated versions of the great classics, adapted versions of the full-length novels. I've read most of the full-length novels, but I like these because there's a picture on practically every other page, and nice big type. The story moves along, and a very fine artist has depicted scenes to show the action.

I love this stuff. I eat it up. I save them. Maybe someday my grandchildren will be old enough to enjoy this—if they can read.

I worry about the education of the American youth more than anyone could know. I listen to talk shows—local and national—and I watch the local elections to see what sort of people get on the school board, what people are dumbing down our kids, and which ones are helping them become self-sufficient, responsible young people who will then become self-sufficient, responsible adults.

Those are the people I like. I look forward to seeing them elected, and I watch how their election campaigns are progressing. I know the good ones, I know the others. But I let elections and politics go because that is not my domain. That is not the reason I'm here. I'm here to help lift people above the political and economic regions of this world. And many of you are helping me do just that.

There are seekers waiting to find the teachings of ECK. A new generation's come in.

Seekers Are Waiting

There has been an upswing in ECK membership among the Canadians within the last two years. Around the beginning of that time, I put out a call to the Regional ECK Spiritual Aides in a newsletter. I said there are seekers waiting to find the teachings of ECK. I said there used to be life in your regions but it's burned out. The people who were there once knew the fire and the power and the inspiration of these sacred teachings. But when they died, it did not pass to the next generation. And so now a new generation's come in. I asked their help.

Now I'm seeing an upswing in the number of new people who are starting to come into Eckankar. So I thank you, all of you who are helping in Canada.

The same holds true in Europe. We're seeing an upswing there too. So I applaud those of you who are helping me find the seekers in Europe.

The growth of new members in Africa is astounding.

ADVENTURE STORY FOR SOUL

Getting back to the books for youth, one of them is a lot of fun: *The Swiss Family Robinson*. It's a wonderful story. A Swiss family is moving to a colony out in the Pacific. They're aboard ship, and there is a storm. The crew abandons the ship and leaves this family—four boys, ages eight, eleven, thirteen, and fifteen, and their parents.

When dawn breaks next morning, the father looks out. The power and fury of the storm has broken, and the ship has been caught up on two rocks. The ship is suspended there until the next storm. So in the meantime, there's a lot to do.

Here is the power and the beauty of the book. It shows the creativity and the ingenuity of this family as they meet the crisis of the moment.

There is a desert island nearby, and the Swiss family Robinson figures out how to get to shore. They use what they find aboard. They don't find rubber water wings. The story takes place years ago when

One of the books for youth, The Swiss Family Robinson, shows the creativity and ingenuity of this family as they meet the crisis of the moment.

all they had were wooden casks and things like that.

So they get ashore. One of the sons finds turtle eggs, and a goose that was aboard ship becomes dinner. That evening the family eats very well.

They're very resourceful, and they go on to have many adventures. I won't tell the whole story; you'll have to read it yourself. I'm not going to give away the ending.

CAN-DO SPIRIT

We're interested in the creative element, because this is the spark of God that God has put into the heart of each human being. Sometimes socialism and welfare put it to sleep, and I cry for that. The teachings of ECK, I hope, will awaken it—awaken the survival factor in every last one of you.

That way, no matter what happens, no matter what comes, you have this can-do spirit. You know somehow there's a way, and as long as there is life, you will do whatever is in your power to make it work. And that's all you can do.

No matter what happens, you have this can-do spirit. You know somehow there's a way, and as long as there is life, you will do whatever is in your power to make it work.

If you can't do it here, if you can't survive in the physical plane, how do you expect to survive in the other worlds? They have the same challenges—and greater ones.

So meet yourself here and now. Unless you do, you're going to meet yourself some other place. And most often, unless you're in Eckankar, you're going to meet yourself again right back here in another life. You'll look in the mirror, and you won't recognize yourself, though, because you'll be wearing a new skin and your mind will be washed of all the past.

LIFE-AND-DEATH DECISIONS

Sometimes people are critical about those who commit suicide. I've given my stand on it. I say it's best to see life through if you can. But if the pain is ever so great that someone says to the doctor, "Please help me out of this life," I will never say a word. Who am I to say, unless I have walked in that person's shoes?

I say it's best to see life through if you can.

Unless I have had his strength or share his weakness, I will never know the reason for that decision. It's not up to me.

Yet these decisions of life and death are taken over very freely by politicians who have no clue what some people go through. They make the laws, so they make a law that says, "Thou shalt not take thine own life." And if someone does, what's the government going to do? Man's law stops at the borders of death; it cannot go beyond. I find this a tremendous divine joke on the human race.

PAYING YOUR DUES

The sacrifices and discipline required for some of you to get to a seminar like this are beyond the imagination of the ordinary person. I understand this, and I respect it. For my part, I go through the very same thing and maybe a little bit more, because I'm carrying a little bit more—many more burdens of people.

As quickly as I can, I pass them off into the ECK Life Stream. But it doesn't come quick. So when a couple of people asked, "Why are you sick all the time?" I said, "You ought to ask, why am I not dead?"

Now I've got to spend six winter months trying to get this body back together. I hope now that we've finished A Year of Spiritual Healing, this will let up.

Many of you have paid your dues. You've paid with your flesh, and you've learned with your heart. No more can anyone do.

When people are so quick to criticize those who take their own life, I just have to say wait. Wait until you've walked a mile in their shoes, and then let's see if you still wear that smile. I'll bet not.

THE REST OF THE STORY

Paul Harvey, a broadcaster who has won many awards, has a radio program called *The Rest of the Story*. These stories are put together by his son, a very talented writer. The son is also a concert pianist; it's a very bright family. Paul Harvey's fifteen-minute program around noon is the most listened-to radio show in America. My wife and I try to catch it when we can. He speaks for middle America. He speaks for me; I don't know about you. But we sure like him.

Later in the day, in midafternoon, comes *The Rest of the Story*. One time Paul Harvey told a story about a very well-known doctor. This doctor had made great advances in the study of the mind, but in his later years he fell victim to cancer.

Operation after operation tore away at his face. He lost the ability to speak well and lost other things that he used to take for granted. He lost his beauty; he lost his ability to hear.

At one point, he went to his doctor and said, "Please give me something to end it all. I've suffered these several years, and I can't take any more." His doctor did not want to comply, but this famous doctor pleaded again and again, and his doctor finally said, "All right, I'll give you something. You can pass from this life very quietly without pain." And so Dr. Sigmund Freud went to the other worlds.

Many of you have paid your dues, and you've learned with your heart. No more can anyone do.

Now who's going to criticize him? I won't. Will you? I hope not.

MORE WONDERFUL BOOKS

Another good book is *The Merry Adventures of Robin Hood* by Howard Pyle. Now, there are many different versions of Robin Hood's story out there. Some supposedly take him from his youth all the way to his death. I didn't ever want that. I just want the happy times when he was a good thief.

Another excellent one is *Heidi* by Johanna Spyri.

The last one I'll mention is by Alexandre Dumas, *The Three Musketeers*. He's a wonderful writer.

If you're anywhere from eleven years on up, you might look into these books. I think you'll have a good read. I like fun books. I like adventure books.

Every night we read stories. My wife reads out loud better than I do. We read all kinds of stories, and I'm the entertainment editor. I beat the bushes for our reading material.

She came to like the Louis L'Amour novels, so we went through the whole Sackett series—wonderful adventure stories. I'd read the whole works years ago, but I've forgotten most of them since. So we began with *The Broken Gun*, and we're working all the way through alphabetically. Next was *The Californios*, and now we're up to *Comstock Lode*.

My wife is very patient. At one point I said, "You know, the story line is pretty much the same as in the other book." And when Louis L'Amour tries to write about the sea—well, he's not Patrick O'Brian.

We read that series too, some twenty novels. Huge! Wonderful command of the English language Patrick O'Brian has. So much so that when he first brought

> You might look into these books. I like fun books. I like adventure books.

his books out, nobody would touch them. A small publisher in England finally picked them up and became very rich through publishing these books. Eventually the word spread to the United States. There is now a very definite cult following of Patrick O'Brian's sea stories. I can't recommend them too highly.

We read all kinds of stories. I can't recommend Patrick O'Brian's sea stories too highly.

Another series of illustrated books I like are the Tintin books by Hergé. They are more available in Europe than here. I raised my daughter on them. After that she wanted to read, so I let her buy comic books. Comic books are shorter; graphic novels tell whole stories.

We have a graphic novel now, *Talons of Time*. And *The Tiger's Fang* is coming. We just got the artwork in. These are created from the books by Paul Twitchell. Mar Amongo, a wonderful artist from the Philippines, made great sacrifices to work on them. We are so very grateful.

HEALING PROCESS

After my car accident in 1991, I had a lot of internal injuries. Whiplash recovery took a year and a quarter. I had ice on my front and back for a time. The doctor said, "Just put an ice pack on once a day." He didn't hurt the way I did, so I put it on every twenty minutes. In time, I went to sleep on the ice, front and back. I was on ice for the better part of a year.

During that time, my immune system went down, because so much damage had been done to the ligaments in the chest. I'm still healing from that. The chiropractor said to get a scan. But I said, "No, thanks. I don't want to do it." I was just becoming sensitive to the electromagnetic radiation. "I can barely get in here," I told him, "and going there would kill me. I'll try to work this out myself."

They would have found the damage; they would have had me go in for an operation; they would have stitched me up, and I would have been better years ago. They would have had to do some work on me that I did not want done, and there would have been risk. I decided to stiff it out, be the lone wolf, do it the hard way. For years, every time I turned wrong there was this huge crunch in my chest. It scared the willies out of people who heard it.

FINDING SPIRIT IN BOOKS

I have a lot of the *Prince Valiant* comics by Hal Foster, which used to be in the Sunday paper. My daughter sent me updates for a while. By then Hal Foster was giving his story ideas to a very capable artist who worked with him. But this artist did not have the vision of the Middle Ages the way Hal Foster did.

In the early comic strips, and continuing up to 1970 or so, Hal Foster did both the story and artwork himself. Absolutely superb. Today I'm able to get him through Bud's Art Books, www.budplant.com.

By the way, I have to say that some of the computer-generated art coming out today is so dead compared to the work that people used to do with a paintbrush.

Another offering that I like is the work by Will Eisner, *The Spirit*. He's the one who began the graphic novel, one of the pioneers who is still drawing.

Eisner stretched the boundaries of what graphic novels could and should be. He's stretched those little, hard four walls that are around each person, pulled those back. His characters walked around and through them in the most wonderful, light-hearted stories.

In the early Prince Valiant comic strips, Hal Foster did both the story and artwork himself. Absolutely superb.

Through it all you'll find the hand of God. You wonder how.

It's in the playing out of karma. In every story you hear, whether it's in a book or on television, there is the subtle playing out of karma. People get along, people do not. People have an instant liking and bonding with each other, or an instant dislike. They hate each other. They don't know why, but it's real.

> *You'll find the hand of God in the playing out of karma. In every story, people get along, people do not. They don't know why, but it's real.*

WE WORK TOGETHER IN ECK

At the Eckankar Spiritual Center, I feel we have the very finest staff that anyone could hope to have. And if you've been out to the Temple of ECK, you will see the new ECK Spiritual Center as it's rising. The moving force behind that is Peter Skelskey and his wife, Sheri, who helps with the design. But when it comes to working with the contractors, there's Peter. He takes his bruises. He even fell off of a ladder once while taking pictures.

The ECK staff takes an enormous beating, and Peter is doing a wonderful job. He did most of the mind and muscle work that led to the creation of the Temple. The ECK Spiritual Center will be a beautiful place, judging by the pictures we've seen.

This doesn't just happen. The wheels in the office don't keep running automatically. Sometimes Peter has to go off-site and handle some insoluble problem that the city has thrown up this time or the builders have thrown up that time. He's a very talented man, so if you see him, shake his hand and give him a gentle pat on the back, because he deserves it.

I'm not saying this to get in anyone's good graces, because I simply don't care about that. I just tell it the way I see it.

Rumi's Poems

I read translations of poems by Jalal ad-Din ar-Rumi. Today we know him as the Persian poet, but he was actually born in what today is Afghanistan. His family fled the Mongol invasion as it swept down into Afghanistan, and they took refuge in what is today Turkey.

Rumi's ancestors were educators, and his father was the head of the local Sufi group. When his father passed on, he passed on the title to Rumi, and Rumi became the head. Rumi was pretty much your average educator and teacher until the age of thirty-seven, when there was a profound change in his life. He met Shams from Tabriz. In Eckankar, we call him Shamus-i-Tabriz.

The translations I especially love are those by Coleman Barks. A friend from Canada got a whole bunch of autographed volumes as a gift for me. One of them is *We Are Three*.

Rumi's life changed when he met Shamus-i-Tabriz, the Mahanta, the Living ECK Master of the times.

Rumi's life changed when he met Shamus-i-Tabriz. Shamus-i-Tabriz was the Mahanta, the Living ECK Master of the times. Rumi was looking for the teacher. Shamus was looking for someone who loved God as much as he. Someone who had the capability, the state of consciousness, to understand what he was all about, what message he had to carry.

At some point, they bumped in to each other. And they recognized each other on the spot. Rumi later said, "What I once thought of as God I met today in flesh."

Rumi's life turned around. He began to speak the many lines of poetry that are today captured in the *Masnavi*. He just spoke this poetry as it occurred to him. He spoke about anything. Someone walked into

246 THE ROAD TO SPIRITUAL FREEDOM

the room, he made it into poetry; someone came into town for a meeting, there was Rumi. He spoke poetry.

At one point a childhood friend and disciple asked, "How long are you going to keep doing this?" Rumi said, "I certainly don't know." The friend said, "If you like, I will write this all down." Rumi said, "All right, if you want to."

This went on for twelve years. His chela was his scribe. Sometimes Rumi would say nothing for several months, then he wouldn't stop talking for days. All the while, his scribe would keep writing everything down. This then appears today in the *Masnavi*.

Very little of this was translated into English. Coleman Barks took the available translations— which were literal translations, meaning very stiff ones—and put them into human language. They're a lot of fun. There's a particularly ribald one, *Delicious Laughter*.

A friend was once going around talking about the other translations and how pious and how mighty was the great Rumi. He was becoming a problem to himself and others. So I sent him a copy of *Delicious Laughter*. I believe that cured him. I never heard from him again.

So, Rumi was a disciple of Shamus-i-Tabriz, the Living ECK Master of the time. And legend has it that one of Rumi's own sons helped kill this high teacher. Rumi was very upset when he heard. But he was a kind man. Even his letters of advice to people have wonderful insight. People sometimes wonder, Did Rumi really write these? Rumi wrote them. They're the kind of letters I write. Sometimes about business, about things that people need to know. I write those letters too, so I know they're true.

Even Rumi's letters of advice to people have wonderful insight.

A TINY BIRD'S
THREE BITS OF WISDOM

Rumi tells this story. One time a man caught a bird in a trap. It was just a tiny little bird, and the little bird said to him, "In your life you've eaten a lot of oxen, you've eaten a lot of sheep, and your hunger is there with you still. Look at me, look how tiny I am. I won't quiet your hunger for even a minute. Let me go, and I will give you three bits of wisdom."

So the man listened. He said, "There's sense to what you say." He opened his hand.

The bird stood on his hand and said, "Here's the first bit of wisdom. Number one: Don't believe an absurdity, no matter who says it."

It then flew out of the man's hand and landed on his roof. Up there, the little bird said, "Number two: Do not grieve over what is past. It's over. Never regret what has happened."

As the man was weighing this, and almost as an afterthought, the little bird said, "I forgot to tell you that in my body there is a huge pearl as heavy as ten copper coins. It was to be an inheritance for you to pass on to your children. It's gone. You let it go. It flew up here."

The man began to wail and cry. While he was wailing, the bird flew off to the branch of a tree and sat there well out of reach. "Oh, stop crying," he said. "Listen. Didn't I just tell you not to grieve for what's in the past? Also, don't believe an absurdity?"

He said, "Now you've heard an absurdity from me. You've heard and believed, and now you won't let it go. Use your head, man. Look it over. My body is so small it doesn't weigh even as much as one coin. How is it going to hold something that weighs ten? My

The little bird said, "Let me go, and I will give you three bits of wisdom."

body can't possibly hold a pearl that size and still be of my own weight."

The man listened. He said, "That makes a lot of sense to me. Tell me number three."

The bird said, "Are you kidding? Look what you've done with numbers one and two." And it flew away.

This is one of the delightful stories that Rumi told. Some are beautiful, some are funny, and they're all enlightening. I recommend them to anyone whose heart is looking for something that he can't find in ECK.

This is one of the delightful stories Rumi told. Some are beautiful, some are funny, and they're all enlightening.

LEARNING THE BASICS OF LIFE

The McGuffey Reader was a mainstay of American education from the mid eighteen hundreds on into the twentieth century. People back then found education very hard to come by. Some of them couldn't complete grade school because of illness, because of work. It held even more true as they got into high school. It was even more difficult.

Numbers one, two, three, and four of the McGuffey Readers deal with the elementary things like learning how to read. I just recently sent for the speller too. I figured, *Why not? I've got all the rest.* So I bought that too. They have wonderful stories, and one of them is this.

There was a traveler seated by the side of the road. He was having a hard time. Fate was frowning on him at the moment, but he still had money. He took off his shoe, got a pebble out. As he was looking down the road, he saw a beggar coming toward him. He knew the beggar was going to want some money.

The beggar came closer, and the traveler noticed that with him was a dog. The two approached, and the beggar asked for a handout. The traveler said,

"You don't have the signs of someone who needs to beg. You aren't blind; you've got both eyes. You're not lame; you're walking well, except you don't have any shoes. You're walking in your bare feet. I see that your socks have worn away around your toes and your heels, and what used to be around your ankles is just hanging there a-flapping in the wind."

The beggar said, "That's true." Then he added, "I'm not like other beggars. I can tell your fortune."

The traveler said, "I don't need your fortunes. I know they're just stories you make up to make people feel good."

"Well, that's true," said the fortune-teller. "That's absolutely true."

The traveler said, "Well, tell you what. If you will tell me the secret of how you became a fortune-teller and what you do, we'll trade that for whatever it is you want. I'll give you a handout for that."

The beggar said, "Agreed."

So he began his story. He said, "Bottom line: people do not want to hear the truth. In the beginning, I told them that I used to be an honest laborer, which is true. I said I put aside the little bit that I could for savings, and that is true. Then I told them I became ill and could no longer work. That is true. But," he said, "nobody believed me. And so I starved. I'd lost everything. I was on the road, and no one would give me money so that I could feed myself. So," he said, "I had to stop at the servants' quarters at all these estates as I passed by."

"When I knocked, the servants would open the door; they would let me in when I asked for a little food and a little drink. And I paid for it with gossip I had picked up along the way. And they traded the gossip of the household with me. Luckily, I have a

The traveler said, "If you tell me the secret of how you became a fortune-teller and what you do, we'll trade for whatever you want."

very good mind. I remember everything that's happening in our countryside."

"Well," the traveler said, "then you must know a little about me too."

The fortune-teller said, "Yes, fortunately, I do. I know you're a jokester, and I know a jokester has a hard time holding a job. And I know you're out on the road now, a little down on your luck, but you have enough to give something to me."

This was the basis for the fortune-teller's telling of a fortune. He had all the gossip. He had the book on every important personage in the country. When one of these rich people called to him to come over and tell a fortune, he could, because he already had the book; and what he didn't know, he filled in. And he filled in happy things, so that his client always was happy.

The traveler said, "I'll keep this in mind, and I'll see. As I go along, maybe I can start picking up some of this gossip myself. And if, in the future, my shoes ever wear out and I'm walking around in socks in the countryside as you are, I shall be able to earn my way and not go hungry and not go cold."

The beggar said, "All right. I did my part of the deal; now do yours."

The traveler was thinking, *I don't actually have everything I need right now to do what he's doing. It's going to take awhile to accumulate all the gossip. Now, should I give him six pence, or should I give him this shilling?* He had both in his pocket, and his fingers went around the shilling, which was worth twice as much. He brought it out, but Virtue held his hand from letting it go. "Virtue"—skinflint, that's what he was.

But then destiny opened his hand, and the shil-

> *The traveler was thinking, Now, should I give him six pence, or this shilling?*

ling fell into the dirt. The little dog ran over, scooped it up, and gave it to his master. The beggar said, "Thank you kindly." The traveler said, "You're welcome."

The beggar, very happy that he had earned his keep, then went on his way. He said he was going to read the fortunes of six wealthy girls in a boarding school, each of whom wanted to know whether her future husband would be a peer of the realm, which meant somebody who got land with a title, or a captain in the royal armed forces.

CLAUDIA SAVED BY THE HAND OF GOD

This next story includes something you can take home in your heart, to help you realize how important it is to imbue yourself with the living essence of the Light and Sound of God. This Light and Sound of God is available in the word *HU*.

"Claudia," from Tennessee, had a morning routine. The first thing she did was her contemplation. When she finished, then she got ready for work. When she got into her car, the first thing she'd do was declare herself a clear channel for God (Sugmad), the Holy Spirit (ECK), and the Mahanta. Then she'd set out on the road, her HU CD in the CD player, playing the HU song. She sang *HU* with all her might as she drove the forty minutes to work.

One day Claudia was driving along the freeway, when the traffic screeched to a halt in front of her.

She hit the brakes and came to a safe stop, but then she looked in the rearview mirror and realized the semitruck behind her would be unable to stop. Worse, she realized her seat belt was unbuckled and there was no time to fasten it.

Claudia looked in the rearview mirror and realized the semitruck behind her would be unable to stop.

Claudia screamed, "God, please help me!"

At that moment she felt a giant hand of God put itself around her and hold her gently in its grip. Now, she knew this as the hand of the Mahanta.

The truck hit the back of her brand-new Toyota Camry and pushed the trunk all the way up to the rear seats. The car was shoved into the car ahead of hers, and the engine crunched back up to the dashboard. Through it all, the CD player kept playing the HU song. And there sat Claudia.

She came out of this state she had been in. The Master had lifted her out of the body. There was a fireman holding her hand. He was the first on the scene.

I have great respect for firefighters; you have to be an adventurous sort. They see and do things that nobody else wants to see and know. They see the things that happen to the rest of us, helping us when we cannot help ourselves.

The firefighter said, "Hold on, ma'am, an ambulance is on the way." Claudia was very calm and detached. She looked at him. She said, "I'm not hurt. I'm OK."

He said, "Have you looked at your car?"

She said, "Of course not. I haven't been able to get out of this seat."

He said, "Well, let me tell you about the car." It looked like an accordion. Right in the middle of it all sat Claudia. When the ambulance came, they insisted she go to the hospital because they were certain there would be internal injuries.

She arrived at the hospital. The doctor did a whole battery of X-rays: no broken bones. No scratches or bruises either. The doctor gave her a handful of pills. He said, "You're going to need these tomorrow, because you're going to be in a world of hurt."

She said, "No, I won't." She went home.

The next morning, Claudia woke up without any pain. She flushed the pills down the toilet, and that was the end of that.

The Mahanta was the hand of God that had saved her life.

A HOUSE FULL OF LIGHT

"Tony" lives in Africa. He became an ECKist in March 2002. At the time, his wife was a Christian. She was an uneducated woman, and she very dearly felt her lack of education. She couldn't read. So whenever he could, Tony tried to encourage her.

Soon, he received his first ECK discourse book. He studied one lesson a month. It's very important to read just one a month. At the end of the third month, he looked back. He said, "This is odd. I used to have all sorts of dreams before I came into Eckankar. Now I haven't had any."

Then he realized why. Since Tony had become an ECKist, their baby girl had started sleeping in their bed. She kicked and tossed and turned all night, and Tony didn't get a minute's rest. His wife slept all night, so she was having dreams. Tony said, "Hasn't something gone wrong, Master?"

Tony is one of those dear, sweet people—a treasure to any woman. And his wife is one of those treasures—one of those blessings to any man. And I'm very happy that they have found each other.

One night Tony's wife had a dream. She woke up and said to him, "It was the most wonderful thing, dear. The whole house was full of light—blue, blue, blue. The whole room is blue too. My dear, I've never seen anything like the beauty of this blue." This is the Blue Light of the Mahanta. Those of you who

The Mahanta was the hand of God that had saved her life.

know it will appreciate it and understand its power. Those of you who have never seen it, may you someday do so.

Tony said to his wife, "Don't worry about your lack of education. The Mahanta will teach you. He will teach you all that you need to know and much more." And she got to learn. In time, she asked to go to an ECK Worship Service. They used to be a two-religion family, and now they are a one-religion family. They're both ECKists.

TONY AND THE SECRET NAME

One day Tony had to go into Port Harcourt to an important meeting with the director of a company. When he finally got there, he found that the director was still in another meeting, so Tony took a seat in the waiting room. The television was on, but Tony didn't bother watching it. He didn't have time for television at home either. He was far too busy, so he never got in the habit.

But on his mind was a question.

In an ECK discourse that I had written, it said that within the first year of study, the new spiritual student, the chela, is going to receive a secret word in the dream state. And this will help him in his unfoldment.

Tony had a problem. He wasn't remembering his dreams anymore. How was the Master going to get through? He had this baby daughter keeping him awake all night, and his wife was getting the dreams. *What about me?* he wondered.

Suddenly Tony's attention was drawn to the television program that was playing, a children's cartoon called "The Ant's Kingdom."

Tony said to his wife, "Don't worry about your lack of education. The Mahanta will teach you. He will teach you all you need to know and much more."

At the very end of the story, the queen says to her subjects, "Do you know my secret name?"

And her subjects say, "No."

So she asks again, "Do you know my secret name?"

And they shout back, "No-o-o-o!"

So a third time—there's always a third time in stories—the queen asks, "Do you know my secret name?"

They say, "No-o-o-o," and she says . . .

Sorry, this is something you'll have to get yourself. I won't tell. But here's a clue. It's tied in with my spiritual name, and I have two. That's the long and the short of it, because one is longer and one is short.

If you're new, ask around, and maybe you'll bump into someone who knows one name or the other. If that doesn't work for you, try singing *HU*. If you decide to become a member of ECK, you'll learn whatever word the Inner Master brings to you, and it may be something quite apart from HU.

In any case, Tony got his answer.

GIFTS OF SPIRITUAL SURRENDER

A chela of fourteen years wrote to me to summarize her years in Eckankar.

It's been a time of gaining some sense of control through surrender of her life to Spirit, she said. She has control of her life, but only through surrender to Spirit. There's been loneliness, sadness, loss—just as in any other life.

But there have been miracles as well, and the Sound, Light, and love of the Mahanta and God. These are really indescribably profound experiences. "I am never alone," she said, "and I gain in strength

There have been miracles as well, and the Sound, Light, and love of the Mahanta and God. Indescribably profound experiences.

and the ability to serve. So, Harold, thank you from the bottom of my heart."

You're welcome.

A READING FROM THE *SHARIYAT*

And may I close with something from *The Shariyat-Ki-Sugmad,* Book Two. It expresses the theme of the heart-of-God talk that I've just given this evening.

Yet we know the butterfly breaks its way out of its cocoon, makes itself a passage, and wings its way into space—thus conquering air, light, and liberty.

So it is with
Soul.

So it is with Soul. Its prison in the body, in which earthly troubles and tumultuous passions keep It confined, is not eternal. After a long series of successive births—the spark of wisdom which is in It being rekindled—It will finally succeed, by the long continued practice of penitence and contemplation, in breaking all the ties that bind It to the earth; and It will increase in virtue until it has reached so high a degree of wisdom and spirituality that It becomes identity. Then, leaving the body which holds It captive, It soars freely aloft where It dwells forever with the Sugmad.

ECK Worldwide Seminar, Minneapolis, Minnesota, Saturday, October 25, 2003

It's very simple. If you set something in motion, it's going to come back.

12
THE LAW
OF RETURNS

*O*n the way here this evening, the conversation in the car turned to the weather. We had better things to talk about, but we talked about the weather. Someone was wondering whether the weather people could really predict with any accuracy.

One of our party had been with the weather service for a while. He said, "Sure." So everyone was kind. No one laughed.

Joan said she'd noticed they've become very much more accurate in the Minnesota area because they are a little bit more open-ended on the forecasts. If it's going to be cold, it's going to be very cold. So the weather people will say, "Wind chill of about forty below." Everybody says, "That's really bad." When it turns out the wind chill's only twenty below, everybody feels good about it. Then it feels like spring, or at least an easy winter. People up here are adapted to the cold.

When the wind chill's only twenty below, everybody feels good about it.

In summer, when it's supposed to be extremely hot, the weather people will say, "It's going to be in the hundreds today with 100 percent humidity." Everybody says, "This is outrageous." When it ends up being only ninety-five, everybody feels better. Yes, we get hot weather in Minnesota too.

I finally said I don't think the weather people have a chance. They do their honest best. It must be even harder in Europe, where they have forecasts that go out two weeks instead of three, four, or five days as they usually do here.

Then I tried to draw an analogy from my experience on the farm. "The weather is like a pig run loose in the pasture," I said. "It's like trying to predict where that pig's going to run next. You don't have a chance."

Someone said, "It certainly shows sometimes that you were a farmer."

I sometimes feel like Ben Franklin. Despite his many accomplishments, he just wanted to be known as a printer. He was a diplomat; he was one of the founding fathers of the United States as well as an inventor, philosopher, and scientist. He also started the American Philosophical Society. He was a special man. But he was also a printer.

The Law of Returns is another way of saying the Law of Karma. It's a nicer way of saying it.

SPIRITUAL ROLE MODELS

The talk tonight is "The Law of Returns," which is another way of saying the Law of Karma. It's a nicer way of saying it. I think it makes a little bit more sense to us here.

Before I get into that, I'd like to mention a book for youth and up—anyone from about age fourteen on. This is *Shane*, and it's a very good book about the American West by Jack Schaefer. It's been published in thirty languages. Someone sent me a copy recently, and Joan and I are reading it in the evening now.

It is a solid novel that reads fast and is highly

interesting. What makes it interesting is it's based on historical fact—unlike many movies and shows on television, which appear to be based on spiderweb-thin plots. There's just no substance to them.

But this is a solid story, lots of fun reading. It shows good people in hard times. When Jack Schaefer wrote this, he was working as an editor, and there was a lot of tension at work. As an editor, he did very little writing. He didn't have to go out in the field; he wasn't a journalist. He felt that would have ruined his writing skills, because sometimes a journalist—especially today—makes up the news instead of reporting the news. It was a little bit that way back then too.

Schaefer was a good man. Mostly he did rewrites, and he ended up writing a whole bunch of snippets here, there, and everywhere to fill in whatever he was working on then.

For relaxation, after years of this, he decided he'd write a short story about something that he really loved. He had been studying the American West for a long time. It grew into this novel called *Shane*. It was published in 1949, right after World War II. And at that time the American people, most of them, had no understanding that the gears of karma were shifting. They wouldn't call it karma, but times were going to speed up. Tensions were going to increase evermore. It would be a whole new world, a hard world. They'd have to give up their laid-back, easy ways of thinking and gear up for an entirely different time.

Shane is about people who have the qualities of nobility. In the foreword by the University of Nebraska Press, the reviewer said Jack Schaefer wrote about noble people who were strong, hardworking,

Shane is about noble people who were strong, hardworking, brave, self-disciplined, honest, and ungalled by self-doubt.

brave, self-disciplined, honest, and ungalled by self-doubt.

I look for role models who allow others freedom, who respect the property rights of others, who are willing to pay their own way.

These are good qualities to carry today, especially for our young people.

Sometimes I look around for role models who allow others to have freedom, who respect the property rights of others, who are willing to pay their own way. It's very hard to find role models of that sort. Just to find out what to look for in everyday life, what kind of person qualifies as a role model, it helps to read a book in which there is a solid hero.

The story is about a boy, Bob Starrett, growing up on a Wyoming homestead in the 1880s. The West had opened already; the homesteaders were moving in on the cattle ranchers. The cattle ranchers were uneasy about it; it meant fences were taking away the open range.

Bob is about eight or nine. One day he is looking out toward the little town, and he sees a cowboy come riding up the road. Then two cowhands, loping past, stop, turn, and study him. This was the way Jack Schaefer tells the reader there's mystery and suspense coming. Something's going on. The first man carries some sort of intrigue. There's something special about him.

So Shane arrives at the farm, and the story begins. It's an engaging, enlightening book with a historically accurate setting. And it's a lot of fun. The story sets forth virtue for our own fast-changing times.

WHY JESUS WAS DIFFERENT

Jesus was a highly developed spiritual being. Easter is tomorrow, so I would like to pay tribute to his memory and what he stands for. His teachings have grown. A study of the growth of Christianity runs from its foundation back in the first century through the second, third, fourth, and fifth centuries, and then it takes a leap at the Reformation.

In the 700s or 800s, long after the fall of the western Roman Empire, the Christian Church of Rome became stronger and stronger. Rome had been the center of the Roman Empire for centuries before that time, and people at the church of Ephesus and other Christian centers had grown used to looking to the Christians in Rome for answers to their local problems. It became very natural for the Christians in Rome, right at the seat of power of the Roman Empire, to speak forth.

During the Roman Empire, it was possible for a Roman citizen to travel anywhere in the Roman world. This was a broad place, and Saint Paul was a Roman, able to travel widely. He had certain freedoms.

An ECKist shared an interesting viewpoint about Jesus. "May" has a friend of the Christian faith, and her friend kept trying to convince her to become a Christian. May said, "It's just not a good fit for me." She tried to explain, and they had a number of conversations about Jesus.

One time May gave her Christian friend an insight that her friend had never thought of. I would say many theologians have never thought of this extremely good point. It reflects the Law of Returns.

May said to her friend, "Soul is like a painting God painted. Each painting is beautifully unique, and God is invested equally in all of us. Soul is an expression of God. In each case, God did Its best in creating us, because it's not in God's nature to turn out a shabby piece of art."

May went on. "God loves us as much as He loves Jesus. The difference—the reason Jesus stands out

May said to her friend, "Soul is like a painting God painted. Each painting is beautifully unique, and God is invested equally in all of us."

so prominently and shines so brightly—is that he loved God back equally."

That's very profound insight on the difference between Jesus and many people.

True Masters all have this love for God, this equal return of the love God gives them. They give this love back to everything around them—to mankind and all living things.

The Law of Returns.

SIMPLICITY OF KARMA

Mike Ditka was coach of the Chicago Bears football team for eleven years.

He referred to the Law of Returns in a way that became very popular. I doubt he was the first to say it, but when he said it, people listened: "What goes around comes around."

We know it as the Law of Karma, cause and effect, action and reaction. What goes around comes around.

Some people were puzzled by what he meant, but for anyone who's acquainted with the Law of Karma, it's very simple. If you set something in motion, it's going to come back.

The Law of Returns is constantly at work around and about us, but many people aren't aware of it.

THE PROCESS OF REFORMATION

During the Reformation, there was quite a debate between Protestants and Roman Catholics. Luther was the first to say man is saved by grace and faith alone. The Catholic position was that people have got to do good works too; otherwise you're going to have people running loose without any sense of responsibility.

This was one of the bones of contention during the Reformation.

True Masters all have this love for God, this equal return of the love God gives them. They give this love back to all living things. The Law of Returns.

But the Reformation started for an entirely different reason. It was a powder keg with a lit fuse, smoldering long before 1517 when Luther nailed his ninety-five theses on the door at Wittenberg. This was a bulletin board, essentially, and people did this rather routinely when they wanted to have a discussion of some sort.

At the time, no one recognized the impact that the ninety-five theses would have in the next few years. Luther didn't either. It was just something he was going to have a discussion about. He wanted to throw it open for debate. It took on a life of its own.

Luther didn't recognize the impact the ninety-five theses would have. It took on a life of its own.

The issue that had been building in the Roman Catholic Church, which the Church was already taking steps to reform, was the corruption of the clergy.

Priests were living with women as their de facto wives, and all sorts of things were going on. But one big issue was the sale of indulgences. The church leaders extracted a huge amount of money from the people. Then they sent it off to Rome to build a cathedral.

This galled a lot of people. Martin Luther was very astute with money. He said, "Why are we sending good German money down to Rome?" This was one of the many little reasons, largely forgotten today, why the Reformation began—why this split happened.

It's important to note that the Roman Catholic Church was already beginning to reform itself. They simply weren't doing it as quickly as some of the Protestants felt they ought to. The question at that time was, how quickly do we proceed with straightening things out?

As the Reformation went on, it gathered steam.

There was Zwingli in Switzerland, and then came John Calvin. Calvin was very straitlaced, very strict. He thought Luther was being far too easygoing.

Of all the Protestant groups, Lutheranism remained the closest in its liturgy, and perhaps doctrines, to the Roman Catholic Church.

Other Protestants were a bit more divergent in their views. In England, the Church of England got itself going because Henry VIII wanted to divorce one wife and marry someone else, so he could have a son. Marriage wasn't seen as a love relationship in those days as it is today. It was an arrangement, especially in royal circles. Kings had to find queens of royal blood, and there was this strange intermixing of nationalities in one country. In England, the House of Windsor is actually German. Until World War I, when it became very unpopular in England to carry a German name, the House of Windsor had been the House of Saxe-Coburg-Gotha. This goes back about three or four generations before Elizabeth II's reign. It began with Edward VII, eldest son of Queen Victoria, who had married the German Prince Albert. German rulership has been in place in England for nearly three centuries. We sometimes find such things strange, but it's very common, this intermingling of nationalities among royalty.

Jim's story about "car-ma" illustrates Maybury's second law: "Do not encroach on other persons or their property."

CAR KARMA

"Jim," whose story is next, said he tried to joke with someone about "car-ma" afterward, but it wasn't the time or place. Because there was a spiritual lesson involved.

This story illustrates Maybury's second law: "Do not encroach on other persons or their property."

Jim was just having one of those days. Work

was stressful. The drive home during rush hour was just impossible. Then there was shopping. Shopping really got him.

When he got home, he had to find a parking spot on the street. Cars were parked along the whole street. He and his wife had grocery bags to carry, so they wanted to park close. Finally they saw one spot between a minivan and a car. A small spot.

Jim started working his vehicle into the spot, grumbling every inch of the way. His wife had to listen to this, thinking, *Pretty soon I'll be in the house, working on dinner. It'll be more pleasant.*

Jim wiggled his way in, inching back and forth, and he bumped the minivan in front of him. He got out and looked at it. There was a little ding in the bumper.

Jim had enough spiritual knowledge, as well as knowledge about how things work out here. He knew he should have left a note with his name and number under a windshield wiper of the minivan. But it had been such a day. "We really don't have the money now," he said. "God only knows how much this is going to cost. I think I'll just take the groceries in. I can't handle any more today."

Jim helped his wife in with the groceries. They went upstairs and started making dinner. He was trying his best to be of some use, but his conscience was troubling him. It wouldn't give him any rest. Finally he told his wife, "I've got to do the right thing. I've got to go down there and leave a note."

So he went downstairs to where his car was parked, and the minivan was gone. Jim thought, *Maybe this is a free ride.* But he knew it wasn't. The Law of Returns gives no free rides. There's always paying back at some point or another, either here or hereafter.

Jim thought, Maybe this is a free ride. But he knew it wasn't. The Law of Returns gives no free rides.

IT'S VERY HARD TO BEAT KARMA

A few days later, Jim was driving, and a humming sound began coming from his front wheel. Soon it turned into a squeal and got so bad it sounded like the wheel was going to come off. He felt he was lucky to get home. He took the car to a mechanic in the neighborhood. The mechanic said, "It's going to cost you $170.00, and we can have it for you tomorrow night."

Jim could get by one day without a car. His wife could help him, or he'd find some way to get to work.

The next day, Jim went in to pick up his car. The chief mechanic, a very peaceful-looking man, went back into the office and started tallying up the separate items on Jim's bill.

While he waited, Jim noticed pictures on the wall behind the chief mechanic. The pictures were of Buddhist lamas and other holy men and deities.

He commented on them, just to make conversation while the mechanic was working.

The mechanic said, "Do you meditate?"

Jim wanted to say something about Eckankar, but before he could, the mechanic enthusiastically said, "Meditation is so important. Whatever your beliefs, meditation is the only way to enlightenment. I hope you and I will achieve enlightenment."

Jim got ready again to say something about Eckankar, but then the chief mechanic went on. "Karma is very hard. I try to stay in the center, but sometimes I sway to the left or the right. It's very hard to beat karma."

The Law of Returns.

The night of his accident, Jim had gone into contemplation before bed and said to the Mahanta, the Inner Master, "I know I'm responsible for this. I know

Jim said to the Mahanta, the Inner Master, "Please let me know when the time comes to pay, so I will understand."

I will pay, but please let me know when the time comes to pay, so I will understand that I'm paying off this particular karma with whatever's happening."

So it was karma with his car. And who was fixing his car but a mechanic who happened to be a spiritually minded Buddhist? This Buddhist had another viewpoint, which would get through to Jim, whereas a Christian or even an ECKist viewpoint wouldn't have, he was so used to them.

Here again, the Inner Master comes forth.

Those of you who have a connection with the Inner Master will find that you have things going for you.

MAYBURY'S TWO LAWS

Richard Maybury's two laws are copyrighted, and he asks simply that if you're going to quote them, you use the exact seventeen words he gives them in: "Do all you have agreed to do, and do not encroach on other persons or their property."

They're in the ECK writings now. I've mentioned them a few times. But they're buried, because we have so many ECK writings. It seems a fitting time to bring them up now, in this talk on the Law of Returns.

"Do all you have agreed to do, and do not encroach on other persons or their property."

Maybury is an economist and an observer of world politics. He gives some of the most astute analyses I've ever seen of the world situation. He calls things well ahead of time. And he even makes suggestions about where to invest in the future because of logistical events that he predicts will happen within a certain degree of probability. He gives the probability.

"Do all you have agreed to do, and do not encroach on other persons or their property."

He's a very humble man; he always allows for the possibility that his guesses could be in error. But surprisingly they're usually not. I'm not peddling commercial things, but the renewal rate for Maybury's newsletter is extremely high, in the high ninetieth percentile. Very few newsletters come anywhere near that. Yet he's a very reserved man, noble, quiet, humble, modest, respectful of other people.

He does a thorough study of anything he writes about, because he needs to. It's in his heart. He made a study of world religions, and he came up with these two laws. He said they are embodied in every good religion around the world.

He boiled things way down—to just two laws. He boiled down the Ten Commandments to two laws. And so many codes of ethics—down to two laws.

> *Maybury said these two laws are embodied in every good religion around the world.*

A HUMBLING EXPERIENCE

As I mentioned earlier, Ben Franklin was one of the founding fathers of the United States. Those were very turbulent times. He had grown up the son of a middle-class merchant, but Ben wanted to run away to sea.

Somehow he ended up in printing, and he found it very much to his liking. A couple of times he got to go out in a rowboat and got seasick. So he was glad he never had a chance to run away to sea, because he wouldn't have made it.

He was a diplomat, inventor, and printer. And he is often pictured standing on a hill, flying a kite in a thunderstorm, lightning flashing. He's holding onto this kite string with a key attached because he is investigating electricity.

The word *scientist* was not coined until 1834. Before then, people who studied the life forces around them were known as natural philosophers. They studied anything and everything that had an impact upon them.

Ben Franklin also learned about the Law of Returns.

As a young man, Ben Franklin had studied argumentation and logic, and he was particularly taken with the Socratic method. This was a method Socrates used, of asking questions and getting the other person to agree on one point, then another point. In other words, get the other person to say yes. Make him concede the little points—because there is no getting around them, they are reasonable, and any person of reason would have to agree it is so. Then keep that up until you win the argument.

Ben Franklin had such an intricate mind; he could think far ahead, like a chess player, and see where he wanted to end up, no matter what moves came between here and there. Every time his opponent in the debate made a point, Ben would be there with another point, using the Socratic method and getting him to agree.

But Ben went too far. He became argumentative.

One time, a Quaker friend took him aside. "Ben," he said, "you're a nice guy, but have you noticed your friends are avoiding you?"

Ben, of course, was now in the position of saying, "Yes"—the other end of the Socratic method.

His friend said, "Now, this may come as a shock to you. You always want to be right, don't you?"

"Yes."

"It's all right to be right," the friend said, "but you won't let it rest there. You have to pound the other guy into the ground. You have to rub it in. Is that right?"

One time, a Quaker friend took Ben Franklin aside. "Ben, have you noticed your friends are avoiding you?"

Here Ben was a little bit hesitant to say yes, even though in his heart he knew it was so.

LEARNING TO RESPECT OTHERS

He thanked his Quaker friend for having been so open with him, and he resolved from that moment on to change his ways. He said he'd never do that sort of thing again. He'd never be so positive in a statement that was open to doubt as he had been in the past. That way, in case he was wrong—and as he looked back, he found out that he had been wrong many times—he wouldn't have to backpedal so far. It wouldn't be so embarrassing. He'd have less face to save.

He set out to make some changes in how he spoke, he said, so that he wouldn't come across as too positive. He stopped using words like *certainly* and *undoubtedly*. Instead he began to use expressions like, "Well, it appears to me" or "I conceive a thing to be so" or "I should think for such-and-such reasons the case would be this or that."

He also found it best never to directly contradict someone, because what did this do? It took something that was very precious to that person—his opinion— and threw it back in his face. This is something nobody likes.

Benjamin Franklin refashioned his speech patterns as a young man. Later in life, people started coming to him for advice.

And so Benjamin Franklin refashioned his speech patterns as a young man. Later in life, he found it very useful, because as time went on, people started coming to him for advice.

He never considered himself a good public speaker, though. Nor was George Washington, the first president and so-called father of our country. Neither of them would ever give a speech on anything that lasted more than ten minutes or so. Thomas Jefferson, another of the founding fathers, spoke of this.

Thomas Jefferson also noted that neither George Washington nor Ben Franklin ever spoke when an issue was still on the table—when people were discussing it and trying to figure it out. At those times, people would get all uptight and emotional. There would be a lot of shouting. Ben Franklin and George Washington would never get into that part of it.

But when things settled down and the central idea was on the table, that's when these two men, if they were going to speak at all, would speak. Their speech would be short and to the point.

In time, Ben Franklin's opinions would be sought on international matters. He became a diplomat. He was in England for a while, then France. People loved him. Taking his friend's advice to alter his manner of speaking had served him well.

HOW TO MAKE YOUR LIFE EASIER

How to Win Friends and Influence People, by Dale Carnegie, is a classic that's been around since 1936. It also addresses the Law of Returns. It doesn't use the phrase, but it does exactly what the title suggests.

From a spiritual point of view, most of the problems people have come from how they treat other people, or from how they don't treat other people. Life becomes unnecessarily difficult, and it keeps them from enjoying everything that's good in it, all that they possibly could enjoy.

So, karmically speaking, it's important to note that a wrong approach in how we do things can make all the difference.

Ben Franklin learned this. He cleaned up his argumentative speech patterns. He got rid of them.

From a spiritual point of view, most problems people have come from how they treat other people, or how they don't treat other people.

And after that, he started making friends and keeping friends. People sought him out.

Carnegie's book is important in the workplace and especially in your family. It tells how to give respect to other people.

It's the same sort of respect you ought to be giving to yourself. Because God loves you. Every moment of your life, you're in the arms of love, in the arms of God.

IN THE ARMS OF LOVE

No matter what happens, it's spiritually because God loves us.

We're speaking about the Law of Returns. Another way of speaking of the Law of Returns would be to say "in the arms of love." Because no matter what happens, it's spiritually because God loves us.

God set up this world. God allows the negative power to exist and to move about, because the so-called Satan is testing you. And what's he testing you with? Not evils that come from out there somewhere, but evils that have come from inside you at some time or another.

There are two kinds of people: the master and the victim. There are lots of victims today.

A master accepts complete responsibility for everything he does. That means paying his own way. And when something goes wrong, he recognizes not just the apparent trigger for it, which might look like someone else coming down on him. A master recognizes where it truly originates.

The victim doesn't. So many times, the victim will adopt a passive role. "I was walking down the street, and this thing fell on me." Or "I didn't do anything; it just happened." They don't recognize that sometime in the past, in this life or a previous one, they themselves created the condition that brought the Law of Return into effect. They set it in motion.

EARNING YOUR WAY

People move through life without understanding this Law of Return. Sadly, we have a society that's becoming ever more dependent on some taking the property of others to survive. And this comes about through people not paying their fair share.

Often the rich are accused of not paying their fair share. But I believe the top 10 percent of earners are paying over 50 percent of the taxes. It's extremely high. A very small percentage of people are paying a very high percentage of the taxes. The bottom 50 percent of wage earners are paying much less than 10 percent.* They're getting a free ride—and more and more so, because people have the victim consciousness.

It's a sad spiritual state of affairs. A form of enslavement. People don't understand this. They think they're getting something for nothing. The more they get of a "free" thing, the more they want of it.

This is why a democracy is always doomed to fail. It failed in ancient Greece, and it has ever since. It's always failed because, as people get more of the power to exercise their will through the laws, they want more of their neighbor's property. And they'll get it.

They'll get it through lawsuits, or they'll get it through welfare when they could be paying their own way and carrying their own weight. When

Victim consciousness is a sad spiritual state of affairs. A form of enslavement. People think they're getting something for nothing.

---

* Figures updated based on statistics for 2011.

someone's on welfare, even the welfare people don't try to find them work. Because the welfare people are on welfare themselves in a way—they need their jobs. And any job in government, basically, is a parasitic job. It does not create something for other people; it sucks away from the productive efforts of others.

DANGERS OF VICTIM CONSCIOUSNESS

I know these are harsh things to say, but I must remind you that there ought to be a good balance between a society taking care of its needy and also providing ways for its people to work, so that the confiscatory taxes do not discourage people from going out and earning their own way. There is a time, and there is a way, but it won't happen.

I see these as spiritual ills, not economic or political ills. They are spiritual ills. There's no need to say this party is doing this or that. It's shared equally in our country.

The heritage of you, as Soul, is so much greater.

It's that victim consciousness. Sometimes it seems rather a harsh thing to say, but the heritage of you, as Soul, is so much greater. The heritage of everyone is so much greater.

People who are of the victim consciousness do not have respect for themselves to begin with, so how can they have respect for others? They can't, and they don't. They may give respect with their lips, but it's not in their actions.

WHERE ECKANKAR IS GROWING

I feel bad when I have to point this out periodically, but I don't hear anyone else doing it often enough. And I don't either.

There's a spiritual sickness in this land. And not

just this land, but in many places.

The countries where Eckankar is making the strongest gains are those where people have the least economic security.

I won't name the countries, or they might feel that I'm looking down at them, which is not the case. I'm looking up at them. Wonderful, wonderful people there. As there are here.

But the weight of materialism in this country puts out the light of spirituality where it does exist.

SIDESTEPPING PROBLEMS

How to Win Friends and Influence People is an excellent book. I think it can help people sidestep many of the problems they run into. The book is full of stories. I like to use stories in my talks too, because stories are more fun. Philosophy is not.

The book is a quick, fun read, but if you're going to read it, I'd suggest you go through it slowly and carefully. Read a page or two a day, and let it sink in. Practice the principles as you go through so that they become a part of you. This makes it more than just a good read, which in time is forgotten.

Take your time, read a few pages a day. Then give it a rest. For a few days, don't even read it. Set it aside and practice what you've learned. It's such a good book.

Here are some of the things to look forward to, some of the strong points that I found about the book myself. I just jotted them down from memory.

Practice the principles as you go so that they become a part of you.

- Excellent reasons for not condemning or criticizing the behavior of others—and what you can do instead.
- What sincere appreciation will get you.

- Learn the power of your smile.
- Why you don't win an argument, and how to avoid the argument.
- How Socrates can help you make a point.
- If it's necessary to point out someone's faults or criticize them, how to do it without being hated for it.

FREEDOM AND HAPPINESS

This book will show you how to work with the Law of Returns, which is something that we deal with in this world—cause and effect.

We're trying to rise above it in ECK to come to the Law of Love, which is much higher. It cuts through a lot of this. But in the meantime, it helps to know how things work out here. It'll make your life a lot easier.

If your life is easier, you'll have more freedom.

What comes with freedom? Happiness. People want happiness, but they go about it backward. They spend their money on things: new computer toys, new cars, new clothes and the like. Trying to find happiness.

If they'd only look for freedom first. Maybe meditate like the Buddhists, or contemplate as we do in Eckankar, which is a lighter form of going within than meditation.

The Law of Love, which is much higher, will make your life a lot easier. You'll have more freedom. What comes with freedom? Happiness.

CAROL'S REWARD

"Carol" is a Second Initiate in Eckankar. She'd done the spiritual exercises for a very long time and had good success. She was Soul Traveling and having dream experiences. They were OK.

But Carol knew there was something more.

What would happen if she changed the way she was doing her spiritual exercises?

She looked at them. "What have I been doing?" she asked herself. "I've got problems that hit me in the daytime, so what do I do at night? I go to the Mahanta, the Inner Master."

She was speaking of the spiritual guide in Eckankar whose full title is the Mahanta, the Living ECK Master. He functions in two ways—inner and outer. As the Inner Master he's known as the Mahanta.

Carol said, "I have my daily problems, and I take them to the Mahanta at night. I say, 'Help me get rid of these.' Basically, I'm always bringing more and more problems, trying to have the Master take care of them."

What would happen if she changed her approach?

So she stopped asking questions of the Mahanta, stopped badgering him. Instead, when she went into contemplation, she just sat and waited with the Inner Master. She waited for him to speak, but if he spoke at all, she could never hear what he said.

This went on every night for over three months. He never spoke. They sat in silence, she and the Mahanta, while she wondered why.

Eventually Carol figured out why. It was so that she could learn to be comfortable with the Mahanta, the Inner Master. Then things began to change. The Mahanta began teaching her. He took her to the various Temples of Golden Wisdom.

Carol always did what I've recommended, and this is to do the spiritual exercises. That's so important; it's your connection with the divine. Patient and persistent was she. So she earned the right to study with the Mahanta and with the other Masters.

Carol realized that this honor was due, in large

Carol did the spiritual exercises. That's so important; it's your connection with the divine.

part, to her shifting her agenda. She had changed from looking out for her own problems, her own goals and aims, to seeking the Master's will. The Master's will is the will of the ECK, the Holy Spirit. They're one and the same—the Holy Spirit, the Sound and Light of God, love in totality, love in expression, the Word made flesh.

What's Carol's reward from this new way of doing her spiritual exercises? A greater sense of joy, love, and freedom in her life. She Soul Travels to the inner planes, and she has gone very far, to the fifth level—well beyond the third heaven that Saint Paul speaks of.

What's Carol's reward? A greater sense of joy, love, and freedom in her life.

DIRECT ROUTE TO THE SPIRITUAL LIFE

Through these experiences with the Mahanta, Carol has received an important understanding. In a letter to me she said, "You're teaching me to separate the urgent from the important. Though the duties of daily life are urgent, nothing is more important than my spiritual practices and presence to you and the ECK."

Carol is finding the very direct route to the spiritual life. It's more direct, in a sense, than the Law of Returns.

Yet the Law of Returns is necessary in so many ways. So I have mentioned a few things that will help you out considerably in your daily life.

As a speaker, I try to be at least polished enough for you to get the message. Sometimes if you have something to say to the people you're speaking to, and their hearts are open for it, you don't have to be polished at all. You can be a Ben Franklin or a George Washington and get by.

I'd like to thank you for having been so gracious

as to give me some of your time this evening. I appreciate it. I hope that in return you have received something to help you spiritually. I'm sure you have, because these talks always help me too. I get a better look at you. I love you dearly. And may the blessings be.

I love you dearly.

ECK Spiritual Skills Seminar, San Diego, California, Saturday, April 10, 2004

The Mahanta, the Living ECK Master will help you see the things you need in your spiritual unfoldment—see the diamonds that are all about you—so that you, the diamond in the rough, may become a polished stone of God.

13
ACRES OF DIAMONDS

his is the Year of the ECK Missionary, the ECK Vahana.

I would like to mention a book by Dale Carnegie. In a previous seminar talk, I mentioned his classic, *How to Win Friends and Influence People.* I've gotten letters from many of you, saying how this has helped you. It's a wonderful book to help you get along better with those around you.

This other book is especially suitable in the Year of the ECK Missionary: *The Quick and Easy Way to Effective Speaking*, by Dale Carnegie.

I read it so that I could become better at the art of communication. If you can speak well or listen well, you can go a lot further in this world than if you don't learn those skills.

I'll mention just a few of the points in the book. They may give you some insight into what's available to help you as an ECK missionary this year.

If you can speak well or listen well, you can go a lot further in this world.

FOR SPEAKERS IN ECK

You may sometime have to give a very short ECK talk. Somebody will ask you, "What is Eckankar?" If you haven't really thought about how to answer that, chances are you're going to say too much.

Dale Carnegie's book has a three-step suggestion.

I'll read all these to you. But I'd forget about step one, and I'd redirect step three a little, because his version doesn't exactly fit the way we do things in ECK.

A short talk is also different from a long talk. In a long talk, you first give an introduction—you tell them what you're going to tell them. Then comes the body of the talk—you tell them. Finally the conclusion—tell them what you told them. That's it.

A short talk's different. In a short talk, you're only going to have about two minutes, so you begin with your example or illustration.

If you're giving an ECK talk, you always try to have a story handy about what ECK has done for you. Some kind of benefit that you've gotten from ECK. This is what people want to hear first. They want to know, What has it done for you?

Unless you do this, you'll go on and on, giving the background of Eckankar and all the definitions for *Sugmad, ECK*, and our special terms. Maybe you'll start to give the address for the Temple of ECK. Then the listener will cut in and say, "I just wanted to know a little about it."

So tell your story first. This is going to take up most of the two minutes.

The next step given in the book—and this is something I wouldn't do for an ECK talk—is to make your point.

I think it's pushy, in an ECK talk, to tell my story and then say, "Here, take this brochure. It'll be good for you." It's like prescribing some kind of medicine. Nobody wants that. I would just tell the story. Leave it at that.

Carnegie says that when you've finished your story, you give the benefit or advantage to the listener. I wouldn't even go that far, because maybe the

People want to know What has ECK done for you?

listener's needs aren't yours. I would just say, "This is the story of what I found in Eckankar. This is what I've found it's done for me, and how I'm a better person today than I was before I found Eckankar."

After about two minutes, stop and wait to see where the conversation goes. Maybe the person has heard enough, even though you might feel it was quicker than it should have been. But if the individual asks for more about Eckankar, answer him. Always be willing to give him an ECK brochure. Say, "Here's a brochure. You can read more about it, and if you like, I can get you a book that would probably be of interest to you."

Then you can be on your way. In parting, you might say, "I'll give you the book next time I see you" or "I can send you a book if you like."

I would just say, "This is the story of how I'm a better person today than I was before I found Eckankar."

THE EASY APPROACH

It's a very easy thing. First tell your story or give an illustration of what ECK has done for you, then say how you're better off than you were before you came to the path of ECK. Very simple.

Dale Carnegie also explains keystone words. I like to call them technical words. They are words we've long used in ECK, and they mean something special to us. There's a whole universe of meaning packed into these terms. But someone new to ECK won't have the ghost of an idea what the terms mean.

Explain these keystone words as you use them. For instance, if you're going to speak about God and use the ECK term *Sugmad*, explain it right away. Say, "That's our word for God." Or if you say "the ECK," explain that it means Holy Spirit. If you use the word *Mahanta*, say, "That's the Inner Master, the Spirit of God that is always with you."

And when you speak about Soul, you can say, "That's who we really are. We are Soul. You and I are Soul. We are not this mind, we are not this body; we are Soul—the only part of ourself capable of returning God's love in full measure."

If you use the word *Vahana*, say, "ECK missionary." Otherwise people won't know what you're saying.

DON'T MEMORIZE YOUR TALKS

This next point is very, very important. Don't memorize your talk. Be it a long or short talk, don't memorize it. That's not to say you shouldn't have the points down pat. You're going to go over them and over them so you know the points by heart and can easily go through them. But don't memorize your talk.

Carnegie explains that memorization comes from the mind. But when you're speaking about key items that you're well-versed in, things you know and love and have rehearsed well, you're going to be speaking from your heart.

And this is what carries to the people in your audience—when you're speaking from your heart to theirs.

AN UNFORGETTABLE TALK

The danger of memorizing a talk is that when you get up there and you give the talk, you're going to forget it. To illustrate this, Carnegie tells the story of Vance Bushnell. Vance Bushnell was fairly new with the insurance company where he worked. It was a very large company once. He'd only been with them a couple of years, but he was good in sales.

> *We are not this mind, we are not this body; we are Soul—the only part of ourself capable of returning God's love in full measure.*

His superiors came to him and said, "Would you like to give a twenty-minute talk at our representative convention?"

Vance was one of those social climbers. This really fed his desire for prestige. He said, "I'd be so happy to." He thought it would get him up the career ladder a lot sooner if he could give one of those unforgettable talks.

It was an unforgettable talk, not quite in the way he had imagined.

Vance rehearsed his talk forty times in front of a mirror. He went over and over and over it, and he went through all the gestures. He worked hard to get everything right. He tried to be what Abraham Lincoln once said he liked—a speaker who looked like he was fighting off a swarm of bees. Which meant like he was really working at it.

Vance got up onstage, and his mind went totally blank. He took two steps backward, and he tried again.

Vance was all set to go. His pump was primed. He got up onstage, and he looked at two thousand faces and four thousand eyes, and he said, "My part in this program is . . ." And his mind went totally blank.

He took two steps backward, and he tried again. He said, "Uh . . . my part in this program is . . ." His mind wouldn't go any further than that. So he took two more steps backward.

He did this a total of four times. Unfortunately, he was on a stage that was four feet high, and there was a five-foot space between the stage and the back wall. The fourth time he said, "My part in this program is . . ." and took two steps back, he dropped clean out of sight.

The audience howled. One man was rolling in the aisle. They thought it was the funniest thing they'd ever seen. They thought it was sheer genius on the part of the insurance company to plan such a comedy act.

Poor Vance was crushed. As soon as he could find a piece of paper and a pen, he wrote up and handed in his resignation. But his superiors wouldn't hear of it. "No," they said, "you're too good a man to let go."

That restored his confidence. He stayed with the company, became one of the best speakers they had, and eventually ended up as the vice president.

LEARNING ABOUT YOURSELF

Dale Carnegie also speaks about a Doctor Russell Conwell and an address he gave called "Acres of Diamonds."

"Acres of Diamonds" presents the idea that your opportunities are not over there somewhere, but right at home— among your friends, family, and associates.

In the early 1900s, Russell Conwell went around the United States and gave this talk about six thousand times. But it wasn't the same talk; it was a different talk each time. "Acres of Diamonds" presents the idea that your opportunities are not over there somewhere, but right at home—among your friends, family, and business associates. That is where opportunity lies.

Conwell would go into a town well before his talk. He'd meet the mayor, superintendent of schools, teachers, merchants, barber, librarian, and everyone else that he could. He'd find out the opportunities in the town and what challenges the town faced. Conwell was a man looking to learn about himself.

Anyone who makes such a thorough study of something is basically looking to learn about himself.

Dale Carnegie did the same thing. He had been a loser as an actor. Finally he got tired of being a loser, and he said, "I'm going to go and find out how people who win go about it." From this he developed the Dale Carnegie study course which he turned into a book that sold millions of copies.

TRUST IN GOD AND TAKE THE NEXT STEP

Russell Conwell had a saying: "Trust in God and do the next thing."

Several young men came to him. They were working in factories. They said, "We want to learn, but we can't. All the college courses are held during the daytime. There's nothing for us."

"Come after work," Conwell said, "and I'll teach you."

Pretty soon those several young men had grown to fifteen, then thirty, then forty-five, then a hundred. Conwell had to trust God that someplace would open up where they could meet. Thus began what would become Temple University, based in Philadelphia. It was built on borrowed funds. When the note came due, one time Conwell was down two thousand dollars; another time, ten thousand. If he couldn't pay back the loan, the land would go to the holder of the note and Conwell's dream would be gone.

But this is where he trusted God.

At the last moment—somewhere, somehow— someone gave him two thousand dollars. That took care of the first time. The second time, when he needed ten thousand dollars—which would be over two hundred thousand dollars today, inflation being as it is—someone wrote a check. The person said, "You helped my brother so much, I just felt compelled today to give this check to you."

Conwell was right at the brink of failure, and his faith in the divine power carried the day.

If Conwell couldn't pay back the loan, the land would go to the holder of the note and Conwell's dream would be gone.

THE STORY OF ACRES OF DIAMONDS

When Russell Conwell was a young man, he joined a group of English tourists traveling to the Middle East. They hired an Arab guide to show them the way along the Tigris and Euphrates Rivers. The guide would take care of the camels and show them the route.

Arab guides in those days felt it their duty to also entertain the people who'd hired them. They were both guide and storyteller.

To the Western ear, their stories never seemed to go anyplace. They just seemed to go on and on and never end. Then the storyteller would switch to another story. It got very tiresome.

Conwell got along well with the guide. When the guide was cursing a camel or something, Conwell never got upset. He just shut his ears and went placidly along, just made believe nothing was going on. When the guide would start another story, Conwell learned that he was better off shutting his ears then too.

The Arab guide caught on. He knew what Conwell was doing, but he didn't say anything.

But one time he began waving his hat wildly, trying to attract Conwell's attention. Conwell studiously ignored him because he was afraid that if he looked at the guide, he would tell another story. He couldn't take one more story. But finally he couldn't help himself. He looked over, and the guide said, "I will tell you a story now which I reserve for my particular friends." He put such emphasis on "particular friends" that Conwell's ears went on high alert. He was listening.

The guide began his story. He said there was a rich farmer, Ali Hafed, who owned orchards, grain

The guide said, "I will tell you a story now which I reserve for my particular friends."

fields, and gardens. He had everything his heart could desire. He was rich, and so he was contented. He was contented, and so he was rich.

One day an old Buddhist priest came to visit. He told Ali the story of creation, how the Almighty had approached this bank of fog, which was all there was in the beginning. He took his finger and began to stir the fog, and it went faster and faster, until it turned into a solid ball of fire. As this fiery ball began to cool, the molten mass within burst through the crust and became the mountains of the earth. That which cooled the quickest became granite. That which cooled more slowly became other things—copper, then silver, then gold. Finally, diamonds.

"Just one of those diamonds the size of my thumb," said the old priest, "and I could buy this whole county." He said, "Ali Hafed, if you had a diamond mine, you could put all your sons and daughters on thrones."

That night Ali Hafed went to bed a poor man. He went to bed poor because he was discontented, and he was unhappy because he thought he was a poor man.

Greed had begun its work on him. Early the next morning he jumped out of bed. The sun had just come up. He woke the old Buddhist priest, who'd been having a wonderful dream. He was very crabby. "What are you waking me for?" he said.

Ali Hafed said, "Tell me where to find the diamond mine."

"Go find it yourself, and let me sleep."

"I don't know where to look."

Finally the old priest said, "All right, I'll tell you if you'll then let me get some sleep. Look for a river

There was a rich farmer, Ali Hafed, who owned orchards, grain fields, and gardens. He had everything his heart could desire.

that runs through white sands and between high mountains. You will always find diamonds there in that sand."

Ali Hafed said, "I'll do it."

LOOKING FOR FORTUNE

Ali Hafed sold his very prosperous farm. He went looking for this fabulous diamond mine.

Ali Hafed sold his farm, and he put his family under the care of a neighbor. Leaving the new owner in charge of what had once been his, this very prosperous farm, he left. He went looking for this fabulous diamond mine, and he didn't find it. He even went to Palestine and didn't find it.

His money was beginning to run out, but he pushed on to Europe. Finally, his clothes were in rags, his money was gone, and he faced starvation. What could he do? He was in Spain then, and he looked out over the ocean, and he saw the giant waves coming in.

He decided it would be a lot better to fall into the ocean than to die impoverished and starving. So he threw himself upon a wave, was washed out, and was never seen again.

At this point the Arab guide broke off the story because one of the camels in back of the caravan was throwing its load.

Conwell said to himself, "What kind of story is this? Here's a story that doesn't have a beginning, nor a middle, nor an end. And the hero's dead."

In a little bit the guide came back, and he took up the story again. This time the story was about the new owner of the farmstead that Ali Hafed had sold.

The new owner had led his camel out into the garden to drink from the stream of water that ran there, and the camel's nose began bumping around in the pebbles at the bottom of the stream. Suddenly the camel's nose uncovered a black stone. It had a marvelous eye of light that reflected rays in every color of the rainbow.

"That's a very pretty stone," said the farmer. "I think I'll take it inside the house and put it on the mantel." Which is what he did. Then he forgot about it.

Some time later, the Buddhist priest came by. He crossed the threshold of the house and saw this many splendored light shining from up on the mantel. "Has Ali Hafed returned?" he asked.

The new owner said, "No, he sold this place to me, and we haven't heard from him since. His family hasn't heard a word from him."

The old Buddhist priest said, "That's a diamond!"

The farmer said, "No, it isn't. That's nothing but a stone. I just got it out of my garden."

"No, no, no, you don't understand! That's a diamond!"

"It's not a diamond, I'm telling you, old man."

"It's a diamond!"

The old priest was so sincere that the farmer was finally convinced. "Come out in our backyard," he said. "Let's go look in the stream."

They went out to the stream and began groping around in the sand. They turned up many more of those stones.

And this was the discovery of the fabulous Kollur diamond mine at Golconda, India. From this mine came two of the crown jewels of England and Russia and many other diamonds as well. This garden was a fabulously wealthy place.

The camel's nose uncovered a black stone. It had a marvelous eye of light that reflected rays in every color of the rainbow.

GOLDEN-TONGUED WISDOM

Conwell knew what the Arab guide was telling him. He said this guide was like a lawyer. You just couldn't pin him down. He didn't want to come right out and say what was on his mind. He had to go to the story and tell it in a roundabout way, then hope you caught it. If you caught it, fine. If you didn't, too bad.

The old guide was saying, "Your opportunities are all back home." It was the Golden-tongued Wisdom, the special voice of God that comes through some messenger.

At the time, Conwell never let on that he knew what the old guide was saying; he just went on with a story of his own. But Conwell knew that the guide was telling him, "What are you wasting your time out here for? Your opportunities are all back home."

That's what Russell Conwell heard, but none of the other travelers in that party heard what he heard. In a way it was the Golden-tongued Wisdom, the special voice of God that comes through some conveyance, some messenger, some fellow human being. Golden-tongued Wisdom meant for the ears of Dr. Russell Conwell only.

And he heard. He went home and did all these wonderful acts of charity to help other people go further on their own way to God.

Some people criticized him. They said, "Here you are, a man of God, talking about material things. It's very unbecoming of a minister." (Because he was a minister.)

But Conwell said, "What more fitting thing is there than to help people help themselves so that they can be happy? What better message can I give them?"

WORDS OF WISDOM

This is what I'm trying to do too—pass along words of wisdom that you can use to build your own life. Because no one else will do it for you. Your opportunities are right at home. They are too close to see. All you've got to do is open your eyes to see them.

This is where the teachings of ECK come in. The Mahanta, the Living ECK Master will help you see the things you need in your spiritual unfoldment—see the diamonds that are all about you—so that you, the diamond in the rough, may become a polished stone of God, a jewel of God, and be able to receive and give this divine love in return.

When this love begins to give, it's not just to God; it's to everyone around you.

When you are giving, you are happy. And when you are unhappy, you are taking from life. Often this means you put yourself before others. Rather than telling people all the great things you know, listen to them and find what they know. Sometimes you learn so much that can help you.

FINDING YOUR OWN TALENT

"Katie" had recently come to Minnesota. She wanted to do something creative. So she went to a creative-arts workshop. But after the session she looked at her own artistry, and she knew that her talent lay elsewhere. "I just don't have this kind of talent," she told herself. She was crushed because she had hoped somewhere, somehow she could find an outlet for the creativity inside her, which was brimming to the surface because she was in ECK.

When you're in Eckankar, the creative fountain is going to open up inside you, and you're going to find some way to give, to let this creativity out.

The creative element that Soul is, is the creative side of God in a sense, the divine spark. This is divinity in expression—something that creates for the good of all.

When you're in Eckankar, the creative fountain is going to open up inside you, and you're going to find some way to give, to let this creativity out.

Katie wanted to find this. All around her were talented, creative people—artists. She could look at their work and see that it was nicely done. Hers, not so good.

GOD, DON'T YOU LOVE ME?

When she'd first come to town, she'd been in the habit of listening to a Christian minister on the radio. This minister, without knowing it, would talk the principles of ECK. The sermons were so good that Katie would listen to them and be uplifted. One time the Christian minister told a story about her attempts to raise tomatoes. No matter what she tried, hers were never as beautiful as those of her next-door neighbor. Her neighbor's were always bigger, with fewer blemishes, and just delicious. The minister's tomatoes never were.

The minister said to God, "God, if you love me, then why won't my tomatoes grow?"

One day the minister said to God, "God, what's the matter here? Don't you love me? If you love me, then why won't my tomatoes grow?"

God came back to her with an answer. "I never asked you to grow tomatoes. I asked you to become a minister."

Katie remembered this story. She'd heard it way back when she first came to Minnesota. So she now asked the Mahanta, "Mahanta, what is going on? Isn't there something I can do of a creative nature? Something where I can let all this out?"

The Mahanta spoke to her. "I ask you to love and serve the Mahanta with your whole heart, and not to worry about anything else. I haven't asked you to do art or music or to write. I just want you to love and serve the Mahanta."

Katie eventually worked at the Eckankar Spiritual Center. There she had her answer. She knew what she was there for—to love and to serve the Mahanta, the ECK (the Holy Spirit), and the Sugmad (God).

WHY DO SOME LEAVE ECK?

Why do some people derail from ECK? Why do they leave ECK when they've been in it so long? Why?

Sometimes it'll be a higher initiate. It doesn't happen often, but once in awhile one will leave. People stay members of ECK after their third year or so at an exceptionally high rate. For the first two years, people are still finding whether or not this is what they want. Many of those stay too. But occasionally, down the road, someone who's been in ECK for many, many years will leave.

"Joseph" is a Nigerian. One day while he was in contemplation, the image of a higher initiate came across the screen of his mind. It was someone he'd once known and respected as an individual who loved God, the Holy Spirit, and the Mahanta, the Living ECK Master. Now this person had turned his back on the Mahanta, the Living ECK Master.

When Joseph came out of contemplation, he looked at a picture of the Master there in his home. "Why?" he asked the Mahanta. "Why do some people derail from ECK? How can the Kal, the negative power or Satan, have such power to take someone as strong as this person and have him leave ECK? Why did God give the Kal power such strength to overcome an individual like that?"

Hardly had Joseph finished his question, when the Mahanta spoke softly, lovingly, and clearly. He said, "Kal is only as powerful as you let him be. It's your choice."

Joseph asked the Mahanta, "Why do some people derail from ECK?"

Joseph realized that there are no outside causes, however convenient it might be to think there are.

ACCEPTING FULL RESPONSIBILITY FOR YOUR LIFE

As you move further along the path to God, you're going to accept full responsibility for everything that happens in your life. Absolutely everything. You won't try to blame someone else for it.

You will look deeply into yourself—if you even need to go to the trouble, if you even want to find out the reason instead of just accepting the fact that you are the initial cause for what's happened to you.

It's just come back, that's all.

The Holy Spirit is giving you a chance to go through some turmoil, pain, or setback so you may grow spiritually.

You can search, but basically it's your contract with the Holy Spirit. When things happen to you that are very difficult, the Holy Spirit is giving you a chance to go through some turmoil, pain, or setback so that you may grow spiritually.

As you grow spiritually, you will be purified and then move on to a higher state of consciousness.

TRUST IN GOD AND DO THE NEXT THING

So often we waste our sympathy on people and gush all over them when they're having hard times. It's not to say we can't have compassion and be there if they need help, but we need not insult their dignity or their pride by offering help where none is wanted. Sometimes help is as simple as just shoveling the snow from their sidewalk, cutting the grass, washing the dishes, or bringing a meal during especially hard times. Doing something of that nature, saying, "Here you go. I thought this might help you."

That will tell the suffering person that you understand, that you really know, you really care.

Then there are people who gush on and on, saying, "Gee, I feel so sorry for you," crying, and all this. But the one who's suffering knows that really no one else can feel the pain as they do. Anything the sympathizer may feel is for himself, not for the sufferer. So do what you can. Cry with the person if that's what is appropriate. But trust in God and do the next thing.

KEEP YOUR OWN HEART CLEAN

People leave ECK because they want something less from the ECK path. They have, right from the very beginning, but they were kidding themselves. They want something less than spiritual unfoldment.

People leave ECK because they want something less than spiritual unfoldment.

They want prestige, perhaps. Perhaps they want recognition for who they are—big stuff. Once they've worked their way up a little bit, they never let anyone forget; they'll go in for dramatic presentations and such.

Not to say that presentations in ECK aren't to be dramatic; they can be. But who can read another's heart but the Mahanta, the Living ECK Master?

Don't try to read another's heart. Keep your own clean. It's a full-time job.

WISHING DOESN'T MAKE IT SO

"Susan" and "Matthew" once gave a workshop on past lives, dreams, and Soul Travel. At the workshop an ECKist said, "I'm not having any luck at all with the path of ECK. Spiritual exercises don't work for me."

These facilitators thought, *How can we get to the bottom of this?* It was a workshop. They were there to help people. So they tried to dig down.

"When do you do the spiritual exercises?" they asked.

They got a blank look.

They prompted the person. "When do you do them? In the morning, at noon, or in the evening before bedtime?" Another blank look.

So they tried another tack. "How many times a day do you do the Spiritual Exercises of ECK?" Same response.

After more such questions, it turned out the woman wasn't doing the Spiritual Exercises of ECK at all.

You may liken not doing the Spiritual Exercises of ECK at all to someone who goes to the river, expecting to get fish, but doesn't throw in a line or a net.

You may liken this to someone who goes to the river, expecting to get fish, but doesn't throw in a line or a net. What do you expect? You get nothing for nothing. Life doesn't give you something for nothing. Wishing doesn't make it so, especially in ECK.

A SHEEP FROM ANOTHER FOLD

"Ann," an ECKist in Switzerland, was giving monthly workshops throughout Switzerland with two other ECKists. One month they were in Zurich, but only one newcomer came to their workshop. There were a number of ECKists there.

One of the workshop facilitators told of someone who had to choose between love and hate. Then the facilitator asked if anyone in the audience had a story to tell along those lines.

The newcomer had beautiful brown eyes. He wore blue jeans, a T-shirt, and a leather jacket and had some tattoos on his arm. But there was sort of a trimmed look about him; he was clean. When the facilitator asked the question, this man laughed very quietly. Then he began his story.

The story was like one you'd hear in an old country-and-western song—a story of heartbreak. This man's best friend had run away with his wife. He didn't particularly hold it against his ex-wife; now he just hated women in general. He didn't do things in bits at a time; he took care of the whole works at once. He painted with a broad brush.

Shortly after that experience, Death appeared to him, and the man knew his son would soon die. And within the year, his son committed suicide.

The father, this newcomer, then went into the woods to do the same thing. He had totally given up. He said, "What have I got to live for? My wife's gone, my son is gone. Everything I love, all gone."

But then he thought he'd give God one more chance.

"God, if you exist," he said, "I need a sign right now." Then he made some kind of a deal with God that he didn't talk about.

The veil opened up between the world of the living and the world of those living beyond this world. I didn't say "the dead" but "those living beyond." Because everything is life. This life is separated from the others by this veil, and he was able to see through it. And mercifully, he was able to see what would be his lot as a suicide. It wasn't a happy one.

Ten minutes later, a voice spoke to him and asked, "Are you making your decision in favor of God, or against yourself?"

That took him by surprise. The message got through.

This man had studied all different religions and done chants of all sorts, but he had gotten no help. One day he was passing by a little church, and a voice said to him, "Stay a little." So he went inside, and when the sermon was finished and the service was

A voice spoke to him and asked, "Are you making your decision in favor of God, or against yourself?"

done, he went back outside and sat on the grass. Jesus appeared to him.

This newcomer asked the ECKists, "Why Jesus? He wasn't exactly my favorite master." But it was Jesus. Jesus took him by the hand, and this great love passed between them.

When he finished his story, the room was quiet.

Finally someone said, "We can't help you with a solution to your problem. But we can tell you about the HU song, the love song to God. It's a mantra above all others."

They told him about the HU song. This beautiful HU song can be sung individually or in a group. When you sing it, you're lifting yourself spiritually.

Ann, one of the ECK facilitators, had this very strong urge to help this man. But the Inner Master's voice said, "Let it be."

Ann was driving home after that session. On the radio came the Beatles song "Let It Be." And the first verse goes like this:

> When I find myself in times of trouble
> Mother Mary comes to me
> Speaking words of wisdom, let it be.
> And in my hour of darkness
> She is standing right in front of me
> Speaking words of wisdom, let it be.
> Let it be, let it be.
> Let it be, let it be.
> Whisper words of wisdom, let it be.

Then Ann understood. This man was a sheep from another fold. He belonged with Jesus because that was his state of consciousness.

Then Ann understood. This man was a sheep from another fold. He belonged with Jesus because that was his state of consciousness. He had to complete a few more courses before he'd be ready for the college of ECK.

That night Ann's heart was filled with gladness. Her job had simply been to set up the workshop, to give the presentation so that this man could make contact with the ECK teachings. Sometime, when he was ready to move on spiritually—and the time would come—he would know about ECK.

BLACK MAGIC—WHITE MAGIC

Singing *HU* is not to change another's state of consciousness, because that's black magic. I know that's cutting the definition of black magic very fine, but that's how we see it in ECK.

Whenever you try to change another to your way of thinking, or your state of consciousness, through prayer or in some other way, that's black magic. And in this respect, black magic and white magic are the same. Some people try to separate the two, but it's changing somebody else's life without his permission. That's black magic, and it's a violation of spiritual law. The violator must someday pay.

The ECK Masters work together. Jesus and the Mahanta work together. And Buddha. They work together. That's how it is. It's the followers who have trouble. They want always to have the most powerful master. People do the most horrendous things to each other in the name of God. They certainly can't do those things, or wouldn't do them, in the name of love. But that's how it is.

When you go home, please give my love to those in ECK who were unable to come. Let them know that my love goes out to all of you. May the blessings be.

Whenever you try to change another to your way of thinking, or your state of consciousness, that's black magic.

ECK Worldwide Seminar, Minneapolis, Minnesota, Saturday, October 23, 2004

On the way home, her coworkers asked Sarah to explain. She said, "I told you I had protection, but you wouldn't listen. I am a member of Eckankar."

14
UNDER THE SPREAD
OF THE
HOLY SPIRIT'S WINGS

*O*ur talk for this evening is "Under the Spread of the Holy Spirit's Wings." I figure that covers just about everything in creation, including all the parts of this talk.

DIFFERENT FORMS OF HEALING

There are as many different forms of healing as there are people. As we go through life, our health changes. Even in the life span of one person, our health needs change from youth to old age.

You may wonder, *How does karma really play out?* You may not see it playing out in your life. But look again. Health has everything to do with karma.

If there was one piece of candy that I didn't try as a youth, I don't know where it was hidden. I ate everything. I had pimply skin and dandruff, and I didn't know where it came from. I used dandruff remover, and all it did was take off more skin. And hair.

You may wonder, How does karma really play out? Health has everything to do with karma.

When you eat things your body can't handle, it's going to reject something. If you're going to take in those sweets or foods you can't handle, the body's going to throw off things like hair. And good health. And youth.

As we get into the fourth and fifth decades of living, we see a remarkable change from when we were in our twenties.

KARMA AND HEALTH

So karma and health are directly related.

Everything we experience relates to what we've done in the past.

When people come into this life with real problems right from birth, they brought this problem from the past. Scientists may call it a genetic defect, but everything we experience relates to what we've done in the past. And this reflects especially in our health.

I don't advise people to eat this or that, because some people's insides work differently than other people's. My mother's into her nineties, and I think she still has her beer a day. She likes candy, but she doesn't eat a lot. That's probably her saving grace. She's doing fine.

FINDING YOUR TYPE

One of the books I want to mention is *Conscious Eating* by Dr. Gabriel Cousens. Basically, he's a vegetarian. I'm not, but I think you may find some interesting things in his book. All healing systems work on symptoms. His is no exception, but it takes a different approach.

One of the very interesting things in *Conscious Eating* is about the *doshas*.

Dr. Cousens talks about three main doshas: kapha, pitta, and vata. Each has its own physical, mental, and emotional characteristics. There's a self-administered test in the book that can help you find out how the three doshas apply to you.

When you read *Conscious Eating*, read the text. Some of the charts have errors; the text is different. Whoever made up the charts must not have read the book.

PROVING IT TO YOURSELF

Conscious Eating only offers suggestions. You've got to do what works for you.

No matter what healing system you try, let it prove itself.

Your final judge is your body. Your body will tell you if you're doing something right or if some part of the system you're trying is not working for you. You learn soon enough. If it's not working, don't do it.

As an example of what you can learn, I've taken homeopathics. They were supposed to trigger a healing crisis followed by marked improvement. But it went a bit farther than a normal healing crisis; it generally took five days for the reaction to settle out—five days of rough road. That's how it is for me, but your experience may be different.

> No matter what healing system you try, let it prove itself. Your final judge is your body.

BRAIN BALANCE

The other book I'd like to mention is entirely different: *The Edge Effect* by Dr. Eric Braverman.

The Edge Effect works with four neurotransmitters. Braverman works from the brain down, because the brain sends messages to all the different parts of the body. If these four main neurotransmitters are out of balance, as they often are, he suggests simple things you can do to get them back in balance.

Braverman's book, like Cousens's, includes a test

to find out what type you are and where your imbalances might be. I wouldn't do both of these systems at once. Pick and choose. If you take two tests, you'll get so confused you won't know which way is up or down.

The Braverman Nature Test determines your dominant nature and whether it's out of balance. He also has another test—which I skipped—called the Braverman Memory Test.

Above all, listen to your body. Listen to your body.

GOOD CORN, GOOD KARMA

Karma isn't everything. Neither time nor deeds can measure what love will do. Love is always the trump card. Love determines a lot of things, and it's more powerful than karma.

Love is more powerful than karma.

A certain farmer would enter his corn in the state fair each year, and each year he'd walk away with the blue ribbon. So a reporter asked him the reason.

"Well, I share my seed corn with my neighbors," the farmer said.

The reporter was incredulous. "How can you? They enter the state fair in competition with you."

"That's so," said the farmer, "but did you know that the wind spreads the pollen from field to field? If my neighbors grew an inferior corn, cross-pollination would degrade mine too. So I must help them grow good corn."

But no matter how good his neighbor's corn was, his was always better. So either his corn was a little bit better, or he knew something else that he wasn't saying.

NEUTRALIZING KARMA

There's another way to deal with karma: neutralize it. That means doing everything in the Master's name.

"Tom" learned about detachment from the threat of looming karma.

He was on his way to meet his wife for dinner. At a stop sign he was waiting for the cross traffic to clear so he could safely cross. But a driver behind him was trying to hurry him—honking his horn, flashing his lights. Tom didn't budge. He wasn't going out into the intersection to get creamed by traffic.

But it did get under his collar. Tom's hostility flared back at the driver behind him. He was reflecting the hostility that this driver was showing him.

After dinner, Tom got back into his car. The car was only four or five months old, and it ran perfectly. But now the car almost didn't start.

Tom was worried. *Now, why is that happening?* he wondered.

Then he remembered the incident with the other driver. The car problem had happened within an hour of when he'd flared up at that driver. It dawned on him: *Could this be connected with an inner thing? Is my anger coming back to me?*

As soon as Tom realized he had caused this karma, he neutralized himself. He made himself clear and open to the ECK (the Holy Spirit) and the Mahanta (the Inner Master).

By putting your attention on the Master and doing all things in the Master's name, you can neutralize karma.

It dawned on him: Could this be my anger coming back to me? As soon as Tom realized this, he made himself clear and open to the ECK and the Mahanta.

RELIGION IN THE ROMAN EMPIRE

Some people ask, "Will Eckankar ever see the explosive growth that Christianity once did?"

I'll answer straightforwardly: No. Not in the same way, although there is very fast growth of Eckankar in different parts of the world.

Conditions were much different in the early years of Christianity. For one thing, there was one united Roman Empire, around the time Christianity ceased to be outlawed. At the beginning of the fourth century, the Roman Empire's religion was paganism—you could worship any god you wanted to worship. This was the way of the empire. All the pagan worshippers would appease their gods by offering sacrifices and doing rituals.

Christianity was outlawed, and Christians were often persecuted throughout the empire. In the local areas people would blame Christians whenever there was a crop failure, pestilence, a flood, or an earthquake. Whenever that happened, the first thing to do was hunt down the Christians and put them in prison or kill them—whatever was handier.

By the end of the fourth century, Christianity had become the empire's official religion, and paganism was outlawed. How did all this come about?

By the end of the fourth century, the tables had turned. Christianity had become the empire's official religion, and paganism was outlawed. A remarkable turn of events.

How did all this come about? The picture changed entirely when Constantine the Great came into office—right after Diocletian. Diocletian loved being emperor so much, he didn't even go through the pretense that Rome was being run under a republic anymore and that he was just the first citizen. He said he was lord and god. He lived like that. And he limited his audiences—he didn't see people very much—although all other emperors before him had been completely accessible to the public.

Diocletian became somewhat special. When he did allow people to see him, they would crawl all the way up to him and never look at him unless he favored them. Then he'd say, "You may get up and then we can talk." But that didn't happen a lot.

When Constantine came in, he was a very strong authority too. He had authoritarian rule—he was basically a dictator, just like Diocletian. No matter what happened, it happened only because the emperor said it could happen.

Constantine was basically a dictator. He flipped from being a pagan to a Christian overnight.

Constantine's Vision

Constantine flipped from being a pagan to a Christian overnight. And this is how it happened.

Diocletian had been a very smart man. He split the Roman Empire into four parts, and he did this for a reason.

Say there was a threat up in the northern border. He was expected to get everybody together and march all his men up there. But then there would be an attack hundreds of miles to the south, and he'd have to go down there. Then all of a sudden, another attack would come in the east, and another in the west. He couldn't do it all.

So he decided on a different method of rulership. There would be two parts to the Roman Empire—East and West. Each part would have two rulers: two rulers in the West and two rulers in the East.

The East was the rich part of the empire. The West was the poorer part. Constantine was in the West.

Constantine wanted to be the only emperor in the West, and his rival there felt the same way. So they

marched their armies toward each other—each
knowing that whoever won this battle, it was going
to be a decisive turning point in his career.

The night before this battle at Milvian Bridge, a
bridge just north of Rome, Constantine had either a
dream or a vision. And in it he saw a cross against
the sun. Early the next morning before the battle, he
had his men paint crosses on their shields. They went
into battle, and they won.

You have to understand the Roman way of thinking. A god had power if he could help you. This vision
of the cross had come to Constantine, so Constantine
converted to Christianity. And it was a real conversion. Some people say he did it for political reasons.
But he had nothing to gain politically; he had everything to lose. It was something he felt deeply in
his heart, and so he made the change. Some even
say that he began to outlaw paganism by the end
of his reign.

All of the emperors who followed him were Christian, except for Julian the Apostate, and he didn't last
long. He had a reign of two years, then he got killed
in battle. Some said the Persians did it, some said
his own men did it. There were a lot of Christians
in the army, especially among the officers, and there
were strong feelings against him. Nobody liked Julian
to start with—neither the pagans nor the Christians.
He had tough sledding.

When they were looking for his replacement, they
asked the next guy in line who was a pagan, "Do you
want the job?"

"You kidding?" the guy said. "I don't want that job.
I don't think this is the time or place for it." So they
asked a Christian. And the line of Christian emperors continued unbroken throughout the rest of the

Roman Empire.

Milvian Bridge was the turning point. Less than seventy years later, Christianity became the empire's state religion. Paganism was outlawed.

CONVERSION OF AN EMPIRE

Will Eckankar see the explosive growth Christianity once did? No, because conditions today are so much different.

Almost twelve years after Constantine became emperor of the West, he also conquered the eastern part of the empire in 324. He chose to rule there because it was the richer part. He moved the capital to Byzantium, which became Constantinople. It was the beginning of the Byzantine Empire, which would last over a thousand years.

Conditions aren't the same today. There was one empire then, one civilization basically, and one ruler. So it only took one vision, or one dream, one conversion.

There were many factors that made the Roman Empire change and embrace the Christian religion so quickly. But it was basically the fact that Constantine and his successors outlawed paganism and made Christianity the official religion.

Many factors made the Roman Empire change and embrace the Christian religion so quickly.

DIFFERENT WAYS TO BE AN ECK VAHANA

A small community in an outlying part of Nigeria did everything it could to reach new seekers. It used some old ways, it used some tried-and-true ways, and it used ways that were completely unexpected.

It was almost like a bird flew into the ECKists' hands and said, "Catch me." This is a double entendre; you'll catch it later.

Each of these three Vahana (missionary) efforts
I'll mention could have been done by a whole group
or just one person.

In one case, a group arranged for a HU Chant in
one of the ECKist's homes. It was pretty much a
standard HU Song. Before they got going, an elderly
woman set the tone for the HU Song when she
declared, "All true religions are really one. All true
religions are really one."

In another case, an ECKist had a whole bunch
of introductory ECK books. He took some to four
young men on motorbikes at a taxi stand. They used
their bikes as taxis, and they were waiting for fares.
So the ECKist approached them and began to tell
them about ECKANKAR. He asked, would they like
copies of this book, *ECKANKAR—Ancient Wisdom
for Today*?

Three of them seemed very willing to listen, but
the fourth man groused.

"There's so much suffering and poverty in the
world," he said. "Why are you people not doing some
philanthropic work instead?"

But the other young men turned on their col-
league. "This man has brought us spiritual food
that has been mostly out of reach," they said, "and
you're grousing about physical food that has always been within reach without solving our basic
problems."

The three started to laugh. This very much
embarrassed the fourth man. The ECKist was able
to give HU cards and books to all of them, including
the grouser.

SARAH'S PROTECTION FROM MAGIC

"Sarah" had the most surprising Vahana story of all.

Sarah is a nurse at a small community hospital in an outlying region of Nigeria. Sometimes, in the course of her work in the hospital, she and the other nurses have to touch dead bodies. It didn't bother Sarah because she knew she had the protection of the Mahanta, the Living ECK Master.

But one day two of her coworkers at the hospital came to her and said, "Sarah, every so often we go to a witch doctor who exorcises the evil that comes from touching dead bodies, because women aren't supposed to do that." They were going to an exorcism, and they said to Sarah, "It might be real good if you came with us."

Sarah tried to tell them about the Master's protection. "I hate to tell you this," she said, "but it won't work in my case." Well, there's no quicker way to get people to urge you to do something than to say you don't need it. Her colleagues wouldn't believe her. They got more insistent than ever. "You'd better come along," they said.

The Inner Master came to Sarah and said, "Go with them." Sarah thought, *OK, if that's going to be the best thing to do, I'll sure do it.*

Then her coworkers said, "Oh, and by the way, you'd better bring a live hen with you. It's part of the ritual."

Sarah went along with all this. If those were the cards she had to bring, she'd bring them.

When they got to the witch doctor, he was very happy to see them. His eyes lit up when he saw the three hens, because as soon as the purification cere-

The Inner Master said, "Go with them." Sarah thought, OK, if that's going to be the best thing to do, I'll sure do it.

mony was over and the women had left, these chickens were going into his cooking pot.

The witch doctor took the first chicken, said some incantations, and twirled the chicken over the first woman's head. The chicken was comatose by the time he'd whirled it around like that. He laid the hen on the first woman's head, and the hen lay perfectly still. Then the witch doctor took it off her head and put it on the ground. The chicken continued to lie there completely still—peaceful and docile.

Then he said, "The bird is docile because it has absorbed the evil from when you handle dead bodies in the hospital." He wanted to drive his point home as long as he was getting paid for it. One for the pot and two to go.

The witch doctor took the second hen, and he got exactly the same results. The hen didn't know what was going on; it just lay on the woman's head, then it lay on the ground.

Finally the witch doctor was ready for Sarah's hen. He took the hen, twirled it over Sarah's head, and said some incantations. Then he put the hen on her head.

But the hen flew off into the bush.

"Well," said the witch doctor, "this hen has had some charm on it. That's why it did that." He looked around at the women, making sure they caught the point—Sarah's chicken was enchanted. It was also better off in the bush than on the ground, let alone the cooking pot. Well, anyway, he still had two chickens.

The witch doctor reached down and picked up one of the still-dazed, docile chickens. He put it over Sarah's head, and he twirled that hen around really

The witch doctor put the hen on Sarah's head. But the hen flew off into the bush.

well. But when he laid it on her head, this second hen flew off into the bush too.

That left only one chicken for the cooking pot. Now the witch doctor's reputation was at stake. If word got out about this, it would be bad for business. So he picked up the third chicken—which was lying there as peaceful as could be. He picked it up, and he twirled it over Sarah's head.

The whole time the witch doctor had been twirling birds over her head, Sarah had been singing *HU* quietly within herself. The witch doctor had no clue. He'd sing his incantations and twirl the hen around her head—and all the while she was singing *HU*.

So the witch doctor put the last docile hen on Sarah's head—and darned if it didn't fly off into the bush too.

The witch doctor was completely beside himself. He could hardly see straight.

Sarah said, "Perhaps you should bring one from your own stock and try it."

The witch doctor became like Popeye saying, "That's all I can stands; I can stands no more."

"Get out!" he shouted, and he kicked all three women out of his hut.

On the way home, the other two women said they'd never witnessed such a thing. They asked Sarah to explain.

She said, "I told you I had protection, but you wouldn't listen. I am a member of Eckankar."

The whole time the witch doctor had been twirling birds over her head, Sarah had been singing HU quietly within herself.

THE POWER OF LOVE

I'm speaking of the power of love. It's stronger than any black magic. It's stronger than any karma. When Sarah was singing *HU*, she did it with love.

HU, sung with love, completely overwhelmed the witch doctor's black magic.

She did it with love for the Master, love for God— love for the Holy Spirit, the ECK. It was sung with love, and it completely overwhelmed the witch doctor's black magic.

Karma doesn't have to happen if you remember to put your attention on the Mahanta and do everything in his name.

ECK Spiritual Skills Seminar, Minneapolis, Minnesota, Saturday, March 26, 2005

The Master can help people. He'll lift you only if you want to come. Sometimes he'll give you a boost simply because you are ready.

15

THE WONDERFUL WAYS OF ECK

Our talk title this evening is "The Wonderful Ways of ECK." ECK means the Holy Spirit. There are miracles around you all the time. All you have to do is recognize them. You have to see what's there, and the ECK will show you, sometimes in the most humble ways. Some of the ways are so humble that people not used to Its way of speaking are going to miss the point.

But many of you understand how It works. You know the silent and the not-quite-so-silent voice in which It speaks. And you're ever thankful that God, or Sugmad, has provided you with the gift of inner hearing and of second sight so you can hear and see Its message as it comes through in the Light and Sound. That's the Holy Spirit, the Light and Sound of God.

There are miracles around you all the time. All you have to do is recognize them.

DORA, BERNIE, AND BIG HARRY

I've been called a lot of things in my time. Some of them have even been good things, and some have been better things. The first thing I want to mention tonight is one of the good things.

I'm going to call this person "Dora." Dora went swing dancing one night, and at one point she found herself dancing with "Bernie." As they were dancing, Bernie said, "Where do you live?" She said, "In Chanhassen." He asked, "Where in Chanhassen?" She gave the cross streets. He said, "Isn't that where the ECK . . . uh . . . ," and he couldn't quite remember the right title. She said, "The ECK Temple? Yes, it is. I live right across from there. And I work at Eckankar."

Bernie was quiet for a little bit. Then he said, "Do you get to see Big Harry very often?"

This struck Dora as extremely funny. She said, "Harold Klemp? I don't see him a lot, but I'm always aware of his presence and aware of his inner guidance."

Bernie thought awhile. Then he said he usually went to Unity Church, but some of the people he knew there would come to the ECK Worship Service at the Temple of ECK. He said, "The reason they like to go to the ECK Temple and to the worship service is because everyone there is so nice. Not fake, but really nice." Then he said that these people call Harold Klemp "Big Harry."

I've been called a big cheese. I've been even called a big cabbage. But I like "Big Harry."

Bernie said, "Do you see Big Harry very often?" Dora said, "Harold Klemp? I don't, but I'm always aware of his presence and inner guidance."

DOORWAY TO THE ECK

Bernie asked Dora, "Do ECKists have a secret handshake or anything?" She said, "No, but we have the HU." Bernie said, "Oh, the HU!" He knew the HU.

Dora dropped me a note. She said she had invited Bernie to an ECK Worship Service, and she had also told him about the seminar tonight. She said, "If he comes to hear you, maybe he'll get a chuckle out of hearing his story." So, Bernie, if you're here, welcome. And if any of you from Unity Church are here, welcome to you too.

We're speaking about the wonderful ways of ECK. You just never know which door the ECK is going to come in, or how It's going to reach you. Even some of the younger people who were born into Eckankar had to come to some acknowledgment and acceptance of ECK. The ECK came to others of us, who weren't born into Eckankar in this lifetime, and awakened us in unexpected ways.

There are those who said, "This is the way. This is the eternal way." And they got on the path, and they never even looked back. Others got on because they were going only a short way, and at first they said, "Oh, this is the path. This is it for me." But then they got off the path because they'd gone far enough. And, as they say in pickup basketball games, "No harm, no foul."

Well, the wonderful ways of ECK.

AMUSAT, A GOOD NEIGHBOR

"Amusat" is a Nigerian, and he's happy being a good neighbor. We have a program in Eckankar where you can tell your neighbor about ECK. It's a form of being a good neighbor.

Amusat was awakened by the Inner Master, the Mahanta, at 3:30 one morning. He woke right up, and he said, "All right, now what?" The Inner Master said, "Get dressed and wait." So he got dressed and waited.

At about ten minutes to four, there was a knock on his door. It was his new neighbor. His wife was in labor, and he wanted Amusat to drive them to the hospital.

Amusat was ready to go. He told his wife where he was going, picked up his car keys, and went straight

You just never know which door the ECK is going to come in, or how It's going to reach you.

out to the car. He drove the neighbor and his wife to the hospital, and they made it in good time.

Afterward the neighbor wondered, *Was Amusat just waiting up for my call?* Here was somebody all ready to go in the middle of the night. He just jumped in the car. So this neighbor called Amusat a good neighbor. Whenever he'd see Amusat, he'd say, "You are a good neighbor, Amusat. You are a good neighbor."

LISTENING TO THE HOLY SPIRIT

Another time there was a book discussion class at a nearby ECK center. Usually, Amusat would go to it. But one particular day, he felt he didn't want to go. Now, ordinarily this would have seemed to him to be one of the tricks of the negative power designed to hold back or slow Soul on Its path back to God. But Amusat had this strong urge to stay home. So he booted up the computer and decided to work on the ECK newsletter they were trying to get up and running for their area.

Just the shortest time after he'd settled down to work, he heard a noise outside. He opened the door and learned that a ten-year-old girl had been carrying boiling water when a six-year-old ran into her and this boiling water spilled over him. He was severely injured. Even worse, the parents weren't home.

So the responsibility fell upon Amusat to get that six-year-old child off to the hospital for treatment. Amusat was able to do it simply because he was home. And he realized that it was another of those wonderful ways of ECK.

After this, all his neighbors, not just his new one, called Amusat a good neighbor.

And this comes from listening, just listening to the Holy Spirit—being aware and following It. And

> *Amusat was able to get that child to the hospital simply because he was home. And he realized it was another of those wonderful ways of ECK.*

in following It, Amusat had done the right thing.

The ECK will never ask you to break laws or do anything that is wrong, nor will the Inner Master. The Inner Master and the ECK are one and the same. The ECK is the macrocosm, and the Master is the microcosm, and they both have the essence of the same thing.

The Master has the essence of the Holy Spirit coursing through him at a certain level of vibration which makes it his level of consciousness. And because of it, he can help people. He can lift them. A Master won't try to push you up into the higher planes; he'll lift you only if you want to come. He won't approach you unless he sees you're ready. Sometimes he'll give you a boost simply because you are ready.

Now we meet "Emmanuel." He's also from Nigeria.

I have to say a word here about Nigeria and its chelas. They are people of the heart. They understand the ECK teachings with their heart. And when they hear of them, they are ready. There are so many Nigerians who are ready for ECK. It is one of those amazing things. You are almost awestruck that there are so many seekers among a certain people. And yet they're there, not just in Africa, but in other places of the world too.

When a seeker is ready, that's when the teacher comes. The Master appears.

EMMANUEL MEETS GOPAL DAS

Emmanuel was born and grew up in a village that was known for black magic and witchcraft.

Here in the United States and in Europe, Australia, and the Western world, we don't have the knowledge of how powerful black magic can be in

In following the Holy Spirit Amusat had done the right thing.

Africa. It is extremely powerful. In this village where
Emmanuel grew up, black magic was rampant, and
a lot of the young men had died. When it took his older
brother, Emmanuel decided to run, to get out of that
place. And he did.

He had this terrible fear. It was just the fear of
living, I suppose, or the fear of not living anymore.
He had no idea what was going on.

He became a Christian, and he looked for answers there. But after a while, he found that daily
he was becoming more dissatisfied with Christianity.
He couldn't understand it. Then after one particular
Sunday program, he came away as confused as he'd
ever been. He prayed to God, and he said, "God, show
me the path. Show me the way that I should go,
because I don't know."

And so he went online and began searching. He
came across a number of Web sites. Among them were
sites for Eckankar, the Rosicrucians, and others. But
he wondered, *Which of these is the right one?* He
didn't know. He wanted to find a religion that would
give him spiritual freedom. And he was asking God,
"Please, please, help me."

Then one night he had a very strong dream. He
and his wife lived in a beautiful city, but it was at
war. So he determined to get in a sailboat with his
wife and sail across the river, to where there was
peace.

As the dream continued, and he and his wife were
in the sailboat, he saw a speedboat coming right toward them. He jumped into the water, and he tried to
swim and push the sailboat to shore so the speedboat
wouldn't catch him. But it caught him. And when it
came up alongside, a man in a white robe jumped into
the water and came swimming up to him.

Emmanuel prayed to God, "God, show me the path." He wanted to find a religion that would give him spiritual freedom.

Emmanuel was wondering, *Is this guy going to hurt me?* But the man didn't hurt him. And then Emmanuel began to feel really good. He decided to swim to the bank of the river and get out. The man in the white robe swam along, then climbed out of the water with him. And they both sat down on the riverbank.

This man said, "On top of the water, I am there. Under the water, I am there. In the sky and above, I am there."

When Emmanuel awoke, he thought, *That must have been Jesus Christ*, because the man had long blond hair and a white robe.

But then Emmanuel went to the Eckankar Web site. He found pictures of the ECK Masters there. And among them, he saw the man who had been in the speedboat. It was the ECK Master Gopal Das.

So after this, Emmanuel enrolled in Eckankar. And as soon as he did, he found that his fear went away. He says, "I now sleep like a baby." He says he only has dreams that are interesting and sweet. So he gave thanks to the Mahanta, the Living ECK Master for having given him the linkup with the ECK.

Emmanuel enrolled in Eckankar. As soon as he did, he found his fear went away.

These are the wonderful ways of ECK. The Holy Spirit will link up with Soul in some way—in this case, through a dream. It will link one up in some way with Itself through the Mahanta, the Living ECK Master.

Some people think this is so much fiction. They will think so until their time comes. And then they find that the Master provides a way they had never seen before and had no access to. It's like a door opens, because it truly is a door into another world. It truly is.

ANTHONY'S MIRACLE

This is a story about yet another Nigerian. "Anthony" was at work one day, and without knowing it, he grabbed a live electrical wire that had thirty-three thousand volts going through it. It knocked him unconscious instantly. But just as fast, the Mahanta, the Inner Master was there and was pushing him back into the body.

Anthony cried out, "I am melting!" because he was out of the body, looking at his own physical body. He saw the lifeline between the human and the inner bodies melting, which would have meant the end of the physical body. He would have died.

But as soon as he became conscious, he found that his body was refilling with energy and was repairing itself.

A coworker helped him up, and then Anthony checked his body; he looked around for damage. He was expecting to be burned here, there, and everywhere, and that he'd have to go to the hospital. But he found only a little burn on his hand where he'd gripped the wire.

Word got around about Anthony's miraculous escape from death, and crowds of people would come to see this man who could not die. They made quite a spectacle of themselves. Everybody would get in line, and they'd look at Anthony like he was a special icon. They studied him, and then they went away satisfied. They had seen "the man who could not die."

The wonderful ways of ECK do everything. In this case, they saved Anthony from electrocution. An electrical shock can kill within two or three seconds. He should have been gone, but he was still here.

As soon as he became conscious, Anthony found his body was refilling with energy and was repairing itself.

"HE'S A WESTERNER"

Speaking of death, the ancient Egyptians had a peculiar convention. They associated birth with the east. Why? Because that's where the sun came up. And where the sun went down, in the west, that was death. When someone died, they didn't really like to refer to it as death. In our culture we use euphemisms like "the dearly departed." What they'd say in ancient Egypt was, "He's gone west" or, "He's a westerner."

Nowadays, some people like to be very careful about every insect. They'll be careful that they don't step on ants. And pretty soon these people get so tripped up that, like the centipede in the fable, they don't know which leg to put forward anymore. We get like that.

I have a rule: Mexican lady beetles do not belong in our home. These things look like other ladybugs, and ladybugs are generally beneficial. But there are a lot of those beetles, and they get indoors and breed like crazy. Joan will always very carefully carry them outside. But the things don't have any sense; they come back. And I then will help them to the far lands. When I report to Joan that there had been a Mexican lady beetle in our home, I just say, "He's a westerner."

LOVE IS FOR RELATIONSHIPS

It's a funny thing. You can be married a long time, and you never really fully understand your spouse. You just love them and accept them, and that's how it is. That's what love is for; it's for relationships.

This goes for relationships between people and animals too. Because animals are little people, sometimes big people. It depends on if it's a horse or a

Love is for relationships. This goes for relationships between people and animals too.

mouse. They're all Soul. And love goes back and forth between any two beings that care for each other a whole lot. This love is sacred. It's divine love. Sometimes people try to belittle people's affection for pets. It just shows where they are.

Animals are all Soul. And love between any two beings that care for each other a whole lot is sacred. It's divine love.

ANN AND THE NURSING DIRECTOR

I'm going to call this next person "Ann." She was an assistant director of nursing at a long-term-health-care facility, and she managed two of the nursing units.

The nursing director came to Ann one time, and he said to her, "You ought to make a plan so we can run these nursing units more efficiently." She said, "All right." She sat down and planned it. She gave the director the plan, and he said, "Excellent! Brilliant!" Then he said, "I'll get back to you. I'll just look through the budget and get back to you with an approval."

Well, Ann waited and waited. Weeks turned into months, and the director still hadn't said anything. But she didn't push it. She just figured he asked for the plan, she gave him the plan, and that was it.

In the meantime, the nursing director was getting more cold and distant toward her.

One day, she drove into the parking lot right ahead of him. When he got out of his car, he asked, "What is that bumper sticker on the back of your car?" She said, "It's an ECK bumper sticker. I'm an ECKist. I belong to Eckankar."

He wanted to know a little about it, and she said, "I can give you a book." He said he'd like that. So she gave him a copy of *ECKANKAR—Ancient Wisdom for Today.* And after a while, he wanted more books, and she gave them to him.

But as time went on, he still remained cold and distant. And Ann found that projects she was trying to get going were becoming more difficult. There was resistance from somewhere, and she wondered, *Where is this coming from?* She couldn't figure it out.

Help from the ECK Masters

The Inner Master had been nudging her. He had been saying, "It's time, Ann. You're going to have to leave this place." Finally one day he came to her and said, "You've got to be out of here by two o'clock today."

She trusted the inner promptings from the Master, and she left a message with the nursing director, with the administrator, with the CEO, and also with the human resources director. She asked if they would meet her in the board room at noon.

This was very short notice, but they all said, "Sure, we'll be there." They were probably wondering, *What's Ann up to now?*

So they met in the room, and Ann said to them, "I very much appreciate the opportunity I've had to work at your wonderful company. I'm very grateful. But, I can't continue working under the conditions I'm asked to, because I'm not able to do my best. And so I'm giving notice right here and now."

Then she suddenly felt that the whole room was full of ECK Masters. They were telling her what steps to take. They said, "Tell them how grateful you've been to work here and also that you want to leave today. And you want to leave by two o'clock." This was without having given notice.

Then the ECK Masters said, "And ask for two months' severance pay." Now, this was a nonprofit

Ann suddenly felt the whole room was full of ECK Masters. They were telling her what steps to take.

company, and they normally gave one month's severance pay to departing employees who gave advance notice. But here Ann was doing the unthinkable. She didn't give notice, and she had the gall to ask for two months' severance pay. To her surprise, they agreed to this. They said, "Come back in an hour, and we'll have the documents drawn up for you to sign."

So she was back at one o'clock, and she got busy signing all the different papers. At two o'clock in the afternoon, she was driving out of the parking lot. She had done exactly what the Inner Master had told her to do.

She had done exactly what the Inner Master had told her to do. Later, Ann saw how the ECK had saved her from the media frenzy.

A week later, there was a job fair. A friend had told her about it. Ann went there, got interviewed for a job, and was hired. Her work would start in a month. This gave her a whole month to sit and digest what she'd been through. And she realized that something wasn't finished with the old job.

One day she came home and turned on the TV, and the announcer was just saying, "A local nursing-home director is being charged with embezzling $1.5 million during his eight-year tenure there."

Then she got the picture. She saw how the ECK had saved her from the media frenzy. But what she probably didn't realize then was that the Inner Master also saved her from likely being investigated herself. She had been the assistant director of nursing, and she might have come under scrutiny too.

But she had been a clear vehicle for the ECK, a clear channel for the ECK. Once she was aware of the inner prompting, once she listened to the Master, then the Master could go in there and begin cleaning house.

And this is what happened to the nursing director himself. He got his house cleaned for him or you might say he got his clock cleaned. Sometimes that's the way it is, and that's how it goes.

The wonderful ways of ECK.

A DREAM WARNING FOR TOBIAS

"Tobias" is from Port Harcourt, Nigeria. He was the chief security officer at a rubber-products factory. The factory would take lumps of latex rubber and process them into other rubber products. But when the factory had a breakdown, these rubber lumps were piling up in the fields around, and it was becoming a real temptation.

Tobias had a dream in which he saw thieves come to carry away these rubber lumps. So he told the company secretary, who was an ECKist and would understand. This wasn't enough to go on, though, so management would not yet put out the money to hire extra security.

A week later, a police officer came up to Tobias and said, "I've heard that some people in the village are going to come here at night and steal a bunch of those rubber lumps." Now word went up to the general administrator of the company very quickly. He arranged for the police to come in, because police can be armed. Private citizens there cannot defend their own property in that way.

So the police were there. And when the thieves came at night, they were quite surprised. They met all these well-armed police, and the thieves took to their heels running.

Tobias realized this was one of the wonderful ways of ECK. Because if the thieves had succeeded, it would have called into question the sort of security he was providing the company. It would not have looked very good on his record.

Tobias, the chief security officer at a rubber-products factory, had a dream in which he saw thieves come to carry away these rubber lumps.

He realized that with the dream, he was able to get set for such an event occurring. And he did not get rattled when things started to move very, very quickly later that week—when the police officer came and told him about the theft that would be attempted very soon.

POWERFUL KEYS TO CONSCIOUSNESS

Every thought, word, or deed either purifies or pollutes the body.

I'd like to mention here a few thoughts I've written about. One of the thoughts is: Every thought, word, or deed either purifies or pollutes the body. Now, this is very important, very powerful, because you're dealing with states of consciousness.

At some point I got rid of all the negative songs I had in my collection. Even if there was only one negative song on a CD, I got rid of it. You have to understand, I listen to country music. And you know how country music is—they always throw in at least one tearjerker on a CD. So I cleared them all out; I gave them away. I figured they would be good for someone, because states of consciousness are different. And then I found myself listening more and more to classical music. But it doesn't have to be classical for you.

If, at some point, you find you need an edge for health or for peace of mind, look at what you're putting out there, or what's around you—what's coming in. Look at whatever your form of music is, or your form of news—whatever ways you let the external world into your internal world.

Because what's coming in is going to go back out there. And then it bounces like an echo; it comes back. It goes out there, and it comes back. And so it strengthens and eventually has a very strong influence on you. And this influence can be either beneficial or harmful. So the choice is yours.

Every thought, word, or deed either purifies or pollutes the body. It sounds like a simple statement, but it's a powerful one.

TRUE SEEKERS ARE HEART PEOPLE

Another thought I had is: True seekers are heart people, so use heart methods to find them.

How do you use love methods, or heart methods? Well, you love everything you do. You just love what you do.

This is certainly true of the African chelas who are out there as missionaries. They love what they do. In Florida, the RESA and an ECKist from Tennessee have such enthusiasm for telling others about ECK that it's infectious—it's catching. People say, "This is wonderful." Some places will have a pizza party as they're planning their missionary endeavor. And it's become fun again.

Missionary work is fun.

And if it's fun, you're going to find people who are alive, who love life as much as you do. It's the old story of birds of a feather flocking together. This is the best way for you to be a Vahana. Love what you do. Whatever way—just whatever way at all.

I'd like to direct your attention to *Those Wonderful ECK Masters*. This book will be very helpful to many of you. It is a powerful book, and it should give you a better understanding of the ECK Masters. They may appear in a dream; they may come in disguise; they may come as themselves. These are the ECK Masters—the Vairagi ECK Masters. They're good people.

I worked on that manuscript a long time; I went

True seekers are heart people, so use heart methods to find them. How? You love everything you do.

over and over it so many times because the ECK Masters deserve the very, very best—as do you. So we try to give you the very, very best there is.

DOING THE SPIRITUAL HOMEWORK

If you do the spiritual exercises with love and put yourself into them, you're going to have the experiences you need.

I think if anyone ever has a doubt about the ECK Masters, they've not been doing their spiritual exercises. I'm speaking about ECKists. Because if you do the spiritual exercises with love and put yourself into them, you're going to have the experiences you need to show you that this is the right way, this is the right path. You will know, because you can't help but know.

Sometimes people come up to me and say, "It isn't working." And I said, "Well, then neither are you." They haven't done their homework, so how do they expect to get a good grade? It defies human reason sometimes that people want something for nothing. And I just say, "Bless them, but they're not ready for ECK anyway. Let them go." And so they may go. I don't care, because they're not ready. In time, they will be. And when they are, then their teacher will appear.

ECK Worldwide Seminar, Minneapolis, Minnesota, Saturday, October 22, 2005

The Breath of God gives us life. It gives us breath. And it's such a blessing to have life. Oh, such a blessing.

16

THE BREATH
OF GOD

High Initiate at the ECKANKAR Spiritual Center said, "Freedom is so hard." And he's so right. He was faced with a couple of conundrums where he was going to have to give up something if he went to the left and give up something also dear to him if he went to the right. What was he to do?

So he said, "Freedom is so hard." He knows he has the freedom to choose to do whatever he wants to do, instead of someone saying, This is what you've got to do.

Well, the youth have asked some very good questions that I think will benefit all of you.

THE MASTER'S FIRST HU SONG

The first question has several parts. "What was your initial impression of singing the HU when you were new to ECK?"

Well, I was blown away, frankly. And I didn't want to cry, because it would be unmanly. The first time I heard the HU sung by a group was at the third World Wide of ECK seminar. I believe it was in Los

A High Initiate knows he has the freedom to choose to do whatever he wants to do, instead of someone saying, This is what you've got to do.

Angeles. This was 1969. The love song to God, the HU, was the most beautiful, beautiful song, or hymn, I'd ever heard. So that was my initial impression when I first heard the HU, when I was new in ECK.

And then the second part of the question is, "What is the best way to explain the HU to a newcomer?" I think the best way is to say, "It's a love song to God that can help you."

HU—THE FABRIC OF LIFE

The third part of this question is, "Has your experience with the HU changed as the Living ECK Master?"

Yes, it has. I'll try to explain. Sometimes I don't have the words. HU is both the name of God, and It's also the Sound of God. That's why we sing the HU. HU is the Sound that underlies all sounds. It's the fabric upon which life lives, breathes, and has its movement.

The ECK, or the Breath of God, the Holy Spirit, makes life possible. Without It there would be no life.

The Living ECK Master is one with the ECK. And there's no difference. So, how has my experience with the HU changed as the Living ECK Master? I really can't say any more beyond that, because to understand, you'd have to be in this position. My apologies. It's the best I can do.

HU is the Sound that underlies all sounds. It's the fabric upon which life lives, breathes, and has its movement.

QUIETING THE MIND

The second question is, "It's very hard for me to sit still. Are there spiritual exercises I can do that are more active than silent contemplation? Is there a way I can do another form of spiritual exercise while I'm learning to be more focused and still?"

There's a French proverb that says, "A good meal ought to begin with hunger." Silent contemplation is the best way. And everyone who hungers for God enough will face the bear and will go through the discipline of quieting the mind and stilling the body.

Now, I do have to say that there are a lot of hyperactive youth today, and also adults. And much of this is from the electromagnetic things that are around them, like cell phones, TVs, and all this.

But this is part of our society. I'm not saying anything against it, but these definitely do affect the individual's energy, where people become more frantic, more frenetic. So doing the spiritual exercises becomes more difficult for them, because they've got to still both mind and body.

When the body is going into contemplation, moving from the physical state into the deeper state, it goes through what I would call several zones of sensation. These are mainly to do with the physical body. All of a sudden you itch, and you try not to scratch. But the itch comes again, so you might as well scratch it. And then keep your attention on the Inner Master, on the Mahanta. Put your attention there, and pretty soon you'll get through that zone.

Then you come to another zone that deals with the mind. These are the mental worlds. Now the mind will try to hop around on you. It will be jumping around the way your body did just a little bit ago.

Paul Twitchell somewhere said it jumps around like a monkey. And it really wants to. Sometimes you can fight it, and sometimes you just watch the monkey jump around. Maybe that will quiet the mind, because it gets old.

So you can do something like this. Try to do the

Everyone who hungers for God enough will face the bear and will go through the discipline of quieting the mind and stilling the body.

spiritual exercise quietly. Accept the body's need to scratch, and just do it. When you get to the mental, or the mind part, put your attention on the Master. Then if the mind jumps around too much, just go with it. Watch it. Pretty soon, the mind gets bored. And then maybe you can break through that way.

So, that's all I can offer on that second question. It does take a lot of discipline—self-discipline. And no one else can do that for you.

THE BEST WAY TO RESOLVE KARMA

"What is the best way to resolve karma between myself and another person?"

Here's a nice one—the third and last question we'll do here: "What is the best way to resolve karma between myself and another person?"

Do everything in the name of the Mahanta, the Inner Master. It's the best way.

Then the individual says, "I realize it has to do with a past life. The past life was a very long time ago. Wouldn't we have already worked out the karma?"

No. You see, that's what reincarnation is all about. This whole world is filled with people, for the most part with Souls who came back because of karma. That's how it is. It's a good kiln, or baking oven. It makes the bread, or the dough, of Soul rise very nicely.

Those are some very good questions from the youth, and you can see that they are putting a lot of thought into what they perceive.

JULIE OPENS HER MOM'S HEART TO HU

An ECKist I'll call "Ginger" missed her flight to Chicago. But she said, "What can you do? You miss a flight. No reason to fret about it; just try to get on the next one." And so she did.

Seated beside her was a very good man, and they had some light conversation. Then the flight attendant came up and said to the man, "Sir, would you be willing to change your seat? There's a mother with her small child sitting in separate seats, and they should be together." The man said, "Why, of course" and got up right away.

So along came this woman with her little girl. The mother's name was "Grace," and she and Ginger took to each other right away. They just had an instinctive liking for each other.

Now, Ginger always asks the Mahanta, "If there's an opening for HU, show it to me so that I can tell somebody about the HU."

So Ginger was talking with Grace. They talked about kid things, and then they talked about parent things. And gradually the conversation moved over into the spiritual area. So Ginger was thinking, *Boy this is the perfect time for the Inner Master, the Mahanta, to send me some kind of message—to let me know this is the time to speak about the HU, this love song to God.* But nothing came.

Then "Julie," the three-year-old, opened the door. She had a book where she could practice her letters, and with the book came a writing board—one of those things you write on with a stylus, and then you just pull the cover sheet up and everything's gone.

The little girl, Julie, held up the board to Ginger. And on it she had put two letters. Now, this is a three-year-old practicing her letters. She could have written any letters she wanted to on this little board. She had written the letters *H-U*.

Of course, Ginger started laughing. She turned to Grace, the mother, and said "This might sound funny, but I was just wondering how to tell you about

Ginger always asks the Mahanta, "If there's an opening for HU, show it to me so I can tell somebody about the HU."

this word *HU*. Julie just wrote it down."

And the mother was quite excited by this because she could see the significance of the timing. It couldn't have been mere coincidence that her daughter had picked out just those two letters.

Julie was a rambunctious and energetic little thing. After a while, she got tired, and she rested her head on her mother's lap. When she did, Ginger, the ECKist, looked at her, talked quietly for a minute, and then sang *HU* to her very quietly. Julie looked at her, smiled, and then sang *HU* with Ginger a couple of times. Then she rested.

HU CALMS JULIE'S STRESS

A further lesson came during a layover. The two adults had taken Julie to a restaurant for a meal. Sitting in a high chair, the little girl became very excited. She started making little noises in her throat that sounded like stress noises. Then suddenly, she breathed HU-U-U-U in a very high little voice. Ginger encouraged her. She said, "Sing or say that word, *HU*, and you'll feel better."

The mother was amazed. She had often heard her daughter make those same little noises at home. And now she realized they were due to stress. But the little girl also knew how to deal with it now. On her own, she was singing *HU*.

Well, the mother still has some doubts about Eckankar. The Inner Master opened the door for her, but only she can walk through it.

TRACY AND THE BREATH OF GOD

"Cara" is an active instrument for ECK, and she was helping lead a workshop on the ECK Masters

Ginger encouraged her, "Sing or say that word, HU, and you'll feel better."

for young adults, eighteen to twenty-five.

"Tracy" was almost that age, so she came. She and her mother were from out of state. They'd heard a little about ECK, so now they came to check it out, and to check out the people too.

The workshop included a spiritual exercise to meet an ECK Master, and Tracy met the ECK Master Yaubl Sacabi. Another ECK Master had taken her to a mountaintop where Yaubl Sacabi was sitting cross-legged, looking straight ahead. Tracy asked him, "How will I be able to afford the college of my choice?" Still looking straight ahead, he said, "All is well."

Then Tracy asked a more detailed question about her purpose in life. The ECK Master Yaubl Sacabi told her, "Be aware of the gentle breeze that's blowing."

Cara, the ECKist, answered Tracy's question about this. She said, "Yaubl was referring to the Breath of God." And at that, both Tracy's and Cara's eyes filled with tears.

Tracy asked about her purpose in life. The ECK Master Yaubl Sacabi told her, "Be aware of the gentle breeze that's blowing."

Later Cara heard that Tracy and her mother had looked the ECKists over and decided it was a good homecoming. So they both became members of ECK too.

REINCARNATION IS REAL

"Lisa" is an Australian, and some time ago she lost her first daughter. The girl was only three months old when she passed away. Lisa was heartbroken. But later she realized that she had repaid karma of a certain kind, both with that Soul and of her own.

Through this, she learned to value life more than she did before. Then, seven years later, she had a second daughter.

Now, when she had her first baby, Lisa made up a little song that she'd sing to her. It was her own zany little song, so no one else would have known it. One day when her second daughter was about seven years old, for some reason Lisa just began to sing this song. Her daughter ran up to her and said, "Mommy, Mommy! That's the song you used to sing to me!"

Well, at that moment Lisa realized there was no death; there is only reincarnation. All this happened before she was in Eckankar.

She also remembered that when she was a child, an ECK Master would come to her—the ECK Master Gopal Das. He used to bring a golden ball, and they'd play with it together. So she had her own remembrances of the ECK Masters from way back when she was just a little one.

The Breath of God. It's all about the Breath of God. It gives us life. It gives us breath. And it's such a blessing to have life. Oh, such a blessing. It's all possible because of this Holy Spirit, the ECK, the Voice of God.

"In the beginning was the Word," said St. John. "And the Word was made flesh, and dwelt among us."

Dave Goes Straight

This next story is about "Dave." I've altered many details in this story, which is also from Cara, the ECKist mentioned previously. Cara was at a business convention, and coming along the hall was a tall black man with the most beautiful, luminous eyes. Cara and this man I'm calling Dave stopped to talk.

Dave told her how hard he worked, and he said he did it for his wonderful family. He had been blessed with a wife, two daughters, and a mother-in-law, and he was caring for them. As soon as he finished his first job at one o'clock in the morning, he'd go to a second job.

Cara said, "You've received the blessings of God.

Cara was at a business convention, and coming along the hall was a tall black man with the most beautiful, luminous eyes.

I want to share the HU with you to pass on to your girls." Dave looked startled, raised his eyebrows, and said, "Yes, I'm a lover of God too." He reached in his billfold and pulled out this battered HU card. He knew HU. Someone had given it to him a couple years ago.

As soon as he knew he was speaking with a fellow ECKist at heart, Dave opened up, and told the rest of the story.

As soon as he knew he was speaking with a fellow ECKist at heart, he opened up, and he told the rest of the story.

He said he'd been in prison for twenty-five years; it was for a major offense. Immediately after his parole, he was walking along a street, and he came to where he could go either left or right. And he wondered, *Should I go left or right?*

Now, of course, this also reflects a crossroads in life. Do you go straight, or do you return to your way of crime? Well, a very strong nudge told him to go right. He went that way, and down the street he saw a white boy being held up by three black men with guns.

So Dave walked right into the middle of it and said something like, "Hey brothers, I've just been there. It's not worth the trip into the pen (penitentiary). Let this kid go. You don't want to go there."

Two of them were convinced, and they left. But the third one was still holding his gun on this white boy. He pulled the trigger, but Dave had moved just quickly enough. He hit the man's arm upward, and the gun went off harmlessly in the air. Then Dave made sure that this thug didn't try to get the gun back. Dave probably took care of things the way they take care of things in prison. In other words, it wasn't pretty.

But what Dave didn't know at the time was that the white youth had been missing, and his father had been searching for him. And just as the ECK would have it—or as somebody who isn't in Eckankar would say, as luck would have it—at the very moment this confrontation was going on, the father showed up. He saw Dave hit this thug's arm and take care of him. He saw the whole thing.

The coincidence is just unreal. So the father came up to Dave, and he said, "Hey, I want to give you a reward for this." Dave said, "No, I don't want anything." The father said, "Here, I'm giving you this three thousand dollars anyway."

It was a lot of money. The father insisted, and so Dave took it. Now, the father was also a very influential businessman. He had inside connections. And he saw to it that Dave's record was expunged. There was no criminal record anymore.

This let Dave get on with his life. In time he met his wife, and he had these two beautiful children. All because he was giving of himself. He was willing to risk his life. He was willing to give his life for another.

This is the way it's explained in *Stranger by the River*. Rebazar Tarzs takes the seeker to one of these grave sites and says, "It is true that when man gives his life for another, he will be saved."

So these are instances of the Breath of God. The ECK was there, and all the coincidences were the ECK working at that very moment. And you just have to be astounded sometimes and say, How? How can these things be?

GUARDIAN ANGELS

This is the story about someone who met the ECK Master Rami Nuri. "Bonnie" tells this story about her friend "Kay." Kay asked her at work one day,

Dave was willing to give his life for another.

"What's the name of your religion again?" So Bonnie said, "Eckankar." Kay said, "You guys believe in guardian angels, right?" Bonnie answered, "Well, yes—ECK Masters."

Then Kay told of what had happened to her twenty-five years ago, when she was seventeen and a half. She was pregnant, not married, and she was on welfare. Her parents let her stay with them. But she only had seven hundred dollars to last out the rest of her pregnancy because she couldn't convince the people at the welfare office that she was pregnant.

It got so bad that she even had to drive the doctor over to the welfare office. He had to say, "I'm a doctor. Here are my credentials. Yes, she is pregnant." Then finally, they put her on welfare.

Well, Kay was always a fighter. No matter what came up, she would always say, "This will not beat me down."

When she was eight-and-a-half-months pregnant, she was on the freeway, driving along in her old car, when she got a flat tire. Eight-and-a-half-months pregnant. She made a good run at it; she got the spare tire. But it was flat too. Now she didn't know what to do. There she was—stuck.

KAY MEETS RAMI NURI

Kay was so aggravated, she gave that old tire on the car a kick. She said, "What else are you going to do to me?" All of a sudden, a white Porsche pulled up, and the driver, a tall man, asked, "Is there anything I can do to help you?"

She said to this stranger, "I suppose you saw me kick the tire." He said, "Yeah. Pretty funny too."

Well, Kay wasn't exactly in a real happy mood.

"You guys believe in guardian angels, right?" Bonnie answered, "Well, yes—ECK Masters."

But she said, "You can drop me off at the nearest phone booth," and she got in his car. She felt very comfortable with this man; otherwise she would never have gotten in the car with him.

This was in the days before cell phones. Believe it or not, there was such a day.

When they got to the phone booth, Kay said, "You can drop me off here, and I can call someone. They'll come and get me." He even gave her money for the call, since she didn't have any.

Kay is a very bright woman. She's always right on top of it. She asked for the man's business card because she expected to pay him back sometime. So he gave her his card and then drove off. The card had the man's name and phone number on it, along with the name of a car dealership that Kay noticed matched the car's license-plate frame.

Kay called her parents, and they came. She didn't want to tell them how she'd taken a ride with a man. You just don't do that. So she just said, "Oh, someone gave me a lift here."

The next day, Kay called the dealership. She wanted to thank the man. Somebody at that car agency answered and said, "Sorry. Nobody by that name ever worked here." Kay said, "But I have his card." "Sorry," they said. And that was it. So then Kay looked for the card.

For all those years, she told nobody about that experience, until the day she told Bonnie.

Kay doesn't lose things. And because she doesn't lose things, she has a very good job now, where she works with her ECKist friend Bonnie. But the card had disappeared. It just wasn't there. Kay looked everywhere for it but couldn't find it.

For all those years, she told nobody about that experience, until the day she told Bonnie. When she heard it, Bonnie said, "I've got some pictures you might want to look at." She had a copy of the glossy sheet with the pictures of a number of the ECK Masters on it, the ones who work out in public.

Bonnie brought the pictures in to show Kay, and she also brought her a copy of the book that had just been released then, *Those Wonderful ECK Masters.* Kay looked at the pictures, and she pointed to Rami Nuri. "That's him," she said. Bonnie asked, "Is the resemblance similar or uncanny?" Kay said, "Well, it's uncanny." And then she said, "Now I'm really freaked out."

Because how could this be? Years ago there was this guy who was supposed to be working at a dealership. He was driving a Porsche; the Porsche had a license-plate frame that gave the name of the same dealership. Everything matched up with his business card. Yet here is a picture of the guy. And this is Rami Nuri.

Yes, freedom is so hard. But life is good.

Yes, freedom is so hard. But life is good.

Everyone has to find his own way to ECK. You can open the door, but only the individual can walk through.

May the blessings be.

ECK Springtime Seminar, Minneapolis, Minnesota, Saturday, April 15, 2006

About the Author

Author Harold Klemp is known as a pioneer of today's focus on "everyday spirituality." He was raised on a Wisconsin farm and attended divinity school. He also served in the US Air Force.

In 1981, after years of training, he became the spiritual leader of Eckankar, Religion of the Light and Sound of God.

His full title is Sri Harold Klemp, the Mahanta, the Living ECK Master. His mission is to help people find their way back to God in this life.

Each year, Harold Klemp speaks to thousands of seekers at Eckankar seminars. Author of more than one hundred books, he continues to write, including many articles and spiritual-study discourses. His inspiring and practical approach to spirituality helps many thousands of people worldwide find greater freedom, wisdom, and love in their lives.

NEXT STEPS IN SPIRITUAL EXPLORATION

- **Browse our Web site: www.Eckankar.org.**
  Watch videos; get free books, answers to FAQs, and more info.
- **Attend an Eckankar event** in your area.
  Visit "Eckankar around the World" on our Web site.
- **Explore advanced spiritual study** with the Eckankar discourses that come with membership.
- **Read additional books** about the ECK teachings.
- See "Contact Eckankar" page 358.

ADVANCED SPIRITUAL LIVING

Go higher, further, deeper with your spiritual exploration!

ECK membership brings many unique benefits and a focus on the ECK discourses. These are dynamic spiritual courses you study at home, one per month.

The first year of study brings *The Easy Way Discourses* by Harold Klemp, with uplifting spiritual exercises, audio excerpts

from his seminar talks, and activities to personalize your spiritual journey. Classes are available in many areas.

Each year you choose to continue with ECK membership can bring new levels of divine freedom, inner strength to meet the challenges of life, and direct experience with the love and power of God.

Here's a sampling of titles from *The Easy Way Discourses*:

- In Soul You Are Free
- Reincarnation—Why You Came to Earth Again
- The Master Principle
- The God Worlds—Where No One Has Gone Before?

355

BOOKS

You may find these books by Harold Klemp to be of special interest. They are available at bookstores, online booksellers, or directly from Eckankar.

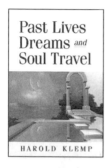

Past Lives, Dreams, and Soul Travel

These stories and exercises help you find your true purpose, discover greater love than you've ever known, and learn that spiritual freedom is within reach.

The Spiritual Exercises of ECK

This book is a staircase with 131 steps leading to the doorway to spiritual freedom, self-mastery, wisdom, and love. A comprehensive volume of spiritual exercises for every need.

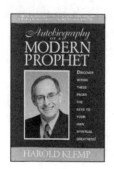

Autobiography of a Modern Prophet

This riveting story of Harold Klemp's climb up the Mountain of God will help you discover the keys to your own spiritual greatness.

Those Wonderful ECK Masters

Would you like to have *personal* experience with spiritual masters that people all over the world—since the beginning of time—have looked to for guidance, protection, and divine love? This book includes real-life stories and spiritual exercises to meet eleven ECK Masters.

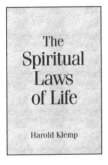

The Spiritual Laws of Life

Learn how to keep in tune with your true spiritual nature. Spiritual laws reveal the behind-the-scenes forces at work in your daily life.

CONTACT ECKANKAR

For more information about ECK or ECK books, or to enroll in ECK membership you may:

- Visit www.ECKBooks.org

- Enroll online at "Membership" at www.Eckankar.org (click on "Online Membership Application"), or

- Call Eckankar (952) 380-2222 to apply, or

- Write to:
  ECKANKAR, Dept. BK 98
  PO Box 2000
  Chanhassen, MN 55317-2000 USA

GLOSSARY

Words set in SMALL CAPS are defined elsewhere in this glossary.

Blue Light How the MAHANTA often appears in the inner worlds to the CHELA or seeker.

chela A spiritual student, often a member of ECKANKAR.

ECK The Life Force, the Holy Spirit, or Audible Life Current which sustains all life.

Eckankar *EHK-ahn-kahr* Religion of the Light and Sound of God. Also known as the Ancient Science of SOUL TRAVEL. A truly spiritual religion for the individual in modern times. The teachings provide a framework for anyone to explore their own spiritual experiences. Established by PAUL TWITCHELL, the modern-day founder, in 1965. The word means Co-worker with God.

ECK Masters Spiritual Masters who can assist and protect people in their spiritual studies and travels. The ECK Masters are from a long line of God-Realized SOULS who know the responsibility that goes with spiritual freedom.

Fubbi Quantz The guardian of the SHARIYAT-KI-SUGMAD at the Katsupari Monastery in northern Tibet. He was the MAHANTA, the LIVING ECK MASTER during the time of Buddha, about 500 BC.

God-Realization The state of God Consciousness. Complete and conscious awareness of God.

Gopal Das The guardian of the SHARIYAT-KI-SUGMAD at the Temple of Askleposis on the Astral PLANE. He was the MAHANTA, the LIVING ECK MASTER in Egypt, about 3000 BC.

HU *HYOO* The most ancient, secret name for God. The singing of the word *HU* is considered a love song to God. It can be sung aloud or silently to oneself to align with God's love.

initiation   Earned by a member of ECKANKAR through spiritual unfoldment and service to God. The initiation is a private ceremony in which the individual is linked to the Sound and Light of God.

Kal Niranjan   The Kal; the negative power, also known as Satan or the devil.

Karma, Law of   The Law of Cause and Effect, action and reaction, justice, retribution, and reward, which applies to the lower or psychic worlds: the Physical, Astral, Causal, Mental, and Etheric PLANES.

Klemp, Harold   The present MAHANTA, the LIVING ECK MASTER. SRI Harold Klemp became the Mahanta, the Living ECK Master in 1981. His spiritual name is WAH Z.

Living ECK Master   The spiritual leader of ECKANKAR. He leads SOUL back to God. He teaches in the physical world as the Outer Master, in the dream state as the Dream Master, and in the spiritual worlds as the Inner Master. SRI HAROLD KLEMP became the MAHANTA, the Living ECK Master in 1981.

Mahanta *mah-HAHN-tah*   An expression of the Spirit of God that is always with you. Sometimes seen as a BLUE LIGHT or Blue Star or in the form of the Mahanta, the LIVING ECK MASTER. The highest state of God Consciousness on earth, only embodied in the Living ECK Master. He is the Living Word.

Peddar Zaskq   The spiritual name for PAUL TWITCHELL, the modern-day founder of ECKANKAR and the MAHANTA, the LIVING ECK MASTER from 1965 to 1971.

planes   The levels of existence, such as the Physical, Astral, Causal, Mental, Etheric, and SOUL Planes.

Rebazar Tarzs   A Tibetan ECK MASTER known as the Torchbearer of ECKANKAR in the lower worlds.

Satsang   A class in which students of ECK study a monthly lesson from ECKANKAR.

Self-Realization   SOUL recognition.   The entering of Soul into the Soul PLANE and there beholding Itself as pure Spirit. A state of seeing, knowing, and being.

Shamus-i-Tabriz   Guardian of the SHARIYAT-KI-SUGMAD on the Causal PLANE. He was the MAHANTA, the LIVING ECK MASTER in ancient Persia.

Shariyat-Ki-Sugmad   The sacred scriptures of ECKANKAR. The scriptures are comprised of twelve volumes in the spiritual worlds. The first two were transcribed from the inner PLANES by PAUL TWITCHELL, modern-day founder of ECKANKAR.

Soul   The True Self, an individual, eternal spark of God. The inner, most sacred part of each person. Soul can see, know, and perceive all things. It is the creative center of Its own world.

Soul Travel   The expansion of consciousness. The ability of Soul to transcend the physical body and travel into the spiritual worlds of God. Soul Travel is taught only by the Living ECK Master. It helps people unfold spiritually and can provide proof of the existence of God and life after death.

Sound and Light of ECK   The Holy Spirit. The two aspects through which God appears in the lower worlds. People can experience them by looking and listening within themselves and through Soul Travel.

Spiritual Exercises of ECK.   Daily practices for direct, personal experience with the Sound Current. Creative techniques using contemplation and the singing of sacred words to bring the higher awareness of Soul into daily life.

Sri   A title of spiritual respect, similar to reverend or pastor, used for those who have attained the Kingdom of God. In Eckankar, it is reserved for the Mahanta, the Living ECK Master.

Sugmad   *SOOG-mahd*   A sacred name for God. It is the source of all life, neither male nor female, the Ocean of Love and Mercy.

Temples of Golden Wisdom   These Golden Wisdom Temples are spiritual temples which exist on the various planes—from the Physical to the Anami Lok; chelas of Eckankar are taken to the temples in the Soul body to be educated in the divine knowledge; the different sections of the Shariyat-Ki-Sugmad, the sacred teachings of ECK, are kept at these temples.

Twitchell, Paul   An American ECK Master who brought the modern teachings of Eckankar to the world through his writings and lectures. His spiritual name is Peddar Zaskq.

Vahana   The ECK missionary; a carrier of ECK or the message of ECK.

vairag   Detachment.

Wah Z   *WAH zee*   The spiritual name of Sri Harold Klemp. It means the secret doctrine. It is his name in the spiritual worlds.

For more explanations of Eckankar terms, see *A Cosmic Sea of Words: The ECKANKAR Lexicon* by Harold Klemp.

INDEX

abundance, 69
acceptance (accepting), 222
  and consciousness, 49
  learning, 26
  more of God's love, 166
"Acres of Diamonds" (Conwell),
  288, 290–93
acting as if, 171
actor, 109
adults, 108
Aeschylus, 190
Africa(ns), 21, 214
Amongo, Mar, 242
angel(s), 193, 217
  guardian, 162
anger, 36, 216
  and neutralizing karma, 309
animal(s), 329–30. *See also* ants;
  bird's-wisdom story; bugs;
  butterfly; cat(s); dog; hawk;
  hen(s); horse(s); insects;
  ladybugs; lesson(s): from a
  squirrel; pet(s)
  and divine love, 51, 129
ants, 51–52
Arab guide(s), 290–91, 292, 294
arrogance, 191. *See also* grocery
  checker's mistake
Athenian(s), 182–84
attachment, 165
aura, 155, 161, 162

balance, 76, 92. *See also* Law: of
  Balance

and finding the neutral force,
  93
going out of, 109
stay in, 98
Barks, Coleman (trans.), 245,
  246
  Delicious Laughter, 246
  We Are Three, 245
Batmanghelidj, F., 3
  *Your Body's Many Cries for
  Water*, 3, 4
beetles. *See* ladybugs
beggar-earns-keep story, 248–51
behavior, 31
beliefs, 89
"Big Harry," 322
bikes. *See* mountain-bikers story
bird's-wisdom story, 247–48
black magic(ian), 303, 317–18,
  325–26. *See also* hens:
  witch-doctor-and-, story
blame, 298
blessing(s), 50, 51
blue. *See also* Blue Light; Blue
  Star; light(s): blue
  man in, 142
  man in a, shirt at bedside,
  117, 119
  someone dressed in, 140
Blue Light, 159, 160, 196, 253.
  See also light(s): blue
Blue Star, 136. *See also* light(s):
  blue
body (bodies), 16, 180. *See also*
  experience(s): out-of-body

body (bodies) *(continued)*
  centers, 116
  effect of thoughts, words,
    deeds on the, 334, 335
  final judge is your, 307
  listen to your, 308
  physical, 117, 155, 156, 328
  Soul, 142
  stilling the, 341, 342
  you wear this, 117
book(s), 231. *See also* graphic
    novel(s)
  Eckankar (*see* Eckankar:
    books)
  for youth, 235–36, 237, 241–
    42, 243, 248
boxes. *See* lost-file story
"Boy Named Sue, A" (Johnny
    Cash), 193
bragging. *See* hen(s): squawking-
    story
Braverman, Eric, 307, 308
  Edge Effect, The, 307
bravery. *See* hen(s): -saves-her-
    chicks story
Breath of God. *See* God: Breath
    of
Broken Gun, The (L'Amour), 241
brothers. *See* mountain-bikers
    story
buckwheat(s), 8–9
Buddha, 303
bugs, 140. *See also* insects
burden(s), 29
bus (driver). *See* kidnapping-on-
    bus story
Bushnell, Vance, 286–88
business card, mysterious. *See*
    flat-tire rescue
butterfly, 256

Californios, The (L'Amour), 241
calculator, 234
Calvin, John, 266
can-do spirit, 238
car. *See also* flat-tire rescue
  -crash-survival story, 251–53
  with flat tire, 7–8

-karma story, 266–69
  problem and neutralizing
    anger, 309
caretaker(s), 16, 17
Carnegie, Dale, 273, 274, 285,
    286, 288–89
  *How to Win Friends and
    Influence People*, 273, 283
  *Quick and Easy Way to
    Effective Speaking, The*, 283
Cash, Johnny, 193
  "Boy Named Sue, A," 193
cashier. *See* grocery checker's
    mistake
cash registers, 234–35
cat(s), 54–55, 189. *See also* face
    of God
  the dogged, 163–64, 165
Catholics. *See* Roman Catholic
    Church
cause
  and effect, 109 (*see also* Law:
    of Cause and Effect)
  you are the initial, 298
CD. *See also* gift: of CD for
    husband; HU: CD
  giving away, 334
"Celebrated Jumping Frog of
    Calaveras County, The"
    (Twain), 187
cell phone(s), 234, 341
challenge(s) to become stronger,
    178, 179
change(s), 21, 23, 166. *See also*
    unfoldment, spiritual
  and a closer spot, 54–55
  resisting (*see* cat(s): the
    dogged)
charity, 35
checker. *See* grocery checker's
    mistake
chela(s), 21, 255. *See also*
    initiate(s)
  in Nigeria (*see* Nigeria(n)(s))
  who misuse ECK, 225
chick(en)(s). *See* hen(s)
child(ren) (childhood). *See also*
    youth

McGuffey Reader(s), 248
McKinley, William, 191
memorization (memorizing), 286
Merry Adventures of Robin Hood, The (Pyle), 241
mind, 118
  centers, 116
  closed, 134
  is very contained, 37
  peace of, 334
  stilling the, 341–42
  travel, 30
miracles, 139, 321, 328
mission(ary) (missionaries), 220, 335. *See also* ECK teachings: telling others about the; Vahana(s)
  for (in) ECK, 79–82, 91
  given in a dream, 198
  of Soul, 18, 144
mistake(s), 111, 147–48
money, 97
Mormon(s), 134, 136, 137
Morrison, Toni, 131, 132
mountain-bikers story, 15–18
muscle testing, 39–40
music
  of God, 220
  heavenly, 169, 170, 196 (*see also* ECK; Voice of God)
  negativity in, 334
  and states of consciousness, 334
Mysterious Stranger, The (Twain), 195
mystery school, 46, 57

nationalities, intermingling of, 266
near-death experiences. *See* experiences: near-death
necessity, 61
newcomer(s), 74, 82, 300–302
Nigeria(n)(s), 96, 313, 323, 325, 328, 333
nursing-director's-embezzlement story, 330–33
O'Brian, Patrick, 241, 242
occupation(s), 67

Ocean of Love and Mercy, 73
old man (Fubbi Quantz), 16–18
opinion(s), 222, 272
opportunities, 294–95
out-of-body experiences. *See* experiences: out-of-body

pagan(s)(ism), 310, 312, 313
pain(s), 298, 299
paper, dot on the, 2
parables. *See* story (stories)
past life (lives)
  in battle at Marathon, 183
  of ECKists in early Christianity, 150
  and karma, 342
  toddler recalls a, 214–15
path(s). *See also* ECK: path of; God: path to
  that allows others freedom, 41–42
  God, show me the, 326
  middle, 98
  people between, 220
  seeking the, 116, 117, 119
  and spiritual shopping, 14
patience, 12–13, 164, 202
patrol officer. *See* traffic-violation story
Paul, Saint, 148–49, 150, 151, 152, 153, 263
peace, 49, 192
  on earth, 195
  of mind, 334
Peddar Zaskq, 122, 126. *See also* Twitchell, Paul
people (person)
  all, teach us something, 26
  creative, 37
  experience God in their own way, 138
  goodness in, 118, 121, 210, 261–62
  heart, 325, 335
  of power, 32, 66
  tired, 206
  who want something for nothing, 336

and the economy, 42
freedom of, 206, 223
good, 32, 270
mainline, 41, 46
in the Roman Empire, 310–13
and spiritual unfoldment, 219
true, 31, 314
we are a living, 75
RESAs. *See* Regional ECK
    Spiritual Aides
resistance, 165, 166, 331
respect, 272, 274, 276
    for others' property (*see* law(s):
    Maybury's two)
responsibility, 49, 56, 83, 268,
    274, 298
    for karma, 224
    for yourself, 233
Rest of the Story, The (Harvey),
    240
resurrection, 215
restroom(s), 59, 60
right, being, 271–72
Robinson, Daniel, 152
role model(s), 262
Roman(s), 149, 152
    Empire, 263, 310–13
Roman Catholic Church, 151,
    264–65
rubber. *See* dream(s): warning in a
Rumi. *See* Jalal ad-Din ar-Rumi
Russian ceremony of love, 61, 62

sales(manship), 34
Satan, 193. *See also* Kal
    Niranjan
Satsang. *See* ECK: Satsang
    class(es)
saving-boy's-life story, 346–48
Schaefer, Jack, 260–61, 262
    Shane, 260–61
scientist, 270
seat(s) of power, 151–52
security officer. *See* dream(s),
    warning in a
seeker(s), 207, 236, 237, 325
    of the path, 116, 117, 119
    reaching (*see* ECK teachings:

telling others about the)
    Rebazar talking to the, 127
    Soul becomes a, 207
    story of a, 71–74
    true, are heart people, 335
    waiting to find the ECK
        teachings, 236
self
    -discipline (*see* discipline(s))
    -esteem, 227
    giving of one-, 348
    help you help your-, 40
    learning about one-, 288
    love your-, 78–79
    meet your-, 56, 238
    the spiritual, 155–56
Self-Realization, 196
service (serving), 9, 46. *See also*
    help(ing)
    is a gift, 138
    to the Mahanta, 225
    organizations, 35
    purpose of, 18
    and sales, 34
    of a widow, 6, 7
Shams from Tabriz. *See* Shamus-
    i-Tabriz
Shamus-i-Tabriz, 162, 245, 246
Shane (Schaefer), 260–61
Shariyat-Ki-Sugmad, the, 57,
    163
Shariyat-Ki-Sugmad, The, 142
    Book One, 126
    Book Two, 18, 90, 98, 256
shirt(s). *See* Klemp, Harold: and
    shirt(s)
sickness, spiritual. *See* con-
    sciousness: victim
silence, sitting in, 279
simplicity, 7, 139
Skelskey, Peter, 244
slave(ry), 181, 186, 189, 190. *See
    also* enslavement
socialism, 233, 238. *See also*
    welfare
society, 90, 190, 341
    and property, 275 (*see also*
    law(s): Maybury's two)